DEADLY LISTINGS

A Day McKelvey Mystery

Amber Adams

AMBER ADAMS

To Mar
For Auld Lang
Syne →

Love
Marie Vernon

ISBN-13: 978-0991421411
ISBN-10: 0991421418

This is a work of fiction and all characters and events are solely the work of the writers' imaginations. Any resemblance to living persons or actual events is purely coincidental. St. Augustine is an actual place, but liberties have been taken in describing various locations in or near the city.

This is Book Two in the Day McKelvey mystery series. Book One, *Above the Fold*, is available at Amazon.com and select retail outlets.

ACKNOWLEDGEMENTS

While today's authors have the vast expanse of the internet at their disposal for research and verification of details, we could not have completed this book without the aid of many dedicated human helpers who gave of their time and expertise. If any mistakes were made in translating their knowledge to the written page, the fault is ours.

We wish to acknowledge the valuable assistance provided by Kathy Delaney and Gail Jones who provided information about real estate procedures, James Ley and Ralph Potter of Terminix, who offered insights into the process of termite extinction, and Joseph McCarty for legal advice regarding trial procedures.

Thanks to Claire Sloan for many hours spent reading and critiquing the manuscript. Thanks also to Nancy Quatrano and John Simmons, who worked on formatting for a "tree book" and an e-book respectively. Their talents make both versions of the book "look right" (a very technical term). Cover art was provided by Katlynn Endicott, and Sharon Buck steered us once again though the social networking jungle.

Special thanks go to the members of the group known as the Ponce Ladies and others who struggled valiantly to save St. Augustine's most historic golf course. They did not succeed, but they have inspired the part of this book that describes in fictional terms a similar event. They are: Dana Birch, Judy Dodge, Nancy Frohardt, Robert Frohardt, Paula Fuller, Mary Gilbride, Peter Grant, Elwyn Hancock, Debbie James, Jean Jones, Connie Lewis, Jo Masuret, Lea Meadows, Pamela Proctor, Rosalie Russo, Lilly Vaill and Dolly Welling.

Marie Vernon and Judy Weber

PROLOGUE

The marble step felt cold under his rear end, but the next-door lady said he wasn't to move.

"You sit right there 'til she comes," she told him. She gave him a pat on the shoulder and started to walk away, but she turned back at the end of the walk.

"Look," she said, "it will be all right. They've got lots of other children there just like you."

Then she hurried off to her job at the meat-packing company. He watched until she got to the corner, thinking she might turn and wave, but she didn't.

She'd said it would be nice there, but Butch Szabo across the street said that was a big, fat lie. "I know this kid got sent there and they feed them slop like stinking cabbage soup and sometimes even dog food. You got to eat it, too, or else you get a beating."

"If it's like that I'll run away."

Butch said that wouldn't work either. "You're five. Where would you go? Besides, you got to wear these ugly gray uniforms so that way if you try to run it's easy for them to find you."

He looked next door at the house that had been his. He wished he could go inside one more time to climb into his mother's bed. Her smell was still there when he buried his face in her pillow.

The next-door lady had said that wasn't a good thing to do, that it was better to let go. Besides, the man had put a big lock on the front door. The younger one had laughed and said, "That'll keep the trash out until we can turn it over."

"It has to be," was all the next-door lady could tell him when he asked why it wasn't his house anymore and how those men could turn it over when it was hooked to the houses on either side.

"Maybe when you're older you'll understand," she told him.

A black car turned in at the corner and came slowly up the street. It crept in to the curb in front of where he was sitting. The driver was a lady wearing a black hat. She looked at some papers then stared over at him before she got out. When she said his name, he stood up and reached for the paper shopping bag with his things.

"Ready?" she said.

CHAPTER 1

A confession: I, Day McKelvey, am a wuss when it comes to other people's love affairs. As a newspaper reporter, I've seen too much of life's seamy side, but I still go all gushy about the blind couple whose seeing eye dogs introduced them, or the ninety-plus oldsters who plan to wed in defiance of The Grim Reaper. So when Everett Peabody asked for my help in wooing and winning his long-lost love, I didn't hesitate.

That Friday, I was giving a final polish to my article for the *Dispatch's* Sunday edition—"Annual Seafood Chowder Contest at St. Augustine Pier"—when Everett stuck his head into my cubicle. My first thought was that some grammatical error or lapse of syntax had brought our reclusive copy editor out of his office cocoon, but judging from the way he hesitated, something other than a misused subjunctive was on Everett's mind. "Uh, Day. . ." he mumbled, "I . . .uh . . I want to buy a house."

I blinked. "You've got the wrong person, Everett. Carl Bailey's our real estate guru."

"It's not like that," he said. "I've already found the house

I want to buy. I just need . . . well, what I need is a woman's opinion."

I frowned, unsure where this was going.

"It's Maple," Everett said. "The house would be for her."

That caught my full attention. The previous month Everett had returned from a visit home to Indiana, beaming like those glow sticks kids wave at concerts. It seemed that he'd reconnected with his old high school sweetheart, Maple Brisby, now a widow, and the torch that had been smoldering all those long years was reignited.

"If this house is for Maple," I said, "shouldn't she be the one to look it over?"

"She doesn't know."

I squinted up at him. "You're planning to buy a house for Maple without her even seeing it?"

"The thing is, all Maple's roots are in her home town, but if I had a really nice place for her, I think she could be persuaded to move here to St. Augustine. I've found this pretty little bungalow in Seagrass Cove, and I was hoping you'd give me your opinion . . . as a woman, that is."

Despite my strong suspicion that Everett could be making a mistake in putting the house before the proposal, I was nevertheless flattered—that was the first time in all my thirty-five years anyone had asked me to help choose a house. Besides, the romantic aspect of it appealed to me, especially as fledgling feelings had begun to develop for the new man in my life, so I said I'd be happy to help.

"The realtor said she'd meet us there at ten Sunday morning." Pleased with my response, Everett returned to his computer screen, wearing the hopeful expression of a little league wannabe who saw a chance of being picked for the team.

After Everett left, Kyle Whitecloud peered across the separation between our cubicles. "What was that all about? Was the Day McKelvey byline in danger of being besmirched by a misplaced semicolon?"

"You won't believe. Our hapless Don Quixote is convinced that if he can offer his Dulcinea a house, she'll up and move to St. Augustine where they'll live happily ever after."

Kyle whistled. "I see. And what is your role in this little drama?"

"Sancho Panza, maybe? I'm going with him to vet out the house that will lure the elusive Maple to his side."

Kyle went off shaking his head and muttering, "Ah, the windmills we men tilt at!"

*****

As promised, at 9:35 on Sunday morning Everett picked me up in his twelve-year-old Dodge Neon. After settling myself on the passenger side, I complimented him on the car's pristine condition. He gave the steering wheel an affectionate pat. "Seventy thousand on the old girl and she still drives like new."

I resisted asking if he'd named the car Rocinante. Like most of the First Coast *Dispatch's* staff, I considered Everett rather stodgy, or, as Kyle Whitecloud put it, a plugger. A confirmed bachelor, he lived alone in a rented two-room apartment, wore the same baggy-elbowed cardigan summer and winter, and thought *It's a Wonderful Life* was the best movie ever made. That is where Everett and I differed—early on my Dad instilled in me a love of old movies and my vote for favorite goes to *Casablanca*. I mean, after all, Ingrid and Bogey—how much better can it get?

"So tell me about this house," I said once we were underway.

Everett said the house was located in a small development on Anastasia Island, across the river from the main section of town. "I was driving around and spotted this SandScapes Realty sign, so I called the listing agent, a Miss Kimmel. She was tied up on Saturday, but said she would meet me at the house this morning."

"Kimmel? Valerie Kimmel?" I asked as he made a slow left turn onto the Bridge of Lions. Everett didn't answer, but leaned forward over the steering wheel to concentrate as we approached a line of bicyclists. Clad in helmets, tight-fitting shorts and brightly colored jerseys, they rode hunched like peasants over their handlebars. It being a Sunday morning there were also lots of joggers and walkers crossing the bridge in both directions, some stopping to gaze down at the flotilla of sailboats lining the piers to the south of the bridge, or those bobbing next to buoys to the north. It was only after we'd cleared the bridge that Everett relaxed his vigilance to ask, "You know this Miss Kimmel?"

"If it's Valerie Kimmel, we were in high school together. I know she works in real estate, so it must be her."

The prospect of catching up with Valerie pleased me. She and I were never close enough to be what today would be called BFFs, but we'd shared a miserable semester in the same high school Home Ec class, a required course that nearly cost me my diploma when I set fire to the butter while attempting to make béarnaise sauce. My comment to Miss Eustis that I saw no real need to learn how to cook when our town had dozens of great restaurants didn't help matters, either. If Valerie hadn't taken pity on my failed effort at chocolate soufflé, and substituted her puffy-perfect one for my globby mess, I would have been doomed to an additional semester in that class, a prospect equally as repulsive to Miss Eustis as it was to me.

After high school, Val and I lost touch. I attended college in Atlanta, where I met and married football star Derek McKelvey. I would have stayed there after my marriage disintegrated because my career with the *Atlanta Journal Constitution* had begun to take off, but then Dad died and Mother seemed to go bonkers. Overnight she transformed herself from a sedate housewife, Doris Richards, into an off-the-wall psychic, changed her name to Zanthia, used Dad's insurance money to buy a shop on St. George Street and began selling crystals, runes and tarot cards. She even held séances and claimed to receive messages from the beyond via a disembodied spiritual adviser named Claude. In hopes of keeping her from going farther off the deep end, I moved back to St. Augustine.

Valerie meanwhile had gone directly from high school to working for a real estate agency, took night classes, earned her license and began the climb to a successful career. St. Augustine being the small town it is, it was inevitable that our paths occasionally crossed. I gathered that she was doing quite well in her career at SandScapes Realty, which was the *Dispatch's* major advertiser in the real estate section. Each Sunday they bought a four-color pull-out devoted exclusively to their listings.

At the east end of the Bridge of Lions, Everett continued south on Anastasia Boulevard several miles to Seagrass Cove. As we wound our way through the subdivision's shady streets, I estimated that the houses had been built in about the mid-1960s. All were designed with the art deco touches that defined that period—rounded corners, flaring rooflines and the steel-framed "picture" windows that had been considered "modern" back then. While those features dated the community's architecture, they also gave it a distinctive charm.

Everett located 23 Oleander Lane and oozed the Dodge to the curb behind a Cadillac Escalade with a SandScapes Realty logo on its side. "Looks like Miss Kimmel's here already," he remarked. "You ask her all the questions about things a woman would want to know."

I assured him that I would.

For a moment, we both stood at the curb, eyeing 23 Oleander Lane. The lot was spacious and attractively landscaped. The sturdy trunks of two live oaks bracketed each side of the modest one-story cottage, its stucco exterior painted pale blue with white trim and a mustard yellow front door.

Everett was beaming as he stared up at the house. "This is perfect," he exclaimed. "Maple will love that bay window. It's exactly like the window in the house where she lives now. That's where she keeps McDuff's cage so he can watch everything that's going on outside."

"McDuff?"

"Her parrot. He talks a little, so she's trying to teach him Shakespeare. Oh this is perfect," Everett exclaimed again. "If the inside is anything like—"

"Let's go find out," I said, and grinned at his eagerness as he hurried up the walk ahead of me.

We mounted the two steps to the small front portico, Everett pushed the doorbell and we waited. "No answer," he said, and punched it again. Chimes sounded from inside, but we heard no footsteps or response.

The realtor's master lock hung unfastened. I reached for the door handle. When the latch yielded, I shoved the door open far enough to peer inside.

"Miss Kimmel," Everett called, leaning into the foyer. "Miss Kimmel, I'm here to see the house."

No answer.

"Maybe she's checking out one of the rooms in the rear," I said, then called aloud, "Valerie, are you here?"

Still no answer.

"Let's go in," I said. "Her car's here and the house door was open, so she must be somewhere on the premises . . . maybe in the garage or the rear yard."

We closed the front door behind us and stepped from the foyer into a cool empty space that would have been called a living room at the time the house was constructed, but which realtors currently dubbed the "great room," a term that always brought to mind an enthroned King Arthur receiving his courtiers.

"Valerie," I called again. The only response was the hollow resonance of my voice in the unfurnished space.

Everett paused in the middle of the room to look around. "This is nice," he said, "the fireplace, the wood flooring, that big window. Don't you think a woman? . . ."

"If Maple is anything like you've described her, she'll like this," I assured him.

We crossed the room to peer through an archway that led into the dining room, not too spacious, but with a nice double window. From there we continued through a door that led to the kitchen. I ran my hand over granite countertops and checked out the stainless steel appliances. "Judging from what I've seen on House and Garden TV," I told Everett, "this kitchen's been newly remodeled."

"That's good, isn't it? She'll like that, won't she?"

"Absolutely. I'm no cook, but even I could appreciate a kitchen like this."

We returned to the living room and started down the rather narrow hallway to our right that led to the bedrooms. All the doors along the passage were closed. I tried the first one while Everett went on ahead. The door I opened was to a characterless room about ten feet by twelve, the kind a real-estate brochure would no doubt describe as an office-slash-guestroom. If Maple was into some hobby—scrapbooking, maybe—she might appreciate having this as a separate space. I started to back out of the room and close the door when I heard Everett's strangled cry, "Day!"

I spun around. Beyond the partially open door he was holding, I could see a woman's legs sprawled motionless on the carpet, her feet clad in black spiked heels.

CHAPTER 2

I sprinted down the hallway and reached Everett just as he sagged and clutched for my arm. His face had taken on an ashy pallor and he was gasping for air.

Immobilized, I stared at where Valerie Kimmel lay askew on the floor, her body rolled up onto her right shoulder. One leg stretched straight, the other knee was bent with the toe of her shoe pointing inward. A black bag, similar to the one I carried when doing research or interviews lay partly open on the floor beside her.

At the sight of the brownish stain matting the back of her ash blonde hair and leaking onto the beige carpet underneath, my knees gave way, and I hung onto Everett, so that for an awkward moment we were supporting each other.

I managed to stammer, "Go outside and call 911." Then, seeing that his face had gone the sickly green of a sliced avocado, I ordered, "Stay out there . . . get some fresh air."

I pushed him down the hall towards the front door then edged into the bedroom. A retching sound came from the front porch, and I struggled to keep my stomach contents intact. A couple of shallow breaths fortified me to stoop and check Valerie for any vital signs, although I was pretty sure there were none. The moment I bent and touched her shoulder, her body rolled toward me as if I had wakened her from sleep, but there was no life in the blank, sightless eyes staring up at me.

Instinctively, I pulled back. "Oh my God . . . Valerie. . ." I whispered in a voice that sounded as if it had been run through a strainer.

More deep breaths were needed to still the thumping inside my chest before I could kneel to check her carotid artery. Her cool skin still gave off a trace of a musky perfume that mingled with the metallic odor from the blood. No pulse throbbed beneath my shaking fingers. Unsure if Everett had been able to use his cell phone before becoming sick, I pulled out my own and dialed 911.

I told the woman who responded that I was sure Val was dead. She took me through a quick check list, starting with the address I was calling from. "Is the person breathing?" . . . "Can you get a pulse?" . . . "Is there bleeding?"

All the time she was quizzing me, I wanted to scream at her to just send someone right away. On wobbly legs, I shoved myself upright and reiterated for the third time that I was sure the person was dead.

"Okay. Stay where you are. Officers are on the way," she ordered.

While I waited, I took a closer look at Valerie's body. Except for the awkward position that would be expected in a sudden fall, none of her clothing seemed disarranged. She wore a neat outfit, an off-white blazer that topped a turquoise scoop-necked blouse and black skirt. A black enamel pin with gold letters that read *Valerie Kimmel, SandScapes Realty* was attached to her jacket's lapel. A band of white on her exposed wrist indicated where there might have been a watch. I noted that she wore no other jewelry except for a small pair of gold earrings. A tiny blotch of blood that had spread onto the blazer's collar sat just below a red scrape on her neck.

I was tempted to check inside her purse, but knew I mustn't contaminate it with my fingerprints. Instead, I swallowed hard, removed my cell phone from a pocket and dialed my editor.

"Esther and I are at the Lazy Sands having brunch," Shel told me. "What's the problem?"

I explained our bizarre discovery.

"I'll get Frank on it right away," Shel snapped. "Meanwhile, gather any information you can and give it to Frank as soon as he gets there."

"Why Frank when I'm right here?" I blurted, even though I knew the answer. A Pulitzer plus years of experience for the *L.A. Times* gave Frank Burke priority on any front page story.

Ever since I joined the *Dispatch's* staff, the man had thrown razor wire around his territory. He raised the barrier even higher after I uncovered the killer who murdered a local college president. That discovery had nearly cost me my life, but had apparently earned me no credits in Frank's book.

Resigned to following Shel's instructions, I went outside to check on Everett. I found him hunched on the front steps, with his head down between his knees. When he heard me approach, he looked up. A sickish odor and his face's pale, greenish tint confirmed that he had up-chucked his stomach contents. "Sorry, Day. I never before saw. . . I just couldn't. . ."

"It's okay," I crouched down beside him. "Wait here and I'll bring you the bottle of water I've got in the car."

Valerie's Cadillac was parked in front of Everett's Dodge Neon and, without thinking I went to it and tried the driver's side door handle. As I'd expected, it was locked.

I retrieved the water bottle from Everett's car. I was handing it to him when a police car swerved to the curb, another close behind. That quickly, what minutes before had seemed a cozy little cottage became a crime scene.

*****

It was afternoon by the time the investigator got around to taking statements from Everett and me. By then I was emotionally drained and wobbly from hunger. Poor Everett looked even worse than I felt. I persuaded the investigator to talk to him first and then let him leave. Everett offered to wait for me, but I told him to go, which he did with a regretful backward look.

The officer taking my report frowned when I told him that I'd tried to open Valerie's car door and had probably left my prints on the handle. Then, seeing how shaky I still was, he assured me, "Natural enough for you to try the car. I'll just note that in my report."

His eyes gave a suspicious flicker when I mentioned that Valerie and I had attended the same high school and were acquaintances. I hastened to add that in recent years I had had only casual contact such as chance meetings at the grocery store or once jogging along beside each other at a Breast Cancer Awareness event.

After the investigator finished with me, Corporal Brad Nortley offered me a ride back to my house.

I was grateful for the offer. On the way, I asked Brad if they'd developed any theories on the crime.

He frowned and caught his upper lip between his teeth for a moment. "Our first guess in cases like this—pretty woman, alone in a secluded location—is a stalker. Another possible, it could be a vagrant who was hanging out there while the house was empty, although we couldn't come up with any evidence to corroborate that—no signs of the bathroom or kitchen having been used. Still, the house's security system is pretty primitive, and it had been disabled. Our officers are going house to house, but so far nobody's seen any unusual activity. Trees block the view from both the adjoining properties and from the street. Anybody could have slipped in pretty easily."

After Brad dropped me off at home, I checked in again with Shel and he assigned me to collect background on Valerie. Even though I was beat and Sunday was my day off—if there was a disadvantage to my job, it was that news happened at any time of day or night—I slapped together a peanut butter sandwich and swigged some orange juice straight from the carton in the fridge and headed back to the *Dispatch* office.

An unusual number of cars were in the *Dispatch's* lot, which meant others had already gotten word of Valerie Kimmel's murder. Other staff members would be working on the story from various angles. I punched my number on the keypad, passed through the lobby where the weekend receptionist was busy answering the phone, and headed for my desk. My hope was that Valerie's background contained some critical clue to the case. I could picture the look on Frank's face if that happened.

Note to self: Such thoughts contemptible. A school friend with all her life ahead of her has been killed, and I'm turning her death into a competition.

In a more somber mood, I began an online search of Val's name. It yielded a number of hits, most of them related to her real estate career, important sales she'd made, her role in various business organizations, awards she'd won. Not too shabby—the previous year she'd been named Top Real Estate Agent of the Year for the entire county.

I pulled up SandScapes Realty's website, a professionally designed paean to the company's professionalism and sales success. *If it's results you want, put your residential and commercial needs in our hands. . .* I was still scanning through it when Kyle stopped by. My long-time friend, Rhonda Williams—we met in kindergarten—was the steady center of my social world, and Kyle served the same function in my working life. Ours was a sort of sibling relationship, Kyle being some four years younger than me. I'd have been proud to have him as a brother—tall, slender, dark-haired, with just enough of his Native American heritage—his father was Navajo—in his features to suggest nobility. Sort of a cross between Dana Andrews and Jay Silverheels. Add to that a quick wit and an irresistible grin. More than one woman had gone into mourning after learning that Kyle was gay.

"Got a call from Shel and another from Frank," he said as he poked around in his cubicle. "The Kimmel murder. You working on it, too?"

"Shel has me doing background on the victim." I showed him the SandScapes website.

"Compton Ballard's outfit," he said. "You have any take on them?"

"All I know about Ballard's business is what I've heard from my friend, Polly Ribideaux. She worked there before opening her own real estate office. I gather she doesn't think too highly of him, but that could be because she resented that he'd taken over from Paul Sands."

"Your friend must be doing okay on her own, judging by the Ribideaux Realty signs all over town."

A little later Carl Bailey, the Real Estate section editor, stopped by and said he'd heard about Valerie Kimmel's death.

"I'll be doing some interviews at SandScapes in connection with the murder case," I told him. "You know anything about this Compton Ballard?"

"As much as I care to," Carl said. "From what I've observed, he's pretty sharp, but not particularly ethical. Case in point, there's this business with the old Coronado golf course."

"I've seen the letters from golfers on the op-ed page but don't know exactly what the hassle is about."

Carl took a sip from the can of cola he was carrying. "The way it's come down, Ballard cozied up to the course's owner who was old and sick and probably not too mentally alert. Then he put together a group of investors and tied up the property with an option before anyone else knew it was up for grabs. Word is that the price his Southwind Enterprises offered is peanuts compared to the course's actual value as development property."

"Nothing particularly illegal about that, is there?"

"Maybe not," Carl shrugged, "but Ballard gave the owner his word that he and his group would keep the Coronado as a golf course, update the clubhouse, make it a first-class facility. Of course his word was only as good as the paper it wasn't written on. The minute the property was optioned, Southwind Enterprises filed an application for a zoning variance. With that property located right along the river, anything they build there will bring top dollar. Chock-a-block McMansions is what you'll see if the variance is approved."

"Think they can swing the zoning change?"

He shrugged again. "Wouldn't be the first sharp deal he's managed to pull off. Before he came to St. Augustine he had to wriggle his way out of a major mess in Atlanta. Seems he colluded with an appraiser and a bank's loan officer to inflate the value of Atlanta's old Moreland Hotel."

"That was Ballard? I was working for Atlanta's *Journal Constitution* then, and I remember hearing about some real estate scandal, but never made the connection."

"The same. The appraiser and the loan officer both did time."

"And Ballard got away with it?"

Carl grimaced. "Sleaze is like Vaseline—everything slides off. Ballard's one of these guys could fall into a cesspool and come up smelling of Eau de Money."

By four-fifteen Sunday afternoon, I was ready to pack it in. I attended to a couple of last items and had just stood to retrieve my bag when on the far side of the room I spotted Skooky Mandel dodging rather furtively into Frank Burke's vacant cubicle . . . a cubicle at least twice the size of mine . . . not that I've measured it.

Skooky was carrying a large manila envelope. The outfit he was wearing, shorts, flip-flops and a t-shirt with a surfer logo, went several notches past the "casual" designation considered appropriate for the office on weekends.

I called to him, "Skook, what are you doing here? Don't you know it's Sunday?" The boss's hapless nephew jerked around as if I'd poked him in the ribs. "Jeez, Miss Day, I didn't see you there," he called across the room.

"You're looking for Mr. Burke?"

Skooky turned back long enough to slip the envelope under others on Frank's desk and then shoved back the lop of blond hair from across his forehead. He crossed to my cubicle wearing the guilty look of a sheepdog with wool around its mouth. "Hope you won't say anything, Miss Day, but on Friday Mr. B. told me to pick up these documents from the courthouse and have them on his desk before I left. Guess I kind of forgot."

Close up, I caught a whiff from Skooky's hair and clothing of an odor that I recognized in my college dorm days—marijuana. I gave him a long stare. "Forgot, Skooky, or got distracted by other . . . activities?"

His lopsided grin acknowledged my guess. "Bunch of the guys . . . I hope you won't—"

"Tell me no more—I can't afford to be your partner in crime."

"Thanks, Miss Day—I owe you one." With that and a wave he was gone.

*****

It was getting late, but I still hoped to get some interviews with Valerie's co-workers. It was one of the times I felt the benefit of living alone—no husband, no child, not even a pet to demand my presence.

SandScapes Realty's office was locked when I got there. I cupped my eyes to peer through the glass door and spotted a woman working at one of the desks. I hit the visitor button on the keypad. After sending me a very suspicious once-over, she rose, went to the reception desk and buzzed me in. When I told her why I was there, she stared at me, mouth agape, as if I'd spoken in some unintelligible language.

"Valerie dead?" she gasped. "I've been at an open house all day. I didn't know."

The woman was too shaken to offer much information. She said she was a new agent and that she hardly knew Valerie at all. "Mr. Ballard's the one you'll have to talk to, but he's out of town," she said.

From my morning spent with the police, I was able to tell her that they had already contacted Mr. Ballard and he was flying back immediately.

It was nearing five o'clock when I left SandScapes. I wanted nothing more than to hole up in my apartment for the evening with one of Dad's old black and white movies. *Portrait of Jennie*, with its melancholy theme, the ghostly presence of a beautiful woman who'd been murdered, would feel right. I could blame any tears on the movie's tragic ending, easier to face than death in real life. But the film would have to wait for another night. I'd promised to meet Rhonda and Polly Ribideaux for dinner at the Harpoon.

As I drove home to change, Valerie's murder made the glittering sunshine, the insouciant breeze swaying the tops of the palms, and the salty sea air streaming in through the Jeep's open windows seem somehow disrespectful of a life brutally cut short. That angered me in a very personal way. Val was of my generation, we shared a past. Even if we were never close friends, she was a part of my life that someone had stolen, bludgeoned to death and left lying alone in an empty room.

That thought stiffened my resolution—the meat of the murder case might be Frank Burke's assignment, but I had known Valerie for many years, known her in a way neither Frank nor the police investigators ever would. Known her in a way that the photographs they took of her body would never reveal. Shel may have given me the soft part of the case to cover, and I couldn't confront Frank head-on, but my Dad was a pilot and he had taught me a thing or two: When you're coming in for landing, you don't fight the crosswind; you use it to carry you in the right direction.

CHAPTER 3

A voice from the bar called, "Day . . . Day McKelvey, over here."

I waved without pausing. The news I was carrying was too grim to dilute with the happy hour crowd's noisy banter. Instead, I hurried into the dining room where Rhonda was seated at a table off to the side. She lofted her Margarita above the table candle and waved me over. "You'll have to catch up."

But after a closer look at me, her smile collapsed. "What? . . ."

I told her.

At the name "Valerie Kimmel," Rhonda's eyes widened in disbelief. Her shocked, "Murdered? You can't mean it," momentarily halted the chatter from nearby tables, and several people craned to see what was happening. Rhonda, oblivious to the attention, went on, "The Valerie Kimmel who we went to high school with? Blonde hair? Cheerleader?"

I slipped my combination purse/carry-all off my shoulder and dropped into a chair. "The same."

Rhonda stared blindly in front of her... "My God. She's our age. I . . . I can't believe it." She went on in a voice as distant as her expression. "I haven't run into Valerie recently, but I've seen her name on real estate signs around town. How . . . how did it happen?"

I told her how Everett and I had found Valerie's body at the house he was planning to buy. "From the looks of it," I said, "the killer was waiting inside the house when she arrived."

"What a scoop for you," she started then clapped a hand to her mouth. "I mean it's awful about poor Valerie, but . . ."

"No scoop, I'm afraid. Shel's assigned the story to Frank Burke."

Rhonda's lips tightened in a sympathetic grimace. "When is your editor going to realize he's wasting a reporter with your background on seafood festivals and senior citizen tango lessons? Although I've got to admit you made that nursing home story zing when you discovered that ninety-year-old lady who'd actually danced with Fred Astaire."

"Considering that Frank Burke guards the crime beat like a junkyard dog, my break will come when we get three feet of snow here in St. Augustine."

"Do you suppose Polly's heard about this?"

I nodded, certain that phone messages and e-mails had been burning up the airwaves to every real estate office in town, including Polly's firm, Ribideaux Realty.

Rhonda, apparently realizing she was still holding her glass in midair, set it down so abruptly the drink splashed onto the tabletop. "Valerie Kimmel," she mused. "Remember how in high school we pretended not to care about Val's sort of popularity, even though we actually envied her?"

"Until that night at the roller rink," I reminded her.

Rhonda's somber nod told me we were reliving the same scene.

It happened during our sophomore year. As usual, Rhonda and I were at the Rainbow Roller Rink that Friday evening along with a crowd of kids our age, spinning round and round the polished floor to the music of the huge Wurlitzer organ. By that time the older crowd Valerie was running with had long since abandoned roller-skating as too childish, too beneath them.

Rhonda's mom had said she'd pick us up at ten, so at a little before, we skated over to the bench on the sidelines and began removing our skates. I had just slipped into my loafers when the door was flung open and Valerie came rushing in, her hair disheveled and her lipstick in a red smear. For a moment she paused and looked about as if panicked, then headed straight for Rhonda and me. She threw herself onto the bench, kicked off one of her shoes, and snatched up a skate I had just taken off.

"Help me!" she pleaded, as she struggled with clumsy fingers to slip her foot into my skate. "If anybody asks, say I've been here all the time."

She'd hardly gotten the words out when a man burst through the door, swept the room with a furious glare, then stormed over to where we sat. He towered over us, eyes blazing and his face skewed in anger. He reached over and grabbed Valerie by the arm, jerking her to her feet. With his free hand, he slapped her across the face so hard that I cringed and Rhonda let out a moan.

"You lyin' little bitch!" he snarled. "Thought you could put it over on me, but you're damned well mistaken." With that came another slap, the sound of it so sharp that not even the music could drown it out.

"Dad!" Valerie screamed. "I was here. They'll tell you. . . ." She looked frantically toward Rhonda and me but we were too stunned to move or speak.

"Get out, slut," Val's father ordered her. "I'm gonna teach you a lesson you'll never forget." He shoved her out the door, while everyone near us stared openmouthed.

Rhonda, as if remembering that same scenario, murmured, "After that night, the roller rink never felt the same."

The bad taste that memory left made me feel glad when the waiter appeared to take my drink order. I'd no sooner given it than Polly strode into the Harpoon. Eyes turned. Polly Ribideaux—Pauline, actually, although she was never called anything but Polly—while not pretty by traditional standards, had the sort of presence that commanded attention. Her tall, erect figure, her sweeping forehead, wide-set eyes and aquiline nose seemed to have come straight from a profile on an ancient Greek coin. The tailored suit she was wearing would have seemed severe for St. Augustine's summer weather, but the subtle colors of a silk scarf softened the look, as did square aquamarine earrings that picked up a sparkle from the candlelight.

My jeans and striped t-shirt felt somewhat dowdy in comparison, but this was a casual get together and I've never felt the need to be dressed up around my best friends. Rhonda, too, had gone casual, with a pert denim vest over a yellow cotton shirt and white capris.

We waved Polly over. Her sober expression told me she'd already heard. "Valerie Kimmel—God, what a shock." She tossed her briefcase onto the extra chair, and swept back her dark hair. "Day, you must have had quite a morning of it."

"When I spotted Val's name on the sign outside the house, I was looking forward to catching up with her. Then to find her dead like that—" I lifted my hands, palms up to demonstrate my bewilderment.

Rhonda looked up at Polly. "With both Valerie and you being in real estate, you must have known her fairly well," she said.

Polly gave a slight snort. "Too well. I'm sorry she's dead and all that, but I can't pretend I ever liked her. I still remember how in high school I got my A in Biology by turning in all the extra credit assignments. There was Valerie who couldn't tell a zygote from a billy goat, and all it cost her was no underwear and a front row seat."

Rhonda and I exchanged glances. Trust Polly not to varnish her opinion, even in the face of a murder.

"Valerie wasn't stupid, you know," Rhonda said. "It was more that she always took the easy way out."

"That didn't change any as she got older," Polly replied. "After all, she was one of the reasons I left SandScapes Realty."

Our server slid a napkin and my margarita in front of me. Polly ordered a gin and tonic, then softened her expression. "I didn't leave there entirely because of Val. After Compton Ballard bought the agency from Paul Sands, I was ready to get out. Paul had been such a straight shooter and Ballard's business ethics were a 180-degree opposite."

"Apparently Ballard hasn't changed his stripes either. Carl Bailey just told me about his scheme to slip through the rezoning of the old Coronado golf course."

"That's typical of the way Ballard works," Polly said. "I was already looking around for something else after he bought the business. Then Valerie started working there, and suddenly the plum listings got handed to her. It didn't take long to figure that with her bonging the boss I'd always get the leftovers."

"All else aside," Rhonda said, "Valerie certainly didn't deserve to die like that."

Polly leaned in to give me an inquisitive look. "How was she killed, Day? I've heard nothing but rumors. Some say she was strangled, others that she was shot . . . ."

I shrugged. "All I know is that the Medical Examiner said there was blunt force trauma to the back of her skull. No sign of a weapon."

The memory of Valerie lying on the floor reminded me of something, and I asked Polly, "Do you remember if Val usually wore jewelry when she was working?"

A squint formed little lines across Polly's forehead. "Even at work Val was particular about her appearance, always coordinated what she was wearing with the right accessories. As I recall, she had some stunning jewelry, the real stuff. Why do you ask?"

"I thought it odd that when we found her she wasn't wearing a necklace. No watch, either, although there was a lighter band of skin on her wrist where a watch would have been. But if stealing her jewelry was the killer's motive, I wondered why she still had on earrings. They looked like real gold."

Rhonda raised an index finger. "The killer may not have wanted to stick around long enough to try to remove them. We all have pierced ears, right? It's not that easy for someone else to take off earrings when the posts go through your earlobe."

Polly removed the slice of lime perched on the rim of her glass and squeezed it into her drink, releasing its tart smell. "Hard to believe someone would kill her for the jewelry. She was smart enough to hand over anything an attacker demanded."

"I hope *you're* careful," Rhonda told her.

Polly blew out an exasperated breath. "Of course I am; Giles sees to that. He's been on the phone to me every fifteen minutes since he heard about Val's death—"Do I lock my car doors?" . . . "Why don't I get a gun permit?" . . . "Maybe I should hire a bodyguard."

Rhonda and I rolled our eyes at each other. Giles Sheffield, ever the devoted husband, could be expected to go overboard where his precious Polly was concerned.

After we'd given the waiter our orders—Polly the grouper, Rhonda and I the grilled shrimp—Polly went on, "Every real estate agent in town is seriously spooked. Some of my agents remember the creep who stalked and murdered three real estate women in Jacksonville."

"That happened while I was working in Atlanta," I said, "but I remember everyone talking about how the man was somebody you'd never have picked from a lineup. Mister Nice . . . another Ted Bundy."

Polly retrieved her lime slice and gave it another squeeze. "One of my agents actually met that man," she said. "According to her, he was well dressed, very polite. Gave a really convincing story about how his company had just transferred him, how anxious he was to find a home so his wife and kids could join him. He even showed pictures of his 'family'."

Rhonda shuddered. "How can women in real estate ever

protect themselves against creeps like that? Especially since most agencies post pictures of their agents."

Polly took a sip of her drink before answering, "Our office has definite procedures. For instance—"

"Wait a minute." I reached for my bag. "Let me get this down."

Polly paused for me to pull out my cellphone and click on the recorder app. "First off," she said, "You never meet with a client without letting the office know where you will be and who you'll be showing the property to. Secondly, any time there's the least doubt about a client, you take along another agent."

"Safety in numbers," Rhonda murmured.

Polly continued, "You always keep your cell phone with you and turned on. You either have a dedicated button for 911 or else you punch in 911 and don't hit 'Send.' That way, in an emergency you can summon help fast."

"What about open houses?" I asked. "You can't control who will show up at those."

Polly nodded. "What I tell my agents is, if you're alone at an open house and a prospect shows up who's making you nervous, you make an obvious call to the office and say, 'I'm at such-and-such an address so bring the contracts here. I'll see you in about five minutes.' That lets the prospect know someone's on the way and alerts the office that there's a potential problem."

Polly ticked off more rules on her blunt, but nicely manicured fingers. "Next thing I teach my agents is, when showing a house to a client, you follow them and keep a distance between you. Never enter a bedroom, den or other enclosed room, but allow the client to enter while you watch from the hallway. Know where each exit is located, and make sure that the doors are unlocked."

"Ready for a fast getaway."

"Right. Along with that, I tell them to park their car where it can't be blocked in and to keep their car keys where they are easily accessible."

When Polly finished, Rhonda sighed, "And I thought selling real estate was such safe, pleasant work."

"Believe me," Polly's manner was grim, "it only takes one scary incident to convince an agent to take those rules seriously. But look, you two—we came here to eat and I, for one, am famished. And tired. This week has been a real downer. Two of my agents on vacation, a closing that nearly crashed, and Friday I practically had to throw two guys out of my office."

"Trouble?" I said.

"Agents for a big New York developer wanting to buy my land, Grandma'am's place. When I explained very nicely that I wasn't even slightly interested, one of them pulled a sheet of paper off my desk, scribbled something on it, folded it ever so carefully, then passed it to me as if he were Santa Claus handing a present to an eager kiddie."

"An offer?"

Polly nodded. "That's when I escorted them to the door and pointed them toward New York. I wasn't named after Grandma'am Pauline to grow up a shrinking violet."

The smiles over Polly's story chased away some of the gloom from the news of Valerie's death. It also brought up reminiscences of the teenage fun the three of us had had at Ribideaux Point, kayaking on the river, swimming from the dock, racing around through the woods. "Only you two didn't play fair, both of you on ponies, me trying to keep up on my bike," I mocked.

Polly clucked her tongue. "Day McKelvey—ever the chicken when it comes to anything with hooves."

Rhonda said. "Val was there a couple of times, too. Remember how she loved my pony and didn't want to do anything except ride?"

"Not that that father of hers allowed her much chance to get away from home," Polly said. "I've always had this nasty feeling—"

She didn't go on, but we knew what she meant.

"The thing I remember most is how your Grandma'am

would call us in for tea on the veranda," I added wistfully. "Her scones were to die for."

During dinner—our shrimp came with the special datil pepper dipping sauce for which the Harpoon was famous—we avoided discussing that tragedy, instead catching up on each other's doings since we'd last met and finding many reasons to smile.

At a time like that, it felt good to have the three of us together, once again sharing our lives, our hopes, even our misadventures and disappointments. Each year that passed, it became more difficult for the three of us to spend time together. College, career changes, the interruptions of marriages (one each for Rhonda and me, two for Polly) divorces (one each for Polly and me), and children (one, Rhonda's son, Kevin) all combined to send us on separate ways. Luckily, there was always the phone and the internet to keep us in contact.

Both Rhonda and Polly knew about my on-again, off-again relationship with Sam Stansfield, and both had tried to advise me that an affair with a married cop was never going to lead anywhere. The truth they offered had been too hard to accept. It had taken Sam's gunshot wound to end it for us. Afterwards, despite my resistance, Rhonda had cajoled her husband into setting up a date for me with Andy Thompson, and she's been cheerleading that still-uncertain relationship ever since.

Looking around the table, I thought once again how odd it was that we'd become so close, each of us as different in personality as in looks. Polly still carried a bit of that stand-offish defiance Rhonda and I saw in her the day she first appeared in the cafeteria at Usina High. Newly orphaned when her parents were both killed while climbing a mountain in Nepal, she'd come to St. Augustine to live with her grandmother, Pauline Ribideaux. I can still recall that cafeteria odor of spaghetti sauce and teenaged bodies and the tang of the mustard on my ham sandwich that first day Polly appeared and stood for a long moment, tray in hand, looking from table to table. Rhonda, with her usual quickness to spot someone in need, signaled her to come sit with us. By the time lunch was over, we had a new friend.

And Polly needed friends. She tended to intimidate the other students with her off-the-charts IQ and her unconcern for social skills. Some people found her abrasive, but that was only because she didn't know how to be anything other than straightforward and honest.

Rhonda, despite her gentle demeanor, was always the stable center of our group—held a stable job as Clerk of the Courts, enjoyed a stable marriage to super-nice Rick Williams, and provided stable mothering to seven-year-old Kevin. Rhonda's beauty is the sort that sneaks in under the radar, a soft sort of prettiness like Katherine Grayson in *Anchors Aweigh.* But anyone who looked closer soon realized that hair a color somewhere between wheat and orange blossom honey and lucid blue-green eyes plus a Georgia peach complexion added up to beyond attractive. She was the tranquil one of our trio, the arbiter of disputes. When there was controversy, she listened without comment and then surprised everyone with an observation that placed the issue squarely in perspective. Some people would say that's because she's ultra- smart, but I'd say it's because of the high-speed connection between her brain and her heart.

And where would I place myself? The physical part was easy—a hundred fifteen pounds, five-four, at least in two-inch heels. My mother, Zanthia, says I should be grateful for hair so blond it's almost white. "That's the *in* color in New York," she tells me. Which doesn't do me much good, seeing that I live in St. Augustine, Florida.

Eyes I list as green on my driver's license, although a certain police lieutenant once referred to them as "opaline" because they tend to change color in different lights.

As for temperament, I have to admit that I tend to spring to conclusions a bit too quickly, and I often fail to conceal my feelings when it might be more diplomatic to do so. On the other hand, I'm not afraid to put myself out on a limb for issues about which I have strong feelings.

Professional qualifications? A keen eye for details, decent writing style, dogged inquisitiveness (which sometimes may be regarded as nosiness) and the ability to read writing that's upside down. I love my job, and *First Coast Dispatch* is a great little regional newspaper struggling to stay alive in the age of techno-readers.

After our dinners were cleared away, Polly, Rhonda and I decided that one dessert to split was all we could handle. We signaled our waiter. "You're in luck, ladies, he said. "Our chef has a special on the Bananas Foster tonight and they're to die for."

I lighted with anticipation. I always enjoy the drama of the waiter wheeling in the platter of sautéed bananas and pouring rum over them before touching his lighter to the dish and setting it on fire. A whoosh of flame, the scent of rum-soaked bananas and anticipation of a special treat—what's not to love?

As we waited for dessert to arrive, Rhonda reached into her bag for pen and pad. "Before we leave, let's decide on the destination for our next getaway."

Our custom of an All-Girls' Getaway for our combined July birthdays started in high school. Over the years it had become an unbreakable tradition, no matter how busy our lives might be—except for that one dreadful year when Polly's first marriage ended in disaster and her beloved Grandma'am died just weeks later.

Polly pretended to be annoyed as she punched in the calendar on her cell phone. "God, Rhonda, it's early June. We decided on the weekend of July 19th and that's still over 6 weeks away. We're all turning thirty-six fast enough. Why speed the process?"

We debated for a while and tentatively decided on a trip to Tarpon Springs, a quaint town on Florida's Gulf side, where sponge divers still plied their trade.

"So Tarpon Springs it is," Rhonda noted in her pad. "I'll check into reservations, find us a nice bed and breakfast."

The Bananas Foster had disappeared and we were in the middle of divvying up the tab when a musical chime interrupted. Polly pulled her cell phone from her bag, checked the number, then held up a finger to us as she answered. "Hi, honey."

Knowing that Giles and Polly's love fest would last forever, Rhonda and I stood, tossed our share of the bill on the table and blew air kisses to Polly and each other. Rhonda headed toward the ladies room. I wove my way back past the bar crowd and out into the still-muggy darkness of the June night.

I was fumbling in my bag for my keys as I approached the far end of the Harpoon's parking lot. Suddenly out of the darkness a male voice ordered, "Hold it right there, Lady!"

CHAPTER 4

Sam Stansfield stepped from between two cars and I staggered backward like a puppet whose string had just snapped. My heart took off on a wild flutter, partly from fright, partly from other emotions. "Jesus, Sam!" I rasped. "What are you doing here?"

He gave a derisive snort. "First off, suppose I were an attacker? You ought to have had your keys out before you left the building and you should be carrying them with the sharp edge outward between your fingers the way I showed you. Second off, what's the idea of wandering alone through a dark parking lot?"

Fright gave way to annoyance. "Did you show up here just to lecture me about keys and parking lots?"

Sam flicked his chin upward. "Seems like you could use a few personal safety reminders. But no, I just happened to be passing the Harpoon, saw your Jeep and thought maybe we could . . ."

"Sam, there is no 'we'. As for the 'could,' that's out, too. I don't think either of us wants to—"

He made a flapping gesture to wave off my resistance. "Hold it, will you? Look, I saw the report that came in on the Valerie Kimmel murder and noticed that you had found the body."

"Actually, it was Everett Peabody, our copy editor, who spotted her first."

"Anyhow, I wanted to make sure you were okay."

"I'm fine." My words sounded stiff and awkward. I knew I should jump into my Jeep and speed away from there before things got complicated again. My head said go, but my feet stayed glued in place. My tongue wasn't working too well, either. I wanted to strike back, "How's Diana?" to remind Sam he was married, but instead I just stood there while the tarry smell of the parking lot's still warm asphalt rose around us.

Sam seemed to read my thought. "Don't know if you heard," he said, "but I've been batching it for over a month now."

"Batching it as in bachelor?" Soon as I asked, I wished I could take back the question. Sam's status, marital or otherwise, was no longer my business. Things between me and Andy Thompson seemed to be going well, and I planned to keep it that way. At least that's what my head was saying. My feet still hadn't gotten the message.

Sam had come into my life two years before and nothing since had been the same. It happened when he was lead investigator on the case of a serial killer and I was reporting on the case for the paper. After a long exhausting night of interrogation, Sam had broken the case and the killer confessed. We went to celebrate with a few drinks. That's when the feelings we'd been repressing broke their restraints. We fell in love. Fell into bed. Fell into a relationship that could lead nowhere. Sam was tied to a bipolar wife who had him convinced that if he left her she'd end her life.

For too long after our affair began, I'd clung to Sam, tethered by the intense emotions our attachment generated. Wherever I was, he was always right there at the edge of my consciousness . . . and my conscience. I allowed him to enter my life to an extent that cut me off from other relationships, from other men, even from my friends.

Unlike Cary Grant and Deborah Kerr in that old classic, *An Affair to Remember,* I did not end up in a wheelchair as atonement for my sins; it was Sam who suffered when he was wounded in a shoot-out. The price I paid was that I wasn't even able to visit him in the hospital—it was his wife who was there at his bedside, her hand in his, his eyes fastened on her.

If it hadn't been for Rhonda and Polly to provide the ballast when my ship of romance capsized, I'd have drowned in anger and remorse. The memory of those awful months stiffened my resolve. "I've got to go," I said. "It's late."

Sam seemed to perceive that any weakening on my part had vanished. "C'mon," he said, "I'll walk you the rest of the way to the Jeep. Sorry if I scared you back there, but I was just thinking about . . ."

One look at my face and he went silent, only touching my arm lightly as we started toward my Jeep. When I noticed he was walking with a slight limp, mixed feelings began churning inside me, the regrets and might-have-beens.

We reached the spot where I'd parked my vehicle. Sam waited next to the driver's side window after I'd climbed in behind the wheel and started the motor. I kept expecting him to try to persuade me to stay or to take him with me. He did neither, and that made it even harder to back out and drive away.

CHAPTER 5

Monday got off to a sluggish start after a night of dreams in which Sam Stansfield featured too prominently. Soon as I arrived at the office, double-shot latte in hand, Shel asked how my background piece on Valerie Kimmel was progressing. I told him I'd phoned to set up an interview with Valerie's boss, Compton Ballard, and while I was at SandScapes I'd be talking to her co-workers. "I've also got to dig out her family history."

Before leaving the *Dispatch* office, I stopped by Everett Peabody's desk. "I'm sorry our trip yesterday had such a nasty ending," I told him.

Everett shoved away from his screen. "That poor girl. How could anyone—"

"Hopefully the police will catch whoever killed her. A shame that it's spoiled your house hunt."

"You liked that house, didn't you?"

"I didn't have much chance—I mean, what we saw seemed nice."

He stared wistfully off into the distance. "I think Maple

would have loved it."

*****

At SandScapes Realty, I parked in one of the marked spaces. At the beach on the opposite side of the boulevard, a family strolled across the sand, the father with a beach umbrella tucked under one arm and a little boy of about three riding on his shoulders. The morning breeze molded the mother's sheer cover-up against her body, and a preteen girl danced alongside, clutching a boogie board.

I slid out from the driver's seat and exited the Jeep, slamming its door shut with a little more force than necessary. At age thirty-five I still hadn't formed the kind of ties that make a family. With Sam, that could never happen. If things worked out between Andy and me, there would be a ready-made family, his two little girls. I tried to picture us heading for the beach, the children in tow. That thought both intrigued and terrified me.

Inside the real estate office, a nameplate on the reception desk identified the somewhat overweight woman behind it— *Cindy Kaufman.* Cindy's back was to me as she babbled excitedly on the phone, pausing to snatch tissues from a floral-patterned box. From her conversation, it was obvious she was giving the person on the other end an embroidered version of her own role in the murder investigation.

While she nattered on with an I'll-be-with-you-in-a-minute wave in my direction, I checked out SandScapes's office layout. The reception desk occupied the right half of the front area. To the left, a cluster of upholstered chairs and a caramel colored leather sofa provided a comfortable seating area for clients. Brochures splayed on a large glass coffee table enticed prospective buyers with color photographs of the company's listings.

Beyond the reception area, four or five cubicles similar to those in the newspaper office lined the right side with two rows of desks in the center. That morning, only about half were in use. Beyond the desk area, a wide hallway led to what appeared to be several private offices. A water fountain and two copy machines occupied the more open area along the room's left side. A repairman was working on one of the machines, crouched down on his haunches. His t-shirt failed to stretch far enough below the waist to hide his broad back, and his low slung jeans provided a generous view of the crack between his cheeks.

The man muttered grunts and curses as he attempted to dislodge papers stuck inside the machine's mechanism. From time to time reached behind him to toss torn and wrinkled scraps in the general direction of a wastebasket. It was not my business, but no one else was witnessing his carelessness, so I took a few steps, bent down and picked up the ink-blackened remnants of what appeared to be some sort of financial records. Careful to hold them with my fingertips, I very pointedly dropped them in the wastebasket. The man turned around and glanced at me, but failed to take the hint. With a tissue from my bag I wiped the sticky ink residue off my fingers and turned back to the reception desk.

Cindy, noticing my impatient expression, hung up the phone. In the process, her elbow bumped her Styrofoam coffee cup, sending a slosh of liquid across the desk to dribble onto the floor. When she leaned over to mop up the spill with a wad of tissues, it was obvious from the dark roots showing along her part that she needed a serious touchup if she planned to continue as a blonde.

I showed her my press ID. "I have an appointment with Mr. Ballard. Is he in?"

Still mopping away, Cindy jerked her head toward the office hallway at the rear. "He came straight here from the airport. You can't see him right now—he's in there with the police detectives." She snatched up more tissues, this time to dab at her eyes. "It's so . . . so *horrible*. You just never know, do you? That could have been any one of us. I'm having my husband pick me up from work, I'm that terrified."

In spite of Cindy's dabbing and her teary voice, it was evident she was basking in the fifteen minutes of fame Valerie's murder had brought her. As a reporter, I'd met plenty of people who, like Cindy, relished the attention that trailed along behind any calamitous event.

"Did you know Valerie Kimmel well?" I asked.

"Oh, indeed yes. Miss Kimmel, she was wonderful. The last person in world you expect to get . . . to get—"

"So you've known her for quite some time?"

Cindy's answer came a little more reluctantly. "I only started here three weeks ago, but I could tell she was, you know, nice . . . somebody special."

I indicated the double row of desks. "Which was hers?"

"Oh, no. Miss Kimmel has . . . she had her own private office." She gestured again toward the rear of the room. "Hers is the middle one on the left between Mr. Ballard's office and our bookkeeper, Harry Ports."

Mention of Valerie's now-vacant office brought more Cindy tears, but between dabs with the tissues she was eyeing me, eager for more questions.

"When did you last see Miss Kimmel?" I asked.

She bobbed her head knowingly. "That would be Saturday afternoon. She was here for a while, then left for a showing, saying she'd be back later. I'm here until three and she was already gone by then."

"Was anyone else here in the office when you left?"

"Most everyone was out. I believe it was just Elaine Descuto and Nick Petroski."

"Are they here now?"

"Mrs. Descuto's over there." She pointed to a small woman with graying hair and a pleasant expression whose desk was midway between the reception area and the rear offices.

"And Mr. Petroski?"

"He called to say he was writing up a listing this morning and would be in later."

I told Cindy she'd been tremendously helpful. At Elaine Descuto's desk, I introduced myself and said how sorry I was for the loss of Valerie.

"It's come as such a terrible shock," Mrs. Descuto said. "I keep looking back there at her office and expect her to come through the door. And to have it happen here in St. Augustine where it's always seemed so safe." As she spoke, Elaine Descuto unconsciously reached for the small framed photograph of four children that sat on her desk.

"Cute family, Mrs. Descuto. How old are they?" I asked, knowing that giving a parent the opportunity to talk about his or her offspring usually helped put them at ease.

"Elaine, please, and do have a seat," she said, her eyes lighting as she pointed to the smallest child. "Emily—she just started preschool this year. Loves it, loves her teacher. All I hear at home is 'Miss Linda this, Miss Linda that' until I'm almost jealous. Next to Emily is Will. He's seventeen and is planning to go to Georgia Tech next year. Alexis is next to him—she's our family athlete, the star of her college's lacrosse team. And the tall one at the end is Denny." Here Elaine hesitated as if needing to find a positive spin for Denny.

"Handsome young man," I supplied.

"He is, isn't he, handsome, I mean. I'm hoping he'll soon go back to college, but when his father left—"

Moisture swelled in Elaine's eyes and she swiped her hand across her cheek. "I'm sorry. This terrible business is all so upsetting to everybody."

I suspected that it was more than Valerie's murder that had this nice woman upset. In fact, I could mentally map out her family's situation—three practically grown children, a husband who'd "found himself" at middle age, or rather found a "her," a failed attempt to mend the marriage with another child. Now here she was in what I estimated to be her mid-to-late forties, obliged to be both mother and father to a son who could not accept the breakup.

Note to self: Good reason not to get carried away with visions of marital bliss.

To steer away from that subject, I asked, "Do you recall anything Miss Kimmel mentioned to you when you were in the office together on Saturday?"

Elaine stared at me across her desktop with a thoughtful frown. "Just that on Sunday morning she was showing a client one of her listings. After that she said she was looking forward to saddling up her horse for a long trail ride."

"Would she have come into the office on Sunday before meeting her client?"

Elaine tilted her head. "More likely she'd have gone directly to the house. Val always arrived early at the site where she was showing a property, made sure the A/C was set right, the lights were on, draperies opened, blinds were straightened, everything in order. If she did come here first, our security system would show whether she checked in that morning. It automatically records who comes in and what time."

"So each time you enter the building it's recorded?"

"Only during hours when the office is normally locked. It's voice recognition and all we have to do is announce our name, not like the old system that required us to carry two extra keys. After Mr. Petroski was hired he suggested the change and, in fact, he even installed it for us. He said our old system was so obsolete that a five-year old could break in. I guess he'd know. He worked for a local security firm before he came here."

I noted the information about the security system records, although I expected the police would have already checked on that.

"How long had you known Miss Kimmel?" I asked.

"I've worked here two years, so I've known her for that length of time."

"Would you mind telling me your impression of her?"

Elaine shifted the folder on her desk then returned it to its former position before answering. "Valerie was very dedicated to her work and a very effective agent. As Mr. Ballard's second in command, she kept the office very well organized. I respected her ability."

I gave Elaine Descuto a ten for diplomacy, and pictured Everett Peabody's horror should he ever encounter the word "very"—his particular nemesis—so many times in one statement. After thanking her, I went on to speak with the other agents.

"Valerie," one agent said. "A shame. No, can't say I knew her well. Most of the time she worked closely with Mister Ballard." The flatness of the woman's tone told me that Valerie had been no favorite of hers.

One of the women offered a more positive assessment of Valerie. "When I was just starting, she gave me some good pointers on make-up and how to dress so I'd look more professional," the woman said.

Generous in sharing her professional expertise with other staff members, I noted.

Another contributed the information that Valerie kept a keen eye on expenses. "We often joked that if a paper clip was missing she'd notice it. And just let anyone touch the thermostat. We could sit here with sweat pouring down our backs and she wouldn't lower the A/C one degree."

Diligent in conserving office resources.

Another agent offered, "She was really into riding. Spent as much time as she could out at Hunting Ridge Stables where she boards her horse. Blue Sky Boy, he's called. A pretty name, don't you think?"

I was pulling up directions to the farm on my phone when the entrance door swung open and a man entered. He was wearing a business suit and carrying a briefcase. His appearance would have been unremarkable—medium build, rather sharp features, brown hair going bald at the crown—except for a deep depression above his left temple. The skin covering it looked as if it had been pulled taut and was paler that the rest of his facial skin. I wondered if he'd been in an accident.

He stopped at the reception desk, pulled a sheaf of papers

from his briefcase and, with an authoritative gesture, shoved it across the counter to Cindy. I was close enough to hear him say, "I want three copies of this pronto. Bring them to me in my office as soon as they're ready."

Cindy rose to take the papers, but pointed to the copiers. "Is this all black and white, Mr. Ports? The color copier is jammed again."

"No. It's color." The man swung around, noticed the repairman, and strode over to the machine and stooped to snatch up one of the sheets littering the floor. When he glanced down at the paper he was holding, his countenance underwent an abrupt change. "What the hell! Who in blazes—" he demanded and turned to Cindy who had followed him to the copier.

His reaction startled Cindy, causing her to draw back. "It was like this when I tried to use it this morning. But we're getting it fixed."

The repairman, now on his knees, glanced up as he dug a few final scraps from between the machine's rollers. "'S okay, boss, I'm done here soon as I put this panel back."

The man Cindy had called Mr. Ports snarled something at the repairman then bent and began scooping all the scraps into the wastebasket. When the last scrap was retrieved, he snatched up the container and hurried off toward the rear offices, ignoring that both Cindy and I were gaping after him.

"Is something wrong?" I asked her.

She lifted both shoulders. "You tell me," she said. "Mr. Ports gets upset if anybody messes around in his office—doesn't even let the cleaning people in there, but I've never seen him go off like that before over some little thing."

It did seem a lot of fuss over a jammed copier, but then the murder was bound to have everyone on edge. Cindy returned to her desk to answer the phone and when she hung up she called to me, "That was Mr. Ballard. He said the officers are leaving and please be ready with your questions as he can only give you a few minutes of his time."

CHAPTER 6

One of the office doors at the SandScapes rear hallway opened and three men emerged. From his photo on the *Dispatch's* real estate pages, I recognized Compton Ballard. He looked exhausted, his eyes red-rimmed and his jowls sagged in fleshy folds. He appeared to be in his late fifties, paunchy, about five-eight or five-nine and well past the point where the custom tailoring of his Armani suit could conceal an expanding waistline.

Of the two men who accompanied Ballard, one was in uniform, the other plainclothes but with that unmistakable air of authority a badge bestows. When they reached the client area, they each gave Ballard a brief handshake then turned and left the building, walking with a brisk stride as if they were doctors intent on delivering a transplant heart.

Now that Compton Ballard was alone, I approached and introduced myself. "Everyone at the *Dispatch* is sorry for the loss of Miss Kimmel," I told him. "I just need to ask you a few questions about her."

He sighed. "You and the whole world. All I've done since I red-eyed it back last night is answer questions. But go on back." He motioned me toward his office. "Be with you soon as I give my secretary this number to call."

I entered his office and before seating myself, took a moment to look around—often surroundings say more about a person than an interview reveals. In Compton Ballard's office, one entire wall of shelves was filled with golf trophies, golf award certificates and framed score cards. A place of honor was given to a golf ball mounted on a base with the inscription, *Hole in One, Satsuma Country Club, July 12, 2008.* Several walls were devoted to signed photos of Ballard with various celebrity golfers he had been paired with in pro-am tournaments. Thanks to my former husband, Derek, who, like many professional football players, was also a golf addict, I recognized a number of the names. I'd also learned from Derek that the fees paid for that honor could be quite steep.

On the wall behind the massive desk that dominated the office's center three framed black-and-white headshots of Compton Ballard were displayed, each poster-sized image a slightly different pose. His Grecian Formula comb-over was prominent in all three.

When Ballard entered, I was still examining the photos. "These are from my press conference when I swung the deal for the Preston Office Complex three years ago." A diamond the size of a Brazil nut glimmered on his outstretched hand as he pointed to the photo on the left, the one in which his chin was cupped in one hand, his face arranged in a thoughtful expression. "That one," he said, "is Ballard listening to a question from the *Wall Street Journal* reporter."

The pointing finger moved to indicate the middle photo where, head cocked and eyes slightly squinted, he held two fingers to his cheek. "Here, Ballard thinks before responding." He paused dramatically before pointing to the third pose, a frowning, head-on shot in which his index finger aimed toward an unseen audience. "Here Ballard responds to the *Wall Street Journal* reporter's question."

Then, apparently satisfied that he'd made a sufficient impression—I got the message from his reverent pronouncement of *Wall Street Journal*—he arranged himself in the maroon leather chair behind the desk and indicated I could take the less ornate one in front. I seated myself, wondering if our entire interview was going to be conducted in third person.

His kingly chair offered Ballard the impression of greater height and substance, an effect that his stocky build and short stumpy legs undermined when he was standing. Perhaps I tend to read too much into such physical manifestations as eye blinks and cheek twitches, but the way Ballard's glance swept back and forth, his eyes never quite meeting mine, convinced me he wasn't all that he represented himself to be. A self-made man was my guess, needing to inflate his achievements to compensate for some lack in his background.

Note to self: Dangerous to jump too quickly to such conclusions, but equally dangerous to ignore them entirely.

"You must be very proud of your accomplishments," I offered for openers. "I gather Valerie Kimmel had been with you for quite some time."

"Valerie is . . . was . . . a wonderful asset to my firm," he said with the most sincerity in his voice I'd heard so far. "Real girl Friday. Smart cookie, too. Times when I had to be gone, like this past week, I could rely on her to take over, handle the office. You should say in your article that she was my personal assistant."

"Did she seem at all nervous or upset at the time you left for Salt Lake City?"

Ballard twisted the hunk of diamond on his ring finger. "I've been wracking my Goddamn brains out all the way back from Salt Lake, trying to figure out what might have happened to her. Only thing I can come up with is this is some pervert looking for an easy target."

"Do you feel Valerie would have been an easy target?"

The question paused him. "Actually . . . no. Val always carried her cell phone, and when she was showing properties she was careful to let someone know where she'd be."

"Did she do that on the day of the murder?"

"Hard to say, it being a Sunday. The cops are checking the security records to see if she stopped by the office before her appointment. If she did, Nick Petroski's the only other agent likely to be in here at that time. Not unusual to find him here at nine o'clock at night or seven, eight of a morning. Not like some of the people who get into this business thinking, hell, I can do real estate in my spare time, work when I feel like it, take off any time I choose."

To pull him back on topic, I asked, "Can you tell me when was the last time you talked to Valerie?"

Again the head tilt, his "thinking" pose. "She phoned me several times while I was in Salt Lake," Ballard said. "Office business. Far as I remember, the last time was late Saturday afternoon. Yes, Saturday. Around two."

"That would have been the day before she was killed?"

He nodded.

"Anything in particular she called about?"

"The usual. Filled me in on progress on a couple of our listings. Talked about which houses our Sunday TV ad would feature. Said her closing on Friday went as planned."

Ballard stopped and sat thinking for a moment. The expression that flicked across his face made me ask, "Was there anything else?"

He shook his head. "No. That was it. But then later that evening, while I was at dinner she tried to call again. My cell phone had a lousy connection, and there was a lot of noise in the restaurant. Far as I could make out, Val was trying to tell me that she'd seen something going on here in the office that upset her, but before she could say more, we lost the connection."

"No hint what she was referring to?"

He shrugged. "Something about the copy machine. I figured either it had jammed or maybe somebody was using it to copy personal documents." He paused and pointed out the door in the general direction of the broken copier. "Val gets . . . that is, she used to get upset about anyone using it for personal stuff, especially the color copier since supplies for that have gone sky high. Same if anyone tinkered with the A/C setting or if any desk lights were left on at night."

Further questions brought little additional information. When I left Ballard's office, I stopped by the reception desk to ask Cindy for a list of all the company's agents. While I was waiting, a middle-aged man with a pale, acne-scarred complexion entered. He carried himself with unusual erectness that gave him an almost military bearing, but his gait was slightly off center. Then I noticed he was wearing a built-up shoe on his right foot.

Cindy informed me that this was Nick Petroski, the other agent who had been in the office with Valerie on Saturday afternoon. I waited until he was settled at his desk, then introduced myself and explained that I was gathering information about Valerie Kimmel for the newspaper. "I'll only take a couple of minutes of your time—" Not giving him a chance to refuse, I seated myself on the chair next to his desk.

After a moment's hesitation, he said, "I doubt I can be of help. Miss Kimmel, she was not someone I knew very well."

He spoke in rather stilted phrases with just the slightest accent. I guessed his age at somewhere in the mid to late thirties His ethnicity I guessed to be Polish, judging from his name. Except for that limp, everything about Nick Petroski seemed precise—the crispness of his collar, the exact centering of his tie, the way he sat at his desk, spine straight and shoulders squared perfectly level. Although wearing civilian clothes, he gave the impression of being in uniform. Tinted glasses made it impossible to tell the exact color of his eyes, either gray or blue. I wondered about the built-up shoe and remembered a friend of Dad's who'd had polio as a child and wore a shoe like that.

"How long had you worked with Miss Kimmel?" I asked him.

He frowned as if considering, then reached for a pen from the Baltimore Orioles mug on his desktop. I noticed he used his left hand and wondered if he was naturally left-handed or whether whatever had caused the crippling of his right foot had also affected that entire side of his body. He placed the pen's tip of it against his chin, a gesture oddly reminiscent of Compton Ballard's pose in photo number two. "About nine months," he announced finally. "I came to work at SandScapes last September. Yes. Nine months." He replaced the pen as if it had done its work and could be retired.

"I understand you were here in the office on Saturday afternoon when she—"

His phone interrupted. With an apologetic nod in my direction, he picked it up. "Yes?" he said. I saw a flush rise from his collar as the sound of his caller's raised voice echoed from the receiver. Nick responded haltingly, "Are you sure?" He looked at me, then turned and lowered his voice. "I really can't talk now. I have someone in my office." A few nods of the head. "Yes, well, we can talk about it as soon as I'm free."

In order not to appear intrusive, while he was talking I checked the framed picture on the desktop in front of me, which, except for the Orioles mug filled with pens, was his desk's only ornament. It wasn't a photograph of a wife or family as I might have expected—it was a framed baseball card. The player looked vaguely familiar, but then I'm not a fan of that most all-American of sports.

Before I could scan my memory for the player's face, Nick hung up the phone and said with an apologetic nod, "You were asking me—"

"I was wondering if on Saturday afternoon you noticed anything unusual about Miss Kimmel's behavior."

He lifted the phone and replaced it as if checking that it was securely on its stand or perhaps to allow himself time to consider my question. "Not that I can recall. She was here for a while and then left, but I'm afraid I wasn't aware of the time."

After a few more questions to which he offered no information of value, I rose and thanked him for his time. As I left, the sloppy repairman had already gone and Cindy was using the machine which now clicked away as it spewed forth the pages she was feeding.

On the drive back to the office I was thinking about my Dad who'd also been a baseball fan like Nick Petroski. He, too, had treasured his baseball card collection and sometimes he and I would lay them all out, lining them up by teams. That's when it came to me—Brooks Robinson, the Oriole baseball player—that was his picture on Nick Petroski's desk. I mentally high-fived myself for the connection.

CHAPTER 7

At the end of a long farm lane a sign lettered in forest green on a white background hung from a post:

HUNTING RIDGE STABLES
Haley Simms, Proprietor
HORSES BOARDED
RIDING LESSONS and PONY CLASSES
English and Western

The Jeep's tires crunched on gravel as I swung the wheel to the right and proceeded past brown four-board fences that bordered fields of summer-browned grass. In the middle of one pasture, several horses were gathered next to a concrete watering trough while others sought shelter from the sun under an oasis of live oaks that cast a shade so deep it was almost black.

Ahead were farm buildings, a rambling ranch house swaddled by giant oaks with a complex of sheds and stables nearby. At the end of the lane I parked next to a riding ring where a girl of about ten or eleven was galloping a dappled pony round and round. Each time the girl leaned forward approaching a jump, my stomach constricted, relaxing only after she'd cleared the jump and straightened in the saddle. My seeress mother, Zanthia, says my fear of horses started with a pony ride at a carnival when I was three. I have no recollection of that event, but to this day I'm a sissy when it comes to any hoofed animal bigger than a baby goat.

A tall, gaunt woman of about middle age stood inside the ring, her graying locks pulled back into a no-nonsense ponytail. Without taking her eyes from the young rider, the woman raised a hand in my direction. As she signaled me, her wrist protruded from the sleeves of the oxford shirt she was wearing atop worn but well-cut jodhpurs and dusty Wellingtons.

She called instructions to the rider in a voice that matched the finishing school tones I'd heard when I phoned to request the interview. The little Jack Russell terrier at her feet scooted his energetic self beneath the fence to challenge me with a high-pitched bark that brought a sharp command from his mistress.

The rider took her final jump, the pounding of hoof beats ended and the woman turned her attention my way. "McKelvey?" When I nodded, she reached across the fence's top plank to take my hand in a strong, boney grip. "Haley Simms, just Haley will do."

"I'm Day. From the *Dispatch*."

"So you said on the phone. You've come about the Kimmel woman. Don't know if I can be of much help, but we'll talk when I'm done here. You go on over to the stables and wait."

Heeding her command, I headed in the direction she'd indicated. The Jack Russell trailed behind, occasionally circling to check me out from the front.

The stable that Haley Simms pointed me toward was an L-shaped structure with a covered walkway fronting a long row of box stalls on either wing. A small, wiry man was breaking apart a bale of hay and stuffing portions into the wall rack inside one of the stall openings. All along the row horses snuffled and tossed their manes, their noses poking expectantly over the plastic straps of the stall guards.

Grizzled hair and an arthritic gait marked the man as in his sixties, possibly even older. If he was aware of my approach, he gave no sign and continued to move down the row, heaping sweet-smelling alfalfa into each rack, all the while muttering to the horses in some language only he and they understood.

With huge watchful horse eyes peering at me from each stall, I remained at a safe distance. After the last hayrack was filled, the man whacked at the front of his jeans, sending dust and slivers of hay flying, then cut his eyes at me in a brief upward glance. "You lookin' for me?"

When I told him that I was a reporter and that I was interested in talking with anyone who had known Valerie Kimmel, he turned without a word, picked up a leather feed bucket, and walked away.

I tagged after him. "Mister . . . uh . . . I'm sorry, I didn't get your name."

"Arch," he said without turning.

"And your last name?"

He mumbled something that sounded like "beagle."

"Sorry. I didn't catch that."

"Fleagle." The word came out begrudgingly. "Arch is all you need call me."

"I just want—"

He turned and faced me. "Whatever the Kimmel woman was doing here was her business. All I ever done was help her saddle up a few times, put her tack away when she was done, stuff like that."

I nearly tripped over the still-circling Jack Russell. "Can you show me which was her horse?"

He flicked an arm toward the far line of stalls. "Down there—chestnut gelding with the white forehead blaze."

At the far end of the row, in the largest of the box stalls, I spotted a horse with a white patch on its face and I headed in that direction. I approached the stall warily. "Hello, horsey,"

I murmured and reached to stroke its nose. Suddenly the huge black beast gave a loud whinny and reared in its stall. I stumbled backward, nearly losing my balance.

Behind me, I heard Arch snicker. "Ganador sure as hell ain't no gelding. Ain't no chestnut neither."

Still quivering inside, I backed farther from the stall. "Is he dangerous?"

"You could say so. Not many that could handle him."

"Why would anyone want a horse like that?"

Another snicker from Arch. "Big, mean horse can make the fellow riding him feel pretty big himself."

Note to self: Is this an analogy with men who drive long-snouted sports cars?

With a begrudging motion, Arch led the way to the third stall from the end. I was relieved to see his face soften as he set the bucket on the ground and reached to stroke the animal's neck. "Steady up there, Sky, dinner's comin'."

The horse snuffled as if it understood.

"His name's Sky?" I asked.

"Blue Sky Boy. She always called him just Sky."

At the mention of his name, the horse whinnied and tossed his head. I reacted with a couple of quick backward steps.

Arch shot me a disdainful look. "Sky don't bite."

I inched forward and with great trepidation reached to stroke the horse's long snout. The skin there was surprisingly smooth and satiny, but when Sky's nostrils suddenly quivered, I jerked my hand away.

Seeing that Arch was about to walk off again, I improvised. "Sky's a beautiful horse. Did Ms. Kimmel come here often to ride?"

"Usually coupla times a week. Sky got so whenever Ganador went out on the trail he wanted to go, too."

I gave a small shudder. "So Miss Kimmel and Ganador's owner rode together?"

Arch scooped up the feed bucket and turned away. "You'll

have to ask Herself." He gave a curt nod toward where Haley Simms was making her way toward the stable. The girl walked beside her, leading her pony by its halter.

The Jack Russell abandoned me to go prancing at Haley's heels. When they reached the stable, the girl led her pony into one of the empty box stalls, and Haley gestured me toward a pile of straw bales under the overhang. "We can sit here while we talk."

I seated myself, shifting to avoid a stiff stubble that threatened to pierce my jeans. "I met Arch Fleagle," I told her. "He seems awfully fond of Blue Sky Boy, but wouldn't say much about Valerie."

Haley gave a wry chuckle and bent to scratch behind the dog's ears. "If you were a horse, he'd have plenty to tell you. Tends to avoid people."

"So what can you tell me about Valerie Kimmel?"

Haley slipped a piece of straw from the bale and creased it between her fingers. "Not much, I'm afraid, beyond that she's been coming here for riding lessons for a little over a year. Most of my students are little girls who are horse crazy until their hormones take over and then it's boys filling their heads. But I also take a few adults."

"Was Valerie a good rider?"

She paused a moment before answering: "When she first came out here, I was sure she would quit by the second lesson. But she sure loves Blue Sky Boy, and once she got into it, she became what I'd call a competent rider. Sat her horse well, but wasn't much interested in perfecting her technique beyond the basics. Later on, after—"

Haley broke off and bent to scratch the dog's ears again before she continued, "Later on she took to trail riding and lots of times came here to take Sky out for a gallop."

"Isn't it expensive to board and feed a big animal like that?"

"Don't think that was a concern for her—her boss paid the bills."

I kept my eyes on my notes to avoid revealing that her remark had startled me. "Compton Ballard? Did he ride, too?"

Haley shook her head. "Don't think the man had ever been on a horse. But every so often he'd come out here to watch her ride."

"So Mr. Ballard was spending money for the horse and its upkeep to come occasionally and watch Valerie ride?"

"Sounds somewhat dotty, doesn't it?" she said. "He told me once about this rich girl, a real good horsewoman, that he fell madly in love with when he was a teenager but she wouldn't give him the time of day. Maybe something in that accounted for his liking to watch his girlfriend ride."

"So he and Valerie were—"

"Whoa up! I didn't mean to imply anything." She rose abruptly, "Got to check that the girl rubbed her pony down good."

She disappeared inside the stall, but returned a couple of minutes later carrying a bridle. She seated herself and began rubbing down the leather with a rag that smelled like car wax. For the rest of our interview, she framed her answers precisely and carefully avoided any further mention of the relationship between Ballard and Valerie.

Still searching for the lead for my article, I remembered Arch's comment about Valerie's horse wanting to go out on the trail with the horse that had given me such a scare, Ganador. That might add interest to my story—friendship between the two horses. "Mr. Fleagle . . . Arch, that is, mentioned that Valerie's horse and the one called Ganador often—"

"Look," Haley snapped, "I don't want other people minding my business and I don't mind theirs. What Miss Kimmel did or didn't do was up to her." She kept her head bent and her eyes on the leather strap she was rubbing.

Her reaction to my question startled me. "Please let me explain," I said. "Valerie was in my high school class. In addition to this being my job, I care about what happened to her. So far, the police haven't been able to come up with any answers to why she was killed, and soon I'm afraid nobody will care enough to find out. But I care . . . I really care . . . Val was . . . she was a part of my life and it's not fair . . . it's just not fair—"

Until I said those words aloud to Haley Simms, I hadn't realized just how deeply Val's murder had affected me. Since discovering her body lying on that bedroom floor, it seemed as if her image was always there, just behind my retina, an image I couldn't escape even in my dreams. I wanted not just to know who had done that terrible thing to her; I wanted revenge on the person who'd stolen away her life.

Haley at first seemed startled at my vehemence, then she sighed and raised her head. "I'm sorry I was so abrupt. This is just for your benefit, not for your article. It probably meant nothing. Alvaro just happened to be here when Val came out one day to check on Sky. I guess they got to talking and—"

"Does this Alvaro have another name?"

"Cardenas."

"Hispanic?"

"From Buenos Aires. Here on business for his father's company. An avid polo player. Had his favorite horse shipped all the way from Argentina. Wants everything the best for Ganador—best stall, special feed, raises the roof if anyone so much as touches his saddles—"

"So he and Val met and became . . . friendly. Where does Compton Ballard fit into this picture?"

"I guess you'd have to say he doesn't." Haley's tone was dry. "I doubt Miss Kimmel told him about Alvaro and she never rode with him when her boss was around."

Haley looked uncomfortable as if she'd said too much. When I saw she had no further information to offer, I thanked her and left.

All the way back to town, my too-fertile brain kept spinning various scenarios. Ballard jealous that Valerie was romantically interested in someone else? As a married man, Ballard had no right to be jealous. Still, a wedding ring didn't guarantee fidelity—who should know that better than I?

From Polly and then from some of SandScapes' agents, I'd gotten the impression that to further her career, Valerie had some sort of sexual involvement with Ballard. From what Haley had told me, Ballard had seen Val as a fantasy substitute for a girl who'd once rejected him. Then along came Alvaro Cardenas, a rich Argentinian, probably with Latin good looks. That he played polo and could afford to ship his horse all the way to Florida spelled money, lots of it. All of which would no doubt look very attractive to Valerie. Could that have made Ballard bitter enough to commit murder? But how? He was in Salt Lake City at the time Valerie was killed. A hired hit man, perhaps?

That scenario seemed ridiculous. *Note to self: Sedate, historic St. Augustine is not Chicago's south side or the Jersey shore.*

But what about this Alvaro Cardenas? I pictured a passionate Latin, dark hair, dark, steamy eyes . . . .

Behind me a horn blared. I cringed as the driver I'd cut off swerved out around me, a finger elevated in my direction.

CHAPTER 8

Mounted on a snow-white horse, I galloped across the broad Argentinian pampas. Fearless, I was riding side-saddle and looked smashing in a bolero jacket over a crisp white blouse, a calf-length black skirt, gaucho boots and a brimmed hat. Beside me, on the huge black stallion, a caballero with flashing eyes and . . . .

The alarm clock shrilled and I opened my eyes to the familiar whisper of the fan rotating above my bed. I lay there a moment longer as my dream image faded.

*****

My first stop Tuesday morning was at the home of a high-school classmate, Amanda Frey, who had lived next door to Valerie when they were growing up. Amanda and her family now occupied a typical Florida seaside cottage in a little enclave of single-story houses a block off the beach. A tricycle sat halfway up the walk and a surfboard was propped against the side of the garage.

Amanda met me at the door with a toddler tucked under her

arm, her free hand clutching a tattered blanket. "Chloe's teething," she informed me as she closed the front door with her foot. "Most kids want a pacifier, but the only thing that quiets her is chewing on her blanket."

She shifted the blanket to Chloe who grasped it and stuffed it into her drooling mouth. With a wry smile, Amanda preceded me into the living room. At the sofa, she shoved aside a *Pat the Bunny* book and a colorful plastic box from the top of which protruded the heads of bugs, each a different color. After brushing away a cluster of what I guessed to be teething biscuit crumbs, she signaled me to sit. "I pulled out the yearbook after you called," she said.

She popped the baby, blanket and all, into her swing, and wound the mechanism. To its steady *click-clack, click-clack*, the two of us examined the Usina High School yearbook for the class of 1995. "It's hard to believe how young we were back then . . . and how ridiculous we looked," Amanda said.

I groaned. "Just dig the dated hair-dos. How could styles change so much in just . . ." I paused to count on my fingers. "Dear God, has it really been 18 years?"

We flipped to the "K" pages. Under her class picture, Valerie Kimmel was described as *Vivacious, loves to dance, always ready for a good time.* Farther on no photos of her appeared among the school's athletic teams, but she was listed as secretary of the Business Leaders of Tomorrow. The Class Prophecy described her as *Most likely to be running her own day spa.*

Amanda turned back to look more closely at Val's photo. "Val had a reputation, you know, as someone who was," she paused to form parentheses with her fingers, "'easy,' but I think that was her way of asking for attention, for love even. She was so needy in that respect."

Recalling the experience with Valerie at the roller rink, I had a pretty clear idea as to why she might have craved love and attention, but I wanted to hear it from Amanda's perspective. "Why do you suppose that was?"

Amanda's eyes darkened and she expelled a regretful breath. "Poor Val. If you had seen what that girl—"

"You mean the father?"

Amanda nodded. "We lived right next door, and I can't tell you how many times my parents called the police. Mostly on Friday nights when he drank up his paycheck. You couldn't blame the sister for leaving home first chance she got."

"I didn't know there was a sister."

"Caroline. She was about ten years older than Val."

"What about Val's parents? Are they still around?"

Amanda shook her head. "The mother died about five years ago. As for that bast—" Amanda glanced across at baby Chloe before amending, "as for Val's father, I believe he lives somewhere near Tampa. Stays perpetually drunk, I hear. When the sister was still around, she did her best to protect Val. I remember one time when Val was about eight or nine she left her bike outside and it rained. The old man started to beat her with his belt when Caroline stepped in and claimed it was her fault."

"What about college?"

"Val didn't have the means for college, but she worked part time and took business courses at the community college."

"Have you seen much of her recently?"

Amanda gave a wry laugh. "With three rambunctious kids, I don't have a lot of time these days for socializing. And Val was so busy once she got into real estate that I doubt she had much free time, either. I did run into her a couple of months ago at the supermarket, and we went to the Essential Bean for coffee. She talked mostly about her horse. And the real estate business, of course. Wanted to know if Dave and I were considering moving to something a little roomier. Like as if!"

"Did she mention whether she was happy in her job? And did she say anything about her boss?"

"Compton Ballard? I got the impression he'd done well by her, judging by her oceanfront condo and that Cadillac Escalade she drove. She was proud of how much control he gave her over running his company. And she was obviously well paid—dressed to the nines. And the jewelry—always had on lots of bling, the real stuff. Some of it a bit too flashy, but I guess growing up with so little, it was her way of showing the world she'd made it."

She paused and thought for a moment. "Or maybe she didn't have to buy it for herself. That day we met she was wearing a really unusual necklace. Hard to describe, sort of a carved cameo with gold filigree edging on a gold chain. When I commented on it she gave me this sort of arched look, as if there was something—or someone—special connected with it. But I had Chloe with me that day, and she started acting up so I didn't get to ask Val anything further."

Before leaving Amanda, I asked if she knew how I could get in touch with Val's sister. "She lives in Ohio," Amanda said. "Columbus, if I remember correctly. Or at least she was living there at the time of their mother's funeral. Her married name is something that starts with a W . . . Walker . . . Walters . . . no, wait . . . it was Wallace."

*****

Back at the *Dispatch* office, I found a half dozen or so Wallaces in the Columbus, Ohio area, but finally reached one who said she was Val's sister, Caroline. I offered my condolences and explained that I was writing an article about Valerie for the local newspaper.

"The police told me she was killed . . . I couldn't believe—"

Her voice had a distant quality as if she were distracted or as if she'd not yet fully comprehended the reality of some shattering event. When she halted for a long time, I prompted, "Can you tell me—"

She interrupted, "I need you to do me a favor."

"Of course, I'd be glad—"

She didn't allow me to finish, as if what she had to say would elude her if she didn't get it all out at once. "As soon as they release Val's body, I've arranged with the Callaway Memorial Home in St. Augustine for her funeral." She paused, then continued in an almost staccato voice. "I want Valerie to look beautiful; I want everyone who sees her to remember how beautiful she was."

"That's very—"

"She'll need a dress. She sent me a picture when she got her real estate award and that's the dress I want her to wear. It was a shade of green that matched her eyes exactly."

"But couldn't you—"

"My husband's seriously ill. He's scheduled to have surgery tomorrow, and I won't be able to leave except to fly down the day of the funeral and back that same night."

In the end, I found myself agreeing to go to Val's apartment on Anastasia Island, getting the key from the apartment manager, finding the dress and delivering it to the Callaway Memorial Home.

In response to my questions, Caroline seemed unable to focus on anything other than the dress and arrangements for Val's funeral. I hung up, a bit frustrated that I'd gotten no new information about her sister's early life and much of what I did know about that was not usable. The *Dispatch* was careful about how deceased people were portrayed, and even baddies were reported on with respect once they were gone. Shel's admonition "Don't make us have to lawyer-up," was always at the back of my mind.

It was after six when I filed my article and headed for home—home being the second-floor apartment of Mrs. Castelli's big old Victorian on River Street. Back when I returned to St. Augustine, I'd felt obligated to stay close by to keep Mother from tilting too far into the occult, but I was smart enough not to agree when she insisted that I share the apartment she occupies above her shop. Instead, I'd rented Mrs. Castelli's second floor on one of St. Augustine's quieter streets next to the river. In the process, I acquired not only a comfortable nest of my own but a love of the landlady, Graciella Castelli.

I looked forward that evening to kicking off my shoes,

pouring a glass of pinot grigio, plopping myself down on my porch and watching the river flow by. The birds would be twittering as they settled for the night, the river breeze would sweep away the muggy heat, and the wine would put my world to rights. After dinner I had one of my favorites ready to pop into the DVD player—*Night Must Fall*. Dad always said this was one of the overlooked classics. I liked the way you could never be quite sure until the very end if Rosalind Russell was a goodie or a baddie—just like in real life.

Upon arriving home, I found a truck marked *Schrader Plumbing* parked in the driveway. Mrs. Castelli had wheeled herself out onto her front porch and was talking with a man whose coveralls bore that same name. As I drew closer, I heard my landlady say, "Nonsense! It's nothing but a few little flying ants. I've seen them before. I'll get Tuck to spray them and they go away."

The man reached up and scratched behind his ear. "That's the problem, Ma'am," he said. His tone indicated he'd been trying to convince her for quite some time. "The spray gets the ones you can see, but that's only the tip of the iceberg. Those little devils just move a few feet away and start a new nest."

Mrs. Castelli saw me and waved me over. "What's the problem?" I asked as I mounted the porch steps.

"Just these little bugs," she said. "I've told this fellow it's nothing I can't handle."

"Are you a pest control person?" I asked the man.

"No, Ma'am, I just came by to fix the leak in Mrs. Castelli's kitchen drain. But when I got down under in the crawl space I seen she's got a much bigger problem."

"I've told you, they're just flying ants," Mrs. Castelli persisted. "This house has been here near a hundred years and never once has there been a termite problem."

The man gave a weary shrug. "I ain't no professional, but if I was you, Ma'am, I'd sure get it checked out. Coupla' them joists on the back side are looking bad. That's all I'm saying."

With that he picked up the toolbox at his feet, tipped his bill cap to us and left.

"Maybe you ought to . . ."

"Nonsense. I'll get Tucker to spray them when he comes to mow. A little Raid and they'll be gone in a day or two. Come join me for dinner after you've washed up. I made a casserole much too big for one person."

As she wheeled back into the house, through the open door I caught a whiff of the mouth-watering aroma from her kitchen. "You're a saint," I called after her. "I was dreading another frozen chicken pie. There's a nice ripe cantaloupe in my fridge—I'll bring that and a bottle of wine."

"Done and done," she said with a backward wave. "See you at six. Maybe a wee game of Scrabble after?"

I grinned agreement even though I knew the game would be anything but "wee" and would go on until ten or later. But it was nice to have some variation from the old movies I relied on to get me through too many lonely evenings. I rounded the house and climbed the flight of wooden stairs leading to my second floor porch. As always, each time I unlocked the French doors to my beloved apartment I gave thanks for the bright, spacious rooms that have been home to me ever since I returned to St. Augustine. From the day the old Victorian house opened its arms and welcomed me, I've awakened each morning thankful to have found such a haven . . . and with the added bonus of a landlady who loves to share the wonderful concoctions she whips up in her kitchen.

I checked the fridge to make sure there was a full bottle of wine chilling. For a sixty-five-year old, Graciella Castelli was no slouch when it came to putting away the wine or outsmarting me at Scrabble. What chance did I stand against a woman who knew xanthoma is a skin disease?

The only bottle in the fridge was half full, but there was time before dinner to pull one out of my storage place and chill it in the freezer. I crossed the L-shaped living room, and opened the door that had been installed years ago to close off the former stair landing when the house was converted from a single family home. Fire regulations dictated that the stairwell be enclosed at both ends and a fire-proof door had also been installed in the first floor foyer at the bottom.

The stair landing and sometimes even the unused stair treads below now served for storing my accumulation of stuff, some of it leftovers from the home I'd shared with my former husband, some discards too good to throw away and other pieces picked up in the course of my yard-sale addiction with the intention I'd someday make use of them.

The landing's light bulb had long since burned out and, with all the boxes and odd pieces of bric-a-brac in the way, it wasn't worth the trouble of replacing it. I groped about and located the wine, which I always stowed close by the door in easy reach.

Just as I retrieved the bottle I wanted—Mrs. Castelli's favorite, a sauvignon blanc—my cell phone shrilled for attention. I hurried to retrieve it from my bag. The number on the caller ID belonged to Andy Thompson. Still holding the wine in one hand, I started to answer, then hesitated. I'd had a few casual dates with other men after my affair with Sam ended, but instinct told me that casual was not an option where Andy Thompson was concerned. I let the call go to voice mail.

I placed the bottle in the freezer, then, unable to erase the guilt of having ignored Andy's call, I dropped into a chair next to the kitchen table and cradled my chin in both hands. I'd once thought that a passionate romance with fireworks spraying glorious colors across my mental sky was essential, but fireworks can fizzle. I was already two strikes down in the game of relationships—my marriage to Derek, then the affair with Sam. If genuine liking and a feeling of content in being together were the signs, maybe Andy Thompson truly *was* Mr. Right. Rhonda, like a little tea kettle whose whistle kept persisting, constantly reminded me of Andy's many good qualities.

Still, Andy's two daughters, Melissa—Lissa for short—and

Dana, made the situation a lot more serious than the toes-in-the-surf of merely dating. Kids were an undertow that could catch you up and sweep you out to sea, ready or not.

On the other side of the balance sheet was the memory of the kisses Andy and I had shared on our recent fishing trip to the Everglades. The intense feeling they'd generated took me by surprise . . . took me places I yearned for but places I wasn't sure I dared venture. Half the time I managed to convince myself that we'd merely given in to the spell of the Glades—warm sun, waves lapping, good fishing. But it went deeper than that. There are kisses and then there are kisses. Those were definitely kisses.

It seemed to have hit Andy the same way. We'd gone out several times since, but took care to withdraw to the safe plateau of "just friends." Meanwhile, the do we? don't we? of sex still hung between us like the blanket that separated Clark Gable and Claudette Colbert in *It Happened One Night*. We'd come close, but each time one of us pulled back, afraid to cross the line. Experience told me we couldn't go on that way indefinitely. Fish or cut bait. Sink or swim. All the clichés.

"Sleep with him first, then check out the kids," had been Polly's blunt advice. "That way you'll know whether it's worth the effort."

"Don't let anyone rush you. When the time is right, you'll both know," Rhonda had countered.

My mother, after much consultation with the Tarot cards, my horoscope, and her spirit world, insisted it was written in the stars that Andy and I were destined for each other. "Wings— Claude spoke of a great pair of wings," my seeress parent pronounced. "So what else could that possibly mean?"

Plenty of advice, no answers.

Staring at the phone didn't solve anything, either.

Suddenly I'd had enough indecision—the maybe's, the would we's, the should we's. I picked up the phone and hit Andy's redial number.

Time to fish.

CHAPTER 9

Traffic on A1A was light as I crossed the Bridge of Lions on Wednesday afternoon. With luck, I'd be in and out of Valerie Kimmel's condo in a half hour. It wasn't a task I looked forward to. As I drove, I fumed on my cell to Rhonda, "Of all the times you couldn't get off work. You know how this whole business creeps me out."

"Don't make it such a big deal. Find the dress the sister described and get out fast."

"Caroline said to look for the green dress that Valerie wore when she got some real estate award. I sure hope there's only one green dress in the closet, so I don't have to go pawing through all of her clothes."

"You'll do fine—gotta go." The line went dead.

At Playa Serena complex, the brick-paved drive was lined with blazing red and pink bougainvilleas. The three-story condo building wrapped around to give most residents a view of the ocean. I stepped out of the Jeep into heat so oppressive it tempted me to race around the building and plunge into the ocean.

Even water at 85 degrees would have felt refreshing to my 98.6 body. Instead, I hoisted my bag onto my shoulder and headed for the entrance.

The condo manager's office was to my left inside the lobby. A sign on the door informed visitors that it was *Open 10 A.M. to 5 P.M.* Obeying its invitation to *Please come in,* I stepped into air conditioning so cold I expected to find icicles clinging to the ceiling. A heavy-set black woman wearing a loose-fitting outfit in Caribbean shades of blue and yellow greeted me from behind a desk. I told her that I needed to speak with the manager, Felipe Lopez, and she summoned him.

Mr. Lopez appeared almost instantly, a short, compact man with brilliantined hair and a matching gleam in his dark eyes. "Ah, yes, Miss McKelvey. Mrs. Wallace phoned to tell me you were coming. We are all heartbroken for the loss of Miss V," he offered in a slight Spanish accent.

"Had Miss Kimmel lived here long?"

"Yes, one of our original tenants. A very particular lady. She always noticed the little things—like if someone failed to shower before using the pool or allowed their dog to wet on the front shrubbery." Then, as if aware he might have given the wrong impression, he added, "And always she had a nice smile for everyone. But of course you know this. You were her dear friend, no?"

Would Valerie have considered me her dear friend? I wasn't sure. "You have the key to her unit?"

With a ceremonious gesture, he pranced over to a locked cabinet, opened it, withdrew a set of keys, and handed them to me. "The police have been here, you know. They searched her condo, so you might find it in disorder. She was very neat, Ms. Kimmel, and she wouldn't like it to be a mess. Maybe the police were looking for something?"

Ignoring his obvious curiosity, I said I had no idea.

Keys in hand, I rode the elevator to the third floor, my feet sinking into the thick, cushiony carpeting with each step down the hallway. At the entry door, a yellow sliver of police tape still hung from the frame. I straightened my shoulders and, after a hesitant breath, ripped off the dangling scrap of tape and unlocked the door.

Inside, I was careful to lock the door and put on the chain before looking around. The condo's view spread past a generous foyer into a spacious living room decorated in neutral shades with teal and rose accents. A pair of sleek sofas in off-white flanked the marble fireplace, but the curves of the traditional wing chairs positioned opposite contradicted the sofas' severe style. Throughout the room, I noticed other instances of that contradiction—all the furnishings and accessories were obviously expensive, but the overall impression lacked coherence.

Or was that envy on my part? The space was huge, easily three times the size of my apartment's living room. Visible through the open archway at one end, a crystal chandelier was reflected on the dining table's polished mahogany. At the living room's opposite end, sliding doors opened onto a patio with an expansive view of the beach.

The condo's air was stale, a reminder that no one lived here anymore. I crossed to the door and slid it open to let the fresh breeze sweep through, then stepped outside for a minute to take in the ocean view. The beachfront vista was breathtaking, but the ocean always seems too vast and impersonal for anyone to possess it. By comparison, the vista of the Matanzas River from my apartment's second floor porch had a comforting intimacy.

I stepped back inside to survey the living room more closely. Some framed photos on a credenza bore the sooty residue of fingerprint dust, and smudges marred the surface of the cabinet's pale, finely grained wood. Valerie appeared in each of the pictures. Several were of awards ceremonies in each of which she stood center, proudly displaying her trophy or certificate. Other shots had been snapped in restaurants and one on a cruise ship. I picked up one to study it closer. In it, Val, in riding habit with her horse Sky, lined up with three other people, all posing with their mounts. I recognized Ganador, his sleek black head tilted towards Sky as though about to nuzzle him. Standing next to Ganador, holding his bridle, was a dark-haired man with aristocratic features and demeanor to match.

"Alvaro Cardenas," I spoke the name in a whisper, in spite of being alone in the room. My eyes lingered on that handsome face a few seconds until I remembered what I had come there to do. The photographs replaced, I proceeded down a short hallway toward what I estimated was Valerie's bedroom.

The first door on the hall opened into a bedroom decorated in soothing shades of pale green and lavender. Both the window drapes and the duvet boasted a trellis pattern with climbing wisteria on a white background. The fabric's cottage prettiness was in contrast to the sleek, modern lines of the room's furniture, which included a modernized version of a four-poster bed, its uprights not wooden but a silvery metal.

I ran my finger through the thick coating of dust on the dresser top, wondering who would see to it that the mess the police technicians had left would be wiped away. And who would dispose of all Valerie's possessions? The sister, I supposed. Or did it even matter now?

To shake off that thought, I stepped past the bed and slid open the first of a pair of mirrored closet doors. A light went on automatically to reveal a spacious alcove lined on either side with precise rows of clothing as well as custom-built shelves and drawers.

From one of the surrounding racks, I lifted a specially designed hanger that held a riding outfit complete with jacket and jodhpurs. Three more such outfits hung in the closet along with a row of starched white shirts. The shelf above held several black hard hats, each with a sliver of brim and a chin strap. The riding boots on the floor were buffed to an elegant sheen, and gave off the rich smell of leather polish.

All the items in that closet appeared to be the more casual outfits of Valerie's wardrobe. "Weekend Wear," a catalog would

probably label the tweed blazers, cashmere sweaters and designer jeans. Shelves held shoes in all styles from beach-going flip-
flops to gym shoes to open-toed sandals and low-heeled pumps.
Since this was obviously not where Val stored her dressier items,
I returned to the bedroom, and checked the other set of mirrored
doors.

That closet was even larger. On the long rack to the left
hung what appeared to be Val's working wardrobe of separate
jackets, skirts and tops, while opposite stretched an array of
dressier clothing including a number of floor-length gowns, each
encased in plastic. The closet was a veritable upscale boutique,
and its array of clothing bore designer names like Valentino,
Vera Wang and Versace . . . all those expensive V's.

I edged further into the closet and was ruffling through
silks and brocades and linens when the lingering odor of Valerie's distinctive signature perfume sent a shudder through my
entire frame. Although subtle, the scent was compelling. I was
struck by an eerie sense of her presence. I even imagined her
voice saying, "What are you doing here in my closet, touching
my dresses?"

The urge to turn and flee from the closet, the bedroom, the
condo, was so overwhelming that it took all my willpower to
overcome the feeling. For the tenth time, I wished Rhonda were
with me. My confidence shaken even further, I determined to
concentrate on the job at hand, find the dress, and scram out of
there.

Partway down a row of what would probably be labeled
"cocktail attire," I spotted a green silk dress encased in plastic. I
removed it from the rack and held it up. The sleeveless gown had
its own jacket with a fitted bodice and long sleeves. Satisfied that
this was the dress Caroline wanted, I carried it from the closet
and laid it across the bed along with the stunning pair of dark
green snakeskin pumps I located. Perfect.

I started to pick up the dress and shoes when the thought
halted me that I should probably collect some underwear. Or

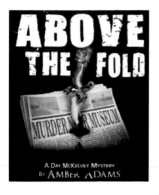

ABOVE THE FOLD

At St. Augustine's Menendez Ball reporter Day McKelvey unknowingly interviews a murderer and his victim. She must dig into past deceptions to expose the killer before he finds her.

DEADLY LISTINGS

Reporter Day McKelvey stumbles on the murdered body of a real estate agent. When she gets too close to exposing the killers she unwittingly becomes his target.

ssary when a person . . . ? That maca-
er shudder. My only intention when I
to interview her for my article, not to
where I had to choose underwear for a

set and found a drawer that held an
ergarments—panties, bras and several
ver much of anything. Touching Val-
strengthened the sense that I was an
ere I didn't belong.

entirely if I let myself think too much,
of lace panties, a matching bra, then
That done, I returned to the bedroom.
resist the urge to take a peek inside the
n suite as the designers on the *Home*
ays referred to a bedroom's attached
oorway, I flipped on the light switch,
r look at the gold faucets, the surround
the shower enclosure large enough to
artet.

bars, a blue blazer that appeared to be
wardrobe hung suspended. I guessed
use steam from the shower to remove
d wondered if that had been a leftover
she could only dream of affording such

he jacket's butter-soft fabric, then re-
and held it against me. Val and I had
The temptation to see how it felt to
esigner label overcame me. My arms
sleeves. A turn left and right in front
s showed that the fit was perfect and
me. Maybe if I gave up my daily lattes
ch a blazer.

ff, I stood sidewise to the mirror, as-

71

"I am pleased to meet you, Ms. McKelvey. I have called the manager every day to find out when the police would be finished with their work so I might search for the necklace. The manager tells me he has not the authority to let me in. Then today, I come here and he says Valerie's friend is in the condo, so I came hoping— "

He paused for a moment like an actor who was uncertain what his next line should be. He must have sensed my ambivalence, because he continued, "You are a woman Ms. McKelvey, you will understand. I was in love with Valerie, so very much in love. I wanted her to come with me to Argentina to meet my family. That is why I gave her—" He straightened his shoulders and glanced around the room, his soulful eyes resting on the photograph I had just studied. "It is . . . it is just so . . . so—"

For a moment, I thought he was going to cry. Moved by his obvious distress, I asked. "What did this necklace look like?" I hadn't looked for any jewelry although I had noticed an elaborate jewelry box on one of the shelves in the closet where Valerie kept her riding clothes.

Alvaro ran his hand through his hair and gazed into the distance as though he were seeing Valerie wearing the necklace. "It was a cameo belonging to my *abuela* . . . my precious grandmother. I had it encircled with gold filigree . . . very fine . . . very tasteful. Even the gold chain that held it was an antique. Not only is it very fine jewelry, it has so much sentimental value for me. Perhaps together we could have a look—"

His request again put me on alert. "You would need permission from the police to remove anything from the condo," I improvised. "The lead police officer on the case is a man named Nortley."

"Yes, I know him. I've spoken to Officer Nortley on the phone. When I heard what happened to Valerie . . . *esta pesadilla* . . . this, how do you say . . . this nightmare, I wanted to know. This Officer Nortley, he tells me nothing. Instead I must come to the station, answer their questions. They offer no respect, as if

I were some ordinary person off the streets." His tightened jaw told how offended he had been at such treatment.

"Did you tell them about the necklace?"

Alvaro drew himself up and gave me a disdainful look. "I am no fool. I could see how they looked at me. Why should I give them an excuse to seize the necklace, hold it as evidence, perhaps to have it conveniently 'disappear'?"

I resented his implication. Not that valuables didn't sometimes turn up missing once police got their hands on them, but these were *our* police he was talking about, not some Argentinian *Gestapo*. My resolve now stiffened, I told him, "Without a warrant from the police, you have no right to search through her things."

Alvaro glowered, clearly offended. He didn't frighten me, but his haughty air of entitlement made me uncomfortable. Perhaps Valerie had liked that sort of male dominance—some women did. I was not one of them.

"And you?" he demanded in a supercilious voice whose tone had lost its ingratiating quality.

"*I* was given permission to pick up the clothes in which Valerie will be buried. That's all. If the police get a description from you, I'm sure your necklace will be returned when the case is solved."

He glared at me for a long moment, then jerked open the door. "Good-bye Miss McKelvey. I loved Valerie." And with that he was gone.

CHAPTER 10

Only the faintest wisp of daylight crept through the blinds when the jangling of the phone wakened me. I shoved aside the sheet to fumble for the light switch. Instinct told me it was Mother's voice I'd hear and instinct was right. In her most Zanthia-the-Seeress mode she breathed, "Day, darling, the most peculiar dream."

I sighed and heaved myself upright. At least this time it was a dream, not some communication from the vaporous Claude, or a hot flash from the Ouija board. "Mother," I groaned, "please make it short. I was hoping for another hour of sleep."

"It's a child," she said, "a little boy. And he's terribly angry."

"What little boy?"

"This dreadful thing that was done to that poor Kimmel girl."

I flopped back onto the pillow. Mother, aka Zanthia, comes up with some bizarre predictions, but this was really off the wall. "Are you saying that a little boy murdered Valerie Kimmel?"

"It's not completely clear, but there definitely was a boy. First his house collapsed, and he was sad and angry, and then he was running from place to place hunting for someone."

"Mother, what could that possibly have to do with—?"

She went on unperturbed. "Valerie was there in the dream. She kept shaking her finger at the boy the way you'd do with a child who's done something terribly bad. I do think the police should follow up on this."

I raised my eyes to the ceiling in a silent petition. "Mother, let me get this straight. There's this mysterious boy—dream boy—and Valerie was scolding him. Did your dream give any clue as to who the boy might be?"

"Of course not, Darling—it was a dream."

I hung up the phone, switched off the lamp, pounded my pillow into shape, and scrunched back beneath the covers, but the train to slumber land had been derailed. The worst of it was, too often Zanthia's weird predictions proved to contain some convoluted kernel of truth. Take the way, even before Polly and her first husband were married, Mother predicted the man would break her heart. At the engagement party Polly's Grandma'am threw for the couple, Mother drew me aside and hissed, "She can't marry that man. His aura's all wrong. People who have that murky orangish-brown are leeches. I must warn Polly."

"Holy Nightshade, Mother," I protested. "Polly's the brightest person I know. She'd never let herself be taken in by a . . . a leech!"

"Day, darling, you can be so naïve at times. Polly's IQ may be 150, but when it comes to love she's as vulnerable as any other woman."

Time had proven her analysis straight on. And now another of Zanthia's stranger predictions. I grinned to myself as I gave up the quest for another forty winks and headed toward the shower. Easy to imagine how the police would react if I reported to them that my mother insisted they go chasing after a little boy in the Kimmel murder case.

After breakfast and before leaving for work, I couldn't resist the urge to call Rhonda and fill her in on my encounter with Alvaro Cardenas. "You are going to be so sorry you didn't go with me yesterday. That Alvaro fellow came by. He said he was looking for an expensive necklace he gave Valerie."

"And did he find it?"

"I wasn't about to let him go snooping around. I told him he'd have to take it up with the police. He wasn't happy about that."

"Did you check around for it?"

"I'd spotted a jewelry box in one of her closets, so after he left I took a quick look but there was no necklace there like the one he described. Lots of bling, though, some of it the real thing."

"While you were on the scene, you really ought to have looked a little harder. If you actually found the necklace, I'll bet there'd be a big reward from Alvaro."

"If Val had a hidden wall safe or put the necklace in some drawer, it will just have to stay there. My only interest was in getting out of there," I said, then added. "When I was in her kitchenette looking for a plastic bag to put her underwear in, I did check the fridge. Thought there might have been perishable food left inside."

"And?"

"Nothing but a bottle of champagne, and a jar of Grey Poupon."

*****

At the *Dispatch* later that morning, Shel Weinstein called me into his office. Wayne Sonderson, the paper's sales director, was there already, his usually somber expression more morose than ever. Shel, too, seemed in an unusually dour mood.

"Sit down, Day," he said. "We've got a problem."

I looked from one to the other. "A problem with?—"

"Compton Ballard," Wayne said. "He's threatening to pull his SandScapes advertising. I need not tell you that's a biggie."

Shel filled in, "Ballard's steamed about the op-ed pieces we've run denouncing his attempt to rezone the Coronado golf course property. Even claims our coverage of the murder is ruining his business."

"Since when do we shape our editorial content because some advertiser—"

Shel raised his hand palm outward to halt my protest. "I can't just tell Ballard to take a flying leap—we're in survival mode here. Our bottom line is bleeding red—in the past month we've had to replace the old Harris press and two of our delivery trucks. On top of that, the price of everything from gas to ink to the syndicated comics has skyrocketed."

"What does this have to do with me?"

Shel glanced toward Wayne before answering. "We thought it might help if you whipped up a personality piece on Ballard for next Sunday's *Life Style* section. Emphasize his civic activities, devotion to wife and kids, career achievements, et cetera, et cetera."

I didn't like the way that smelled. The impression I'd gotten of Compton Ballard told me the proposed article would serve to further stroke his over-large ego. On the other hand, this had to be as distasteful to Shel as it was to me. "We're not looking for a white-wash," he said, "just a piece that emphasizes Ballard's positive aspects."

It was no secret around the office that loans from Arnold Mandell, Shel's brother-in-law and father of our office gofer, the hapless Skooky Mandell, were all that was keeping the *Dispatch* afloat. Mandell Senior's recent plunge into a sure-fire investment scheme had nearly drained the family money pool. If the paper folded, there went the livelihoods of more than fifty people and their families. The bottom line was we'd have to hold our noses and kowtow to Ballard. It was one of the few times I wished I was in some other line of work.

Note to self: Chocolate, the cure for all ills. I detoured by the snack room to pick up a Snickers bar. Kyle Whitecloud was there, punching the button for peanut butter crackers. He looked around when I entered and whistled. "Uh-oh. Do I sense distress on M'lady's face?"

"I hate it," I snapped. "Shel wants me to cobble together an article that will depict Compton Ballard as St. Augustine's outstanding citizen."

Kyle's packet of crackers tumbled down into the tray and he stooped to fish it out. "So Shel asked you to take one for the team?" he said.

I grunted and fumbled in my bag for coins.

"Here, I've got it," Kyles pulled several quarters from his pocket. "What'll it be?"

I pointed to the Snickers.

"That bad, huh?" he said, forcing me to grin in spite of myself.

Snickers in hand, I was headed for the door when Kyle added; "I've got a copy of the Medical Examiner's preliminary report on Valerie Kimmel. Stop by my cubicle if you're interested in having a look."

"Sure Frank won't throw a hissy?"

Kyle grimaced. "You two—some days I feel like I'm the Gaza Strip."

I gave him an apologetic shrug. Kyle and I are good enough friends so that we can harass each other without any ill feeling. Later, I leaned over his desk as he flipped open the blue-bound medical report. "Looks as if the M.E. came up with the same conclusion the police have had all along," he said. "Valerie enters the house; she's attacked from behind by a person or persons unknown. Time of death estimated to be approximately half to three quarters of an hour before discovery of the body—that would be you and Everett. Also, based on analysis of stomach contents, she was killed two hours after her last meal, breakfast. That puts her death at around 9:30 A.M. or shortly after, which fits with the time she left her condo according to a neighbor."

"What does the report say about how she was killed?"

"Apparently by a single blow to the back of her head. Death probably instantaneous, the result of countercoup bruising resulting in intracerebral bleeding."

In response to my inquisitive look, he supplied, "Countercoup—after a hard blow, the brain bounces off the opposite side of the skull. Like getting rear-ended in a car accident."

"So someone hit her from behind hard enough to do that kind of damage. But with what?"

"The report says 'unidentified hard object with possible striations.' Seems odd."

"How so?"

"Doctor Cartwell usually has a pretty firm opinion on the murder weapon, or he at least offers some possibilities like a baseball bat or a tire iron or a two-by-four. Give him the tiniest irregularity in the wound and he can generally nail the implement that did the damage."

"How about sexual assault? Any evidence?"

"Appears not. No semen. No contact evidence."

"That's bad."

When Kyle looked at me strangely, I amended. "I mean bad as in that makes it harder to nail the killer on DNA."

"If he's caught."

"Let's hope that 'if' becomes a 'when' and soon," I said. "Every real estate agent in town is freaked over Valerie's murder."

I turned to leave, but Kyle halted me, "You're in for Trivia tonight, aren't you?"

"I may be late. I've got to get cracking on my research for the Ballard article. Then afterwards I promised Mother I'd stop by her shop."

"Ah, Zanthia. St. Augustine's most intriguing woman."

"Try St. Augustine's most annoying mother."

"C'mon, Day. Your Mom's an original."

"Original as in space case," I grumbled. "You won't believe her latest."

I filled him in on Zanthia's dream about a little boy connected to Valerie's murder. When I finished Kyle laughed and shook his head. "Give her a hug for me."

*****

"Darling, we've simply *got* to do something about this hair." Mother—Zanthia—lifted a strand from my neck and stared at it critically. "Understandable that it's a mess—your sun sign is in the air element."

I pulled away. "Don't tell me my hair has its own horoscope."

She ignored my protest. "It's simple feng shui, dear. Your moon is traveling through an opposing element."

"Aha, I get it. The heavens are screwed up, so I'm cursed with split ends. But what brings on this sudden interest in my hair?"

She gave me the look you'd give a child who's just posed a ridiculous question. "Your big occasion, of course."

I stared at her blankly.

"Everything points to the coming weekend when Venus is in your house," she said, as if that were explanation enough. "Besides, Claude saw wings again. It all adds up. Your pilot is coming and something special is about to happen."

I gaped at her speechless. Did the woman have my phone tapped?

"So this is what we must do—"

"*We*, Mother?"

"It's all arranged. I called Ambience. So lucky, Giles Sheffield is going to work you in even though he's booked solid on Saturdays."

"Mother, I never asked to be 'worked in.' I'll stop by Janine's shop sometime next week and let her give me a trim."

"Day, dear, don't be difficult. Janine's a lovely girl, but she's a Capricorn. Your appointment is for eleven Saturday morning. It's paid for in advance, but you'll want to tip. The morning appointment will give you plenty of time to get ready afterwards. I think that nice outfit you wore—"

CHAPTER 11

At Trivia on Thursday night I seated myself next to Carl Bailey, the *Dispatch's* real estate editor. Carl was chowing down on one of the Whistle Inn's Monster Burgers. I gestured toward the lava flow of catsup drowning his French fries. "Your daily vegetable allowance?"

"Nope." Carl held up a slice of dill pickle. "Got cucumber."

"And I suppose a Margarita counts as fruit?"

"You got it—just have to pick your drinks." Then Carl's round face sobered. "Sorry you got caught up in Wayne's backlash from Ballard."

I signaled the waitress that I was ready to order, then turned back to Carl. "Are you hearing anything new from your real estate contacts? About the murder, I mean."

"Plenty of speculation," Carl said between bites. "According to one rumor, it was Ballard's wife taking revenge because Valerie was having an affair with her husband."

"Not unless the killer was a hired gun," I said. "The police confirmed that Eloise Ballard was with her husband in Salt Lake when the murder occurred. Besides, from what Polly Ribideaux told me, the Ballards have a mutual understanding—she doesn't interfere with his extramarital affairs, he doesn't interfere with hers."

"Nice marriage, huh?" Carl grunted. "Can't you just picture my wife's response if I suggested an arrangement like that?"

I laughed. "Knowing Lainie, by morning, you'd be lying on a morgue slab wearing a toe tag."

Carl grinned. "But seriously, there's something peculiar going on over at SandScapes."

"Such as?"

Carl speared a French fry with his fork and dipped it in the pool of catsup on his plate. "Don't know. Yesterday I was talking to Corey Rudd, president of Rudd Homes. He was telling me about this guy, Harry Ports, SandScapes's accountant. Seems Ports showed up in Rudd's office coupla' days ago looking for a job."

I tried to recall the features of the man who'd gone ballistic about the scraps of paper the copier repairman had littered over the floor at SandScapes. That day Ports had looked much as I'd expect of an accountant—a well-tailored business suit, a starched white shirt and neatly patterned tie. More unexpected had been the prominent cleft on the left side of his forehead, a hole so deep it appeared as if part of the bone beneath it had been removed. His reaction to the mess the repairman had made was peculiar, too, his eyes literally blazing as he scooped up the torn scraps.

The oily enticement of Carl's French fries tempted me, and I borrowed one from his plate. "So—people switch jobs all the time," I said.

Carl shook his fork at me in a mock threat for my thievery. "Maybe so. But according to Rudd, this Ports guy got real uptight when Rudd asked him for details about his job at Sand-Scapes. Rudd said he got the impression Ports is in a hurry to distance himself from his connection with Compton Ballard."

"Maybe Ports thinks Ballard has something to do with the murder."

"Or could have to do with some shady deal Ballard's pulling and Ports doesn't want to get dragged into it," Carl said.

We'd have gone on speculating about Ports' reason for wanting to leave SandScapes, but just then Jake, our Trivia director, announced the first question: Name the month and year of the strongest earthquake ever to occur within the continental United States.

Unsure of the answer, our *Dispatch* team huddled and conferred. Only Everett, seated at the far end of the table, had a look of assurance as he cupped his hand to his mouth and whispered, "December, 1811. New Madrid, Missouri."

Some of those around the table looked doubtful. There were murmurs of "What about California?" From nearby tables we could hear lots of whispers of "April, 1906," which told us the others were also focusing on the San Francisco quake. Randy Worrell, sports editor, wanted us to change our answer, but the majority ruled, and Everett's answer proved correct. Our rival, the Registry Bank's team, also got it right, so we started the evening with a tie, but determined it wouldn't end that way. "Bring it on, we'll *dispatch* you!" was our battle cry.

"Registry Rules!" they countered.

Caught up in our rivalry with each other, we totally ignored a group that had recently joined the game, the residents of the Allende Senior Home. As a result, they managed to rack up considerable points, bet everything on the final question, and got it right. As they passed our table on the way out to their van, a sweet little gray-haired lady paused her wheelchair to murmur, "So sorry, darlings, that we cleaned your clock tonight."

Chastened, we salaamed her.

The game over, I was about to leave when Everett caught my arm. "I got a letter today," he said. "From Maple."

An un-Everett-like gleefulness lit his face, the expression that might be expected from someone who'd just won the lottery.

"She said she's been thinking about me ever since my visit. Said it didn't seem right when we've known each other so long and we get along good yet we live so far apart."

"You must have made quite an impression. So do you think this means she might consider moving here?"

His glee diminished a bit. "She doesn't say so directly. Fact is, she mentioned how rooted she is in her old home and how hard it would be to leave her family and friends. But that shows she's considering it, don't you think?"

Not wanting to contradict the hopefulness in his eyes, I said, "So are you going to tell her about your house hunt?"

He shook his head. "I still want that to be a surprise."

*****

On Friday morning I stormed into Shel's office and slammed down the publicity still Ballard had provided of himself. Shel, seated behind the desk, pulled back as if he thought I was about to attack him. Which I was, in a sense. "Shel, I can't do this. You've got to give it to someone else."

"What's the problem?"

"For one thing, I don't see any way to skim over that hotel business in Atlanta. It's public knowledge that Ballard colluded with a banker to kite the appraisal on the old Moreland Hotel, then mortgaged it at double the actual value. When they got caught, the banker took the rap while Ballard squeaked by on a technicality, with the aid of some very expensive legal help. No wonder Atlanta got too hot for him."

Shel grimaced. "What did he say when you asked him about that?"

"That's the problem—he's refused to give me any further interviews. When I call, he's out and doesn't return my calls. His home phone's unlisted. The only information I've been able to get is from his puff bio on SandScapes's website. According to that he's lily white—got his start in real estate in Charlotte, North Carolina, started small, built good will, grew the business, et cetera. It all sounded a bit too glib so I've done some checking."

"And?"

I showed Shel the print-outs of several websites I'd searched. "This traces him back to 1983 when he first applied for a business license in Charlotte. And get this—not as a realtor but operating as Friend-N-Need Loan Company, one of those places that charges astronomical interest to people desperate for cash. The closest he came to being a realtor at that time was making quick loans at exorbitant rates for homeowners about to lose their property to foreclosure. "

Shel frowned. "Not a nice business, but not necessarily illegal."

"True, I didn't find any charges against him there. But the thing that really puzzles me is that his bio states his age as fifty-nine. It could be a year or so out of date, so he's either late fifties or early sixties, which would mean he would already have been thirty or older in 1983. That made me wonder where he was previous to that, but I couldn't find a trace of him in Charlotte or anyplace else in North Carolina—no school records, nothing."

Shel looked thoughtful. "You also have to wonder where the dough came from he used to start that loan business. He'd have needed some fairly serious capital to get it going. Of course it could all be on the up and up." Shel sounded more hopeful than convinced. "Anyhow, talk to Ballard again, check out his earlier career, then wrap it up. We need to make this Sunday's edition."

*****

Cindy, SandScapes' receptionist, put me on hold, then returned after a long interval. "Mr. Ballard is extremely busy just now," she informed me. "He said to tell you he has no time for the press." With that, she hung up.

Ticked off and determined, I got in the Jeep and drove to the SandScapes office. In their parking lot, the sun's rays glinted off the rear window of a plain black sedan with government license plates that was parked in the slot nearest the entrance. I stopped short, wondering why the Feds would be involved with Valerie's murder. In cases like hers, local law enforcement often

called on the FBI lab for DNA sampling and possibly for pro-
filing, but generally at this stage, only local law enforcement
would be handling the actual investigation.

Inside the real estate office, the staff was gathered in little clusters, speaking in hushed voices and casting speculative
glances toward Ballard's closed office door.

"He's in conference. Can't be disturbed." Cindy, who just a
few days before had bubbled over with information, had turned
oddly uncommunicative.

I piled on an ingratiating smile. "Then maybe you can help
me," I coaxed. "I need background information on Mr. Ballard
for a feature piece in the *Dispatch's* Life Style section. Our photographer's coming by here later to take some pictures. I'll be
sure to tell him to get a shot of you."

"What kind of stuff do you need?"

"Just a few facts about where Mr. Ballard grew up, where
he went to school, that sort of thing."

"Oh. Like what you'd call a bio. We got something like that
in the file. Mr. Ballard gives it out to the clients he handles himself, the ones with big expensive properties to buy or sell."

"Perfect. So can you find me a copy?"

"No prob. Matter of fact, I mailed one out for Mr. Ballard
just yesterday."

Once I had possession of the handsomely bound booklet,
I decided to press my luck by asking Cindy if she knew what
was going on in Ballard's office. "I noticed the government car
outside," I said.

She cast a glance around the office to see if anyone else was
listening before leaning closer. "Don't know," she said, speaking
barely above a whisper, "but the boss has been real upset ever
since those guys showed up. And Mr. Ports—he's the company
accountant—they've got that poor man run ragged, digging out
all kinds of records."

I had expected her to say that the men were investigating
Valerie's murder, but this sounded more like a financial audit,

which fit in with Carl Bailey's comments at Trivia. Just then one of the staff approached the reception desk. Cindy straightened and said loudly, "I really can't say anything about that, Ms. McKelvey."

Back at the *Dispatch* office, I examined Ballard's bio. No cheapo typed resume, it was printed on glossy paper and bound in a thick maroon cover with SandScapes's logo embossed in gold. It even smelled expensive. The pamphlet opened with a professional photo of Ballard seated behind his desk in his best presidential pose. The information inside confirmed much of what I'd already learned about his business, all properly sanitized and considerably inflated. For instance, his Friend-N-Need Loan Company was presented as "a major mortgage brokerage." The resume also revealed that Ballard had been born in Raleigh, North Carolina, attended high school there, then Duke University. It also stated that after eight years of military service, including two tours of Vietnam, he had been honorably discharged from the U.S. Army.

That pretty well deflated the image I'd been constructing of a manipulative phony—Vietnam veterans and Duke graduates might not be exactly sacred cows, but they grazed in the same pasture with Eagle Scouts and kindly grandmothers. Still, I had what I needed to complete my article. I highlighted the important items, and began typing.

CHAPTER 12

Ridiculous as I find Zanthia's far-out predictions and premonitions, there are times I suffer from that same trait. There I was, happily settled into my usual booth in the Essential Bean, sipping my usual mid-morning latte, while the soothing odor of well-brewed Columbian swirled about me. Engrossed in my newspaper, I was hardly aware when the bell above the door tinkled. A hand touched my shoulder and even before I glimpsed polished boots and a flash of tan uniform, I knew who was standing there.

Annoyance shot through me like an unwanted elbow in the ribs—two chance encounters in one week was too much coincidence. Sam must have sensed my reaction because he immediately pulled his hand away. "Just grabbing a coffee to go," he said in the same brusque tone he'd use in addressing a suspect. He seemed about to move on, then halted. "I read your piece on the murdered girl," he said. "Nice job. Are you covering the crime beat now?"

I gave a brief snort. "Frank Burke's not about to let me

touch the hard stuff."

"Too bad, especially after the terrific job you did on the case where the college president was murdered."

"Thanks," I murmured.

The murder he referred to had taken place the previous February but was still St. Augustine's main topic of conversation. Murders are rare in the historic town, especially one where the victim is clad in 16th century Spanish costume. But that case was past, and Sam standing by the booth was all too present. I stirred my latte, hoping he'd leave, while the part of me that lacks a brain wished he'd stay.

He must have caught my ambivalence because he slid into the booth opposite me. "Maybe I can give you a one-up on Frank," he said. "There's a little something we've held back from the press."

I understood immediately what he was talking about—in a crime investigation, police often keep in reserve some vital clue that will help to pin down the perpetrator. They might not reveal that a footprint found near the crime scene can be matched with a particular brand of shoe, or that unusual fibers were found on the victim's body. If my suspicions were correct Sam was dangling some such protected information as a lure.

Note to self: This is wrong on several levels. Sam will be committing a crime by sharing restricted information. I'll be encouraging him to think we still have a relationship.

Sam read my hesitation. "Look, no strings. But I figure this case means a lot to you, having gone to school with the victim and everything."

Curiosity, lifeblood to a reporter, won out. Still, I felt guilty that I was allowing Sam to jeopardize his job in a pathetic attempt to grab my attention for a few minutes.

He gave a light tap on the tabletop with his fingertips. "Here's the deal. Our forensic pathologist has pretty well nailed that Kimmel died from a blow to the back of her head. Weapon was a heavy object, swung with great force."

So far, that was nothing new. The same information was in the report Kyle showed me.

Sam's next words made it more intriguing, "He also told us that the blow was delivered by a lefty." Sam swung his left forearm in an arc, imitating the killer's movement.

I considered for a moment—when Alvaro stormed out of Valerie's apartment had he used his left hand to open the door? Or would that depend on the side of the door on which the knob was located? And Ballard—when he was showing off his golf trophies, I was fairly sure he'd pointed with his right hand.

"Knowing the killer is a lefty eliminates about 85 percent of the population," I said, "but that doesn't bring you much closer to identifying him . . . or her."

Sam tapped the table again, this time more forcefully. "You haven't heard the best part. We have a positive ID on the type of weapon he or she used."

I waited for him to continue. Instead, he said, "Tell me, how are you and . . . what's his name? . . . Andy something? How are you two—"

Furious, I jumped up. "Okay, thanks for the information about Mr. or Ms. Left Handed. And good luck in catching him or her. Now I have to go."

"Day, wait, I'm sorry." Sam grasped my wrist. "That was totally out of line, and I apologize. Sit down for just a minute and I'll tell you the rest."

I started to pull away, then released a huge sigh and sank back into my seat.

"The weapon was a Hi-Lite brand flashlight. Big heavy sucker, fourteen inches long, a lot like the ones we cops carry."

"How did the pathologist ID it?'

"You know how on some flashlights the part nearest the lens is wider than the shaft? This one was like that, and it had distinctive striations that left wound marks." He gestured toward my bag. "You got a piece of paper in there? I'll show you exactly what the head of the flashlight looks like."

I handed him paper and a pencil, and he drew a curved surface and started to sketch in some vertical marks. We were both leaning intensely over the sheet of paper and failed to notice that someone had approached the booth until the sound of a throat clearing caused me to look up to find Frank Burke's accusing face staring down at us.

*****

I didn't need to hear the conversation between Shel and Frank Burke to know what had been said behind Shel's closed office door. I could read it on Shel's face when he approached my cubicle later. He was carrying a square plastic box piled with letters, the kind of container that the post office uses to deliver mail in quantity.

"What?" I said when he placed it on my desk.

"New assignment."

"New, as in—"

"Look, Day, you know how Frank is about the crime beat. I gave you the background piece on the victim and the profile article on Ballard. But now Frank's steamed . . . says you're interfering . . . getting inside information from police sources."

"Okay. So I have a . . . friend . . . who's close to the case. He was talking to me about it, but that's got nothing to do with Frank."

"Let's not make waves where Frank's concerned. Besides, I need someone good on this." He gestured toward the letters.

"This being what?" I muttered, feeling demeaned and totally pissed off at Frank.

"You know about the proposed rezoning of the old Coronado golf course?"

I gave a wary nod, already suspicious of where he was heading.

Shel pasted on his this-could-be-great-stuff smile. "The members of the Coronado Ladies' Golf Association have launched a campaign to halt the proposed rezoning. They've been hounding me with letters and phone calls."

"What's wrong with the op-ed page for that?"

"We've got to give them more ink. Their president, Zelma Beauclaire, is a pit bull and she's got her teeth into this cause."

"You do realize it's Compton Ballard who's brokering that deal?"

"I know. That's kind of sticky, but it's all being done under the name of Southwind Enterprises, so I figure you can downplay his role in this."

"Shel, I don't know diddly about golf. Why not give it to somebody on the sports page?"

"You'll do a great job on this." Shel was still smiling, but I knew better than to continue the argument.

I sat staring at the box of letters he had dumped on me. My mental picture of the Beauclaire woman and her ilk was a group of ladies sitting on the Coronado's clubhouse veranda in their little flowered golf skirts, sipping gin and tonics, and complaining about their scores. Of course they were ticked at having to give up their club. Now our editor expected me to make a story out of their hopeless effort to stop the developer who threatened their playground.

What made the assignment so maddening was that it was Frank's fault I got stuck with it. It had been that way ever since I first came on board the *Dispatch*. Not that I wasn't warned— when Kyle recommended me for the job, he'd explained the situation. "Frank Burke was a hotshot on the police beat for the *L.A. Times* until he reported on some dirty tricks within the police department. When Frank refused to back down on his exposé, things got real nasty. His wife was a teacher. One afternoon she got into her vehicle in the school's lot, turned the key, and the car exploded."

"My God!" I gasped. "Was she?. . . "

"Killed her instantly. Also took the leg of a kid standing nearby. They say Frank went berserk for a while. Luckily, the cops got to the killer before he did. But after that, he couldn't bear to stay there, so he gave up his job and came east."

Kyle's sobering account made me understand Frank's perpetual gloominess, but I still didn't see why he had to take his anger out on me. It wasn't fair. I got along fine with most of the staff, but his negativity put a pall on the pleasure I took in my job.

At noon, I left the office to meet Rhonda for a quick lunch. From the direction of the square, horns were blaring and I hurried to see what was going on. When I got there, King Street presented a logjam of vehicles in both directions as a procession of cars inched its way around the square's perimeter. Each vehicle sported a bright yellow banner with *SAVE THE CORONADO!* spelled out in purple letters. Traffic signals were ignored and no other vehicles were allowed to squeeze past. A delivery truck driver leaned on his horn and yelled out his window, "Move it, you idiots!" and a few other unprintable epithets.

A grey van headed the motorcade, a female voice trumpeting from its rooftop speakers, "Citizens of St. Augustine! Do not allow greedy developers and their political cronies to steal our town's oldest golf course. Save the Coronado!"

I spotted Rhonda's aunt, Eloise McFarland, behind the wheel of her ancient Cadillac El Dorado. Other women were waving from the open windows of their Oldsmobiles and Buicks and the occasional Mercedes. Lucinda Downing from Zanthia's séance group and several others were on foot, passing out flyers and *SAVE THE CORONADO!* bumper stickers to the gaping crowd that clogged the sidewalks. The tourists laughed and pointed, agog at the strange event taking place in the nation's oldest city. Some aimed their camera phones toward the spectacle, and I could just imagine them explaining those shots to their friends back in Sheboygan and Topeka.

Rhonda was already waiting in front of the cathedral by the time I squeezed through the throng. "What a hoot this is." She pointed to a man gesturing excitedly from the steps of Government House. "Mayor Korman is having a total meltdown. He's demanding that the police step in, but the gals have traffic blocked and police cars can't get through."

Miles Arkin, the *Dispatch's* photographer, appeared in the square, along with a film crew from a Jacksonville TV station. Rhonda and I continued watching until the procession of cars turned and began inching north on Avenida Menendez. When they were mostly out of sight, she turned to me and asked, "The Pie?"

I nodded, and we strolled up St. George Street toward where the warm, yeasty smell of the Pie In the Sky Café spilled onto the street.

"So give," Rhonda demanded as soon as we'd put in our orders and claimed a table by the window. "What did your mother say when you told her you had another date with Andy?"

I rolled my eyes ceilingward. "Telling her wasn't necessary—Zanthia's spirits had already delivered the news. Now she's trying to micromanage the entire evening. Insists I've got to buy new shoes."

Rhonda laughed. "Oh, come on—Zanthia's not that bad. And when it comes to style, you've got to admit she's always dead on."

"I know—I just like to gripe sometimes. Andy is flying up from Ocala Saturday evening. He asked if I'd make us a dinner reservation. I figure afterwards we can go someplace to listen to music, maybe the Turtle Tavern or Benny on the Beach. After that, I guess it's back to the airport."

Rhonda tilted her head and gave me a scrutinizing look. "Am I missing something here? You sound rather lukewarm about this date."

"No, not at all," I denied. But a moment later I admitted, "Well, maybe."

Rhonda's eyebrows lifted. "I thought you and Andy were really hitting it off."

"It's just that after four dates we seem stuck, no farther along than that first evening, the date you and Rick arranged for us."

"But didn't you say your fishing trip to the Glades was—how'd you describe it—'beyond great'?"

"That's just it—things there got a little too intense for both of us. Since then, we've seen each other three times, but never alone. It's always restaurants, movies, clubs, anyplace where we're surrounded by other people."

"Safety in numbers—is that your idea or his?"

"Both, I guess. The crazy thing is, Andy and I can spend hours talking, we've got lots of interests in common, we've read the same books, he knows more about old movie stars than I do, we both like Arrowsmith—"

"Sounds great. I don't see the problem."

I watched a couple with a child walk past the Pie's window. The little girl—about four, although I'm lost when it comes to estimating kid's ages—tugged at her mother's hand to pull her toward a display of hats in the shop window opposite. "Politics, religion, world events—those topics we can handle," I told Rhonda. "It's the personal stuff we seemed to be avoiding. Whenever we start to get close, things get awkward, and one or the other of us backs away."

Rhonda's knowing smile curled around her straw. "Sounds to me like the old 'elephant in the room' syndrome."

"A pachyderm in the parlor, for sure. But how do we get past that?"

"Maybe you should give Andy a chance to know you better, let him see you on your home territory. Instead of a restaurant, invite him for dinner at your place, just the two of you."

"Me? Cook? That's a laugh. I don't think all the candlelight in the world can make a hamburger on the grill and frozen fries into a gourmet dinner."

"You don't have to make like Julia Child," Rhonda said. "What about your bouillabaisse? Rick says he'd dump me for you in a flash if you'd promise to make it on demand."

I fished from my plate a sliver of tomato that had escaped my sandwich. Rhonda had zeroed in on my one culinary accomplishment, a dish my Dad and I used to prepare together. "Bouil-labaisse," I mused. "I'd have to pick up fresh clams and mussels. Maybe halibut or grouper and some local shrimp. Bouillabaisse takes a lot of seafood—"

Rhonda gave me one of her looks. "Think of it as bait," she said.

CHAPTER 13

On my return from lunch, I sat at my desk, thinking of ways to make Frank Burke suffer, something non-fatal but painful, like hemorrhoids. Even the nifty pair of Jimmy Choos Rhonda had helped me find at the outlet mall couldn't compensate for the humiliation I was suffering. No thanks to Burke, I'd been demoted to writing about an irate bunch of women golfers.

That Valerie's funeral was scheduled for later that afternoon did nothing to improve my disposition. Still fuming, I snatched up the phone and punched in the number I'd found for the president of the Coronado Ladies' Golf Association.

"Zelma Beauclaire here," a brisk, recorded voice announced. "If your call's a legitimate one, I'll be happy to talk with you. If you're selling something, I don't want it. If you're looking for a donation, write me a letter. If you're calling to complain that my cat has peed in your flowerbed again, I know who you are, so don't waste your time and mine. Leave your name and number after the beep."

At the beep, I stammered my message.

While waiting for Zelma Beauclaire to return my call, I checked for mention of her in the *Dispatch's* files. Her name showed up attached to practically every charity and volunteer group in St. Augustine, most often in an administrative position—the hospital's Pink Ladies, the Literacy Council, the Bright Lights Theater, and the battered women's shelter for starters. Lots of mention in the Society pages as well. *Registry Bank President Elmer Beauclaire and wife, Zelma, at black tie dinner. . . The Beauclaires embark for Panama Canal cruise. . . Elmer and Zelma Beauclaire guests at Governor's Ball.*

With all her other activities, it was beyond my comprehension how a 72-year-old woman found the time or the energy to play golf. I studied a photo of her that appeared on the "Happenings About Town" page. The only adjective to describe Zelma Beauclaire was "square"—square jaw, square shoulders, square hips. Even her white hair was cut blunt and square to just below her ears. Shel had described her as a "pit bull" and I could glimpse a hint of that pugnaciousness in the way she stared directly into the camera lens.

Some time later, my phone rang. When I picked it up a voice barked, "About time the *Dispatch* is getting on this. What do you want from me?"

"Mrs. Beauclaire? . . . "

"Yes. What's on your mind?"

Put off by her brusque manner, I struggled to keep from sounding equally snappish. "I'd like to meet with you to hear how your group plans to fight the rezoning of the Coronado."

"Glad to lay that out for you. Let me see—" She trailed off, and I could hear pages rustling.

She came back. "No free time this week. Tell you what; meet me at the Bridge Club next Tuesday morning, six-thirty sharp."

"You said Bridge Club? But I don't—"

"Bridge Club. That's what we call ourselves—bunch of us who do the Vilano Bridge every morning. We start from the parking lot at Camachee Cove. Six-thirty sharp." Without giving me time to confirm the appointment, she hung up.

*****

Later that day, Polly, Rhonda and I settled ourselves in the fourth row of folding chairs in the Calloway Funeral Home's viewing parlor. The solemnity of the recorded music and the heavy scent of funeral flowers—chrysanthemum odors dominating the more delicate scents—discouraged conversation. Most of the seats were filled, partly due no doubt to the curiosity seekers violent death always seems to attract.

A group of agents from SandScapes was seated two rows in front of us. Elaine Descuto turned to give me a brief wave. I recognized several others, Nick Petroski, a Jane somebody and Cindy the receptionist, who was once again mopping her eyes. I could just make out the deep forehead dent in the man seated at the end of the row, Harry Ports, the neatnik who'd gone off on the copier repairman.

Until that moment, I'd forgotten about the scrap of paper I'd found in Val's jacket. Alvaro's unexpected appearance and the somewhat macabre aspect of my errand there had driven it completely out of my mind. Harry Ports was SandScapes' company accountant. What if Valerie had discovered Ports was embezzling from the company? What if Ports had murdered her to keep her from reporting his thievery to Ballard?

Just then a large woman passed down the aisle while fumbling in her purse. As she passed the SandScapes group, she dropped something; a handkerchief or a tissue, and Ports bent to retrieve it for her. I noticed two things: He used his left hand and there was a black tattoo mark on the web between his thumb and index finger. A marking like that seemed strange for someone so fastidious.

"Day," Rhonda nudged me. "Why do you keep staring at that man?"

"Oh. Just . . . I don't know." I made a conscious effort to turn my attention elsewhere, but the more I thought about it, the stronger the feeling grew that Harry Ports had to be somehow involved in Val's murder. Maybe if I got in touch with Sam . . . .

That line of reasoning brought an abrupt reminder of what had happened in a previous murder case. That time, I'd been dead certain of the killer's identity and had persuaded Sam to switch the focus of the entire investigation, a move that had nearly cost him his job when my suspicions proved untrue. In addition, my accusation had caused a lot of trouble for the man I mistakenly identified, and he'd never entirely forgiven me.

I reined in my runaway imagination. After all, just because the man had gotten upset over a few scraps of paper hardly made him a murderer. I'd do some further checking on Harry Ports, but unless and until I had concrete evidence, there was no point in telling anyone.

Compton Ballard entered just then and made his way to the row in front of the SandScapes group. He was accompanied by sedate-looking middle-aged woman who'd had the foresight to wear a pashmina shawl against the funeral home's overly-ambitious air conditioning. Ballard was the person I should be looking at more closely as a possible murderer. He may have been in Salt Lake City when Valerie was killed, but there was always the possibility of a hired killer. What about jealousy of Alvaro as the motive? That scenario shouldn't be discounted.

I stole a surreptitious glance to the rear and recognized several of our high school classmates, Amanda Frey among them. In my rearward glance, I also spotted a tall woman wearing what had to be a thirty-year-old Chanel suit, a classic, but oddly out of place here in Florida. It took some mental adjustment to recognize her as the riding instructor, Haley Simms. She acknowledged me with a slight nod, then glanced away.

I was rather surprised to see Arch Fleagle seated next to Haley, his hair carefully combed and parted and wearing a neatly pressed plaid shirt—perhaps he wasn't as insensitive as I'd thought. I also looked around to see if I could spot anyone tall, dark and Argentinian, but as far as I could tell, Alvaro Cardenas was not present.

I was relieved to see Corporal Tim Robb standing at the rear of the room wearing civvies. Not that I couldn't handle running into Sam again, but it was less stressful that he wasn't the officer assigned to be present.

More people filed in, and just as the piped-in organ music slowed to a more somber tempo, the funeral director escorted a middle-aged woman to a seat in the front row. Her graying hair was permed into tight curls and her wrinkled face was innocent of cosmetics. I pointed her out to Rhonda and Polly. "That must be Caroline Wallace, the half sister . . . Val's mother's daughter by her first husband," I said. "I interviewed her by phone."

"She's certainly not the fashionista that Val was," Polly kept her voice low. "That dress had to be in style about the time Reagan was in office. Was she able to give you any information about Val?"

"She was twelve years older than Val," I whispered back. "Apparently they were never close, especially after Caroline married and moved to Ohio. She told me about a puppy Val once rescued, but that was about all she had to offer."

The minister, an elderly man with stooped posture and scant wisps of gray hair encircling his scalp, moved to the podium. After an excruciatingly drawn-out prayer, and scriptures offering the guarantee of eternal life, he embarked upon a generic eulogy.

My mind refused to stay focused and wandered to the dinner I'd planned for my date with Andy the following night. What wine with bouillabaisse, red or white? I had some nice merlot stashed in the stairwell, but maybe the pinot grigio would go better. Should I offer him a choice of salad dressings, maybe ranch and Italian? I'd have to get cream for coffee, or would half and half be better? And did he drink regular or decaf? Last time we were out . . .

A nudge from Rhonda brought me to attention. The funeral director had begun easing his way toward the front. At the first evidence of a pause, he thanked the minister and asked if any others would like to come forward and share their reminiscences of Valerie.

An embarrassingly long silence followed. Compton Ballard's wife nudged his arm. He hesitated, then stood and made his way to the front of the room. Unlike the confident egotism he had displayed when I met him in his office, Ballard presented a tense, preoccupied aspect. A dark swoop under each eye gave him the appearance of a man who had spent too many sleepless nights. Several times he paused to grope for the appropriate words but managed to describe Valerie as a valued employee and close associate.

During Ballard's remarks, I was reminded of Frank Burke's criticism the previous day. "So you've checked out all this stuff in Ballard's bio about Raleigh, Duke, and his army service?" Frank asked.

That he'd taken his shot at a staff meeting in front of everyone set me boiling. The article was scheduled for the Sunday edition and there hadn't been enough time to check all the records. I had to bite my tongue to keep from reminding Frank that we were the *First Coast Dispatch*, not the *L.A. Times*.

Lost in my snit, I was unaware when Ballard returned to his seat that no one else had claimed the podium. Rhonda leaned across me to give Polly a meaningful glare. When Polly ignored her, Rhonda rose from her seat, and walked to the front of the room. She gave a short, moving speech about how in high school Valerie had raised school spirit in her role as head cheerleader. "Rain or shine, win or lose," Rhonda said, "Val was there at every game rooting on our teams."

Beside me, Polly released an amused snort. "And humping the coach on the side."

Rhonda's short upbeat talk seemed to loosen inhibitions, and several people who had known Valerie from school or from work came forward to speak. Cindy, the tearful receptionist, stumbled to the podium, but watery sobs consumed her words.

When it seemed there were no more eulogies, a man sitting in the last row stood and shuffled his way toward the front. At first, his shabby clothing and slouched posture made me mistake him for a street person who'd wandered in by mistake. But when he turned to face the audience, in spite of the damage time and alcohol had done, I recognized him as the same man who'd dragged Valerie from the skating rink.

I heard Rhonda catch her breath. "The father," she whispered.

The man grabbed the podium to steady himself, then swept the audience with the same blazing bloodshot eyes I remembered from that long ago night. "Um here," he mumbled, "Um here 'cause Val was my li'l girl. Shome people . . . shome people might think cause . . ."

At that he lost his line of thought and stood teetering. The room went totally silent for an excruciatingly long moment until the funeral director stepped in and took the man's arm. "Mister Kimmel, we all regret—"

Val's father shook him off, then turned toward the coffin and mumbled, "I love you, Valerie. You hear that? Love you . . ." Again at a loss, he stopped in mid-sentence, and this time allowed the funeral director to lead him to a seat.

Amid embarrassed murmurs, Val's sister stood and haltingly offered a few remarks that provided a sad little ending for the ceremony. "Valerie and I were too far apart in age to really be close," she said. "By the time she finished elementary school, I was already married and moved away. But she was a good person and I wish I had known her better when she was alive."

With that the sister sat down. This time Polly had nothing sarcastic to say.

When the service ended, I stopped on the way out to say hello to Corporal Tim Robb.

"Nice piece you wrote on the murdered girl in the *Dispatch*," Tim said.

"The case keeping you busy?"

Tim shrugged. "You know how it goes. You pick up anything while you were talking to people about her?"

"Nothing you don't already have," I said, then, still suspicious that Ballard could have had a role in Valerie's murder, I decided to probe a bit. "One thing puzzles me, though—I got the impression from talking to several of the agents that Valerie and Compton Ballard were . . .you know . . . close. But when I interviewed him, he didn't seem terribly upset that she was dead. At least not on a personal level."

Tim made a face as if he'd bitten into something bad tasting. "This is just between you and me—" he glanced behind him before going on, "but I talked to one of Ballard's buddies. He said that not long before Valerie was killed, he and Ballard were having a few drinks, and Ballard got to talking about her. 'She's just a little something I got on the side,' Ballard bragged. 'I keep her thinking that when I retire she'll take over as company president. That's not going to happen, of course, but that way I know she's got the company's interests at heart.' "

A wave of disgust and anger washed over me. The sanitized article Shel insisted I write would further elevate Compton Ballard's status—the old "lipstick on a pig" syndrome. Instinct told me there was something about Ballard that didn't square with what I'd observed about him. It was too late to do anything about Sunday's edition, but I wasn't finished yet.

CHAPTER 14

Distant rumbles came from the sullen bank of gray clouds sweeping in from the southwest as Rhonda, Polly and I made our way to the Essential Bean after leaving the funeral. The thunderheads threatening rain failed to dispel the muggy heat, and we were all sticky and uncomfortable by the time we were seated. As if the heat had drained our voices, we were quiet until the Bean's air conditioning had done its work and icy frappuccinos were in front of us. Then I scolded Polly for her disrespectful remark about Valerie and the coach. *"De mortuis* and all that."

"It was true," Polly protested. "Besides, just because she's dead doesn't turn her into a saint. When you two give my eulogy, I want you to let it all hang out. I'd rather be remembered as a real person, warts and all."

"Enough about funerals and eulogies," Rhonda said with a shudder. "Let's talk about something more cheerful, like Day's big date with Andy tomorrow night."

I rolled my eyes. "Andy and I are just getting together for dinner."

Polly swished her straw through the whipped cream on her frap. "Spill all," she said "What time is he picking you up? Where are you going for dinner? What are you wearing?"

I made a face at her. "You're worse than my mother. Soon as Zanthia knew Andy and I were going out, she started turning it into the prequel to a wedding. 'Day, dear, you've simply got to do something with your hair.'"

Polly laughed. "As usual, Zanthia's right on target." She reached over and lifted a strand of hair from my shoulder. "What did you cut this with?—a pair of blunt garden shears? What are you doing with your hair?"

"Matter of fact, I'll be seeing your husband tomorrow morning for a cut and style. All courtesy of my own dear mother. She went to Ambience, made the appointment, and prepaid so I couldn't turn it down."

"Not to worry—Giles will whip out his magic scissors and voila! You'll come out downright glamorous."

"Speaking of whom," I said. "What's the latest at the Ribideaux-Sheffield love nest?"

Polly actually blushed. "He is so incredibly sweet. Remember I told you about the little Derbyshire cream pitcher I saw in Swift Antiques' window? I don't know how Giles found out I had my eye on it, but when I came down to breakfast this morning there it was next to my plate."

I rolled my eyes ceiling-ward, a habit I seemed to be acquiring. "So here's a guy who not only does all the cooking—gourmet meals, yet—irons his own shirts and never leaves wet towels on the bathroom floor. Are you sure Giles is for real?"

Polly grinned. "He's real all right—I mean all the essential—"

I raised my hand to stop her. "Do not go there. As a woman who hasn't . . . well, you know . . . in months, I don't think I can bear to hear all the titillating details."

Shortly after, Polly had to leave for an appointment. Rhonda and I sat for a few minutes longer. "Can you believe?" I mused.

"Who would have thought Polly would turn out to be Myrna Loy to Giles's William Powell?

"You and your old movies. If Valerie Kimmel's life were a movie, who would you have chosen to play her?"

I thought for a moment. "Teresa Wright, maybe."

"I don't remember her."

"Where have you been? She won an Oscar for *Best Years of Our Lives.*"

"Day, dear, we don't all spend our evenings watching old black and whites. I hope after this date with Andy you won't have all that much time for them either."

I rolled my eyes again—it was turning into an addiction. "I can see exactly how the script would go if you were writing a movie for Andy and me."

"*It Happened One Night,*" Rhonda quipped.

I laughed. "According to Polly, with Giles and her it happens every night."

Rhonda tossed her napkin at me. "Here were are fresh from Val's funeral and talking about Giles's equipment."

"Sex and death," I said as we both rose to leave. "Not all that far apart, you know."

*****

Saturday morning I stopped by Mother's shop before going to Ambience. As always, The Other Side's distinct atmosphere greeted me—the splash of fountains, the tinkle of wind-chimes and the pervasive scent of incense. Mother——Zanthia—was demonstrating to a customer the meaning of the rune stones she'd spread atop a glass display counter. "This one signifies wisdom. Very potent, but also potentially dangerous. Some things are better not known."

"Ah, yes," the woman agreed. "A little learning . . ."

I waited while the customer paid for her purchase and departed, happily clutching the parcel containing the stones, then braced myself for an immediate interrogation about my upcoming date. But Zanthia's attention seemed focused elsewhere. "I had the most vivid dream last night," she said. "I dreamed that Zelma Beauclaire was arrested. I could see her clearly as anything, peering out from behind bars in that hideous orange outfit criminals are forced to wear."

That supposition evoked a snort of laughter. The idea of Zelma Beauclaire, the woman for whom the term "Society Matron" was coined, behind bars was too ridiculous to contemplate. I was still chuckling to myself and was caught off-guard when Mother switched abruptly to the subject I'd anticipated. "Now, darling," she trilled, "About your date tonight—even though the moon is in a highly auspicious quarter, you must be careful."

I squinted at her. "Careful?"

"This morning I saw in the cards that there would be a crisis before the evening was over. But when I did the cards again, it appeared the crisis would be quickly resolved, so I figure it probably just means that you'll forget the salad dressing or allow the bread to burn. I do wish you'd learned to cook."

*****

The mingled odors of nail gel and hairspray greeted me as I checked in with Ambience's receptionist and seated myself on one of the black leather chairs in the waiting area. Ambience, the town's premier salon, strove for elegance with textured plaster walls, black shampoo capes bearing a scrolled "A" logo, and a modernistic S-shaped reception desk.

Giles Sheffield's station was near the front of the shop. He gave me a short wave of recognition, then turned back to his customer. Last month's Vogue topped the pile beside my chair. I picked it up and began reading ads for designer clothes I'd never buy. A few pages into the magazine, the bell over the shop door jangled and Mother's gossipy friend, Corinne Randall, came in. I pretended an intense interest in a Vera Wang sheath.

The receptionist informed Corinne that her operator was running fifteen minutes behind schedule at which Corinne plopped her substantial self into the chair adjoining mine. "Oh, Day," she exclaimed, "your mother told me all about how you were coming in today for a cut and style. 'Zanthia,' I said to her, 'that's the very time of my appointment with Evelyn.' And here we are."

I smiled. With Corinne there was no need to do more; she'd supply her own dialogue.

She bubbled on. "And aren't you lucky to have Giles doing you? Zanthia must have worked some special magic to get you in. He's always booked weeks in advance. Dotty's business has doubled since he came—even has customers driving all the way down from Jacksonville. A genius with the scissors, that man. Of course he's dreadfully expensive and only does cuts and color, no perms. I'd try him, but Evelyn's been doing mine for years, so I wouldn't feel right about making a change."

Corinne's ramblings blended with the hum of dryers and the murmur of conversations from the various stations, and I tuned out until a nudge from my too-willing informant forced my attention. "Zanthia tells me you've been going out with this young man who flies. Something to do with fish and animals and things. And I understand he's had you up in his plane with him. All the way down to the Everglades, Zanthia said. That sounds like a lovely ride. Of course when Albert and I were dating we never did anything fancy like flying, it was all in this old Pontiac of his and I can tell you that car—"

I reflected that in certain situations deafness might be considered a blessing.

"Ms. McKelvey," the receptionist announced, "Giles is ready for you now."

I wanted to kiss her.

Draped in a cape and enthroned in Giles's chair, I faced my mirrored image as he lifted and examined my tresses. "Nice texture," he said, "but, dear girl, you've allowed this to become rah-ther too long."

As always, Giles' attempt at an upper-class British accent intrigued me. His was almost convincing, but thanks to my addiction to the Britcoms, I caught the little slips that betrayed traces of Liverpool and Manchester rather than Kensington or Hyde Park.

"I keep my hair this length so it's easy to pull it back out of the way," I explained.

His expression—as if he'd decided that the vichyssoise was not up to his standards— dismissed my reasoning. "I would say it's time to go for a softer, more feminine look, one that will frame your features more appropriately."

"But I don't have time for a lot of fuss," I protested. "I like that I can climb out of the shower, grab my blow dryer, and minutes later I'm ready to go."

He smiled, revealing the one slight flaw in his appearance—typical British lack of good dentistry. "We will keep it simple, but not quite so . . . utilitarian."

He picked up his scissors and for the first time I realized Giles was left-handed. Or was I becoming obsessed with left-handedness since Sam's revelation about the flashlight? I'd noticed Harry Ports' left hand at the funeral, and even became aware when the counter guy at the Essential Bean handed me my latte with his left hand, and there was Everett as well, all left-handed. As if that proved anything except Val's murderer could have been any person within the fifteen percent of the world's left-handed people.

Soon, under Giles's skilled fingers, my hair began to show possibilities of being something more than simply a convenient cover-up for my scalp. Half an hour later Giles announced, "And now, look in the mirror at the new glamorous you."

It was flattery, of course, but I did look good with the new style. I wondered if Andy would notice; if he had Sam's detective eye for details.

On the way home from Ambience, I couldn't resist frequent glimpses in the rearview mirror. At the grocery store, I selected a fresh baguette of French bread and salad greens. As I loaded my purchases onto the checkout counter, the bag boy James, gave a little whistle. "You're looking nice, Miss Day. Must have big plans for the weekend."

I smiled acknowledgement, feeling a certain smug confidence that my "date" that night with Andy might well turn into "weekend."

At the seafood market, I chose the freshest, leanest fish available—grouper and flounder along with lobster, shrimp, and mussels. Crab meat, too, since it was in season. The store had just gotten in a fresh batch of scallops, so I added those to my list.

As Tony was weighing my purchases, he also complimented my new hairstyle. On my way to the car, I ran into Will Faber whom I hadn't seen since high school. His "Wow, you're looking great" sent my confidence meter soaring. When I flipped on the radio on the way home, Alicia Keys was singing "How it Feels to Fly." Maybe Mother was right—all the omens were in place.

CHAPTER 15

By the time I dropped the grocery bags onto the kitchen counter, Rhonda's idea that I prepare dinner for Andy began to seem more and more tricky. I felt confident about the bouillabaisse, but what if having dinner here in the apartment turned out all wrong—too domestic . . . too intimate . . . too everything?

Even my new hairdo could make the evening seem contrived. What if . . .

Then from somewhere inside my head, a voice that sounded oddly like Rhonda's muttered, *Get a grip, for Pete's sake. It's a simple date. He'll like your apartment or he won't. He'll like the bouillabaisse or he won't. He'll like your new hairdo or he won't.*

Still not certain, I left the kitchen and walked from room to room, trying to see my place as Andy would see it. The second floor of Mrs. Castelli's old Victorian had been my home for three years. Visitors climbed the outer stairs leading to the second floor rear porch. Simple wicker furniture with bright cushions made it my favorite spot for Sunday morning coffee and newspapers, watching boats go by, or enjoying the view as dusk spread its misty cloak across the Matanzas River.

From the porch, guests entered through French doors into the large airy living room where seating was grouped around the brick fireplace. For dining there was a small pine drop-leaf table and a pair of Windsor chairs with cushioned seats. I'd kept the furnishings simple; some from Mother's attic, others were various yard sale and antique shop purchases. My two indulgences, pretty fabrics and local art, created splashes of color throughout the room.

At one end of the living room, an arched opening led to the small galley kitchen whose windows faced the street side of the house. A hallway to the right of the living room led to my bedroom whose windows faced the river, and a bath as well as a guest room/office sat on the street side.

My inspection circuit left me feeling calmer. Andy would see me on my home territory, and that would be fine. The hairdo?—I checked a mirror and that looked fine, too.

I returned to the kitchen and had just taken down from the shelf the notebook with the bouillabaisse recipe when I remembered that the wine would need to be chilled. Back in the living room, I opened the door to the landing above the enclosed stairwell and again was forced to grope about in the unlit space for the right bottle. Again I was reminded that I needed to ask Tuck to replace the light bulb that hung over the stairs. Last time I'd attempted to store a box on one of the top steps, I'd nearly tripped over the Easter basket and the box of Christmas ornaments I'd stowed there.

I found the wine I wanted and closed the door. No time now to worry about light bulbs, I had a dinner to prepare.

Reading through the list of ingredients in my notebook swept me back to the time when I was a child, those Sunday evenings when Dad used to shoo Mother from the kitchen. He'd tie on his special "Dad's in the Kitchen" apron and begin chopping away at the wooden board next to the sink. The pungent aroma a heap of diced onions piling up under the knife's snick, snick soon brought tears to both our eyes. "It's so sad," Dad would joke. "These poor, poor onions."

I knew he was just being silly, but I still laughed every time.

I remembered, too, how, when the olive oil in the bottom of the big kettle began to sizzle, Dad would lift me onto a stool next to the stove. My job was to drop in the chopped onions, scallions and garlic. As soon as they turned golden, Dad would add the mound of bright red diced tomatoes. He and I would take turns stirring, and soon the enticing smell wafting up from the kettle would fill the entire house.

That afternoon, I followed Dad's recipe, carefully measuring in the ingredients. The original recipe called for stewing off several pound of fish heads, bones and trimmings for the soup base. I cheated a bit by substituting bottled clam juice. Nearly as flavorful, and a lot less time consuming. Next came the seasonings—parsley, bay leaf, thyme tied in a cheesecloth bag for later removal. A few judicious grinds of black pepper. Last and most important, the saffron. More stirring and the oniony smell became transformed and sophisticated.

Then it was time for what Dad called "our secret ingredient." Carefully, I slid a knife blade around the circumference of an orange and removed the peel in a single spiral. The rind's sweet, tart pungence grabbed at my heart and the long-ago memory forced me to dab my eyes with my sleeve. With the spiral of orange peel added to the simmering ingredients in the kettle. I tasted the base, added more pepper and a tad of sea salt. I allowed the mixture to simmer for a few minutes more before turning off the burner. The mixture would be reheated and the seafood added just before serving.

When planning the dinner earlier in the week, I'd decided that, in addition to the soup, all I needed was the salad and a loaf of crusty bread. Those I could manage. That left dessert, and there I found myself stymied. Ice cream didn't seem quite right, but anything that had to go in the oven was totally beyond me—shades of my failed high school attempt at chocolate soufflé.

Mrs. Castelli came to the rescue. "Leave dessert to me," my landlady advised. "Tucker brought me some limes from his tree when he came to mow the other day. A fresh key lime pie, not too sweet, a little tart—perfect with seafood."

I stooped to plant a kiss on her cheek. "You are an angel."

"Ha! If I was an angel I'd have wings to get around instead of these wheels." She laughed as she propelled her wheelchair across her kitchen floor. "You'll need to pick up a can of sweetened condensed milk for me from the grocery store and some whipping cream. And do you have eggs in your refrigerator?"

I thought for a moment. "I believe I do. How many do you need?"

"Oh, I don't need any for the pie. But you might want to have some on hand. Just in case."

I was half way up the stairs to my apartment before I caught her meaning.

*****

From inside the airport lounge I spotted Andy's plane on final approach, the Cessna 182 whose ownership he shared with three other pilots. Now that I'd made all the preparations for dinner at my apartment, I began to feel a little silly. What had I been thinking? Even Mrs. Castelli saw this "dinner in" as a big seduction scene, a transparent ploy. And who knew if Andy liked bouillabaisse, or key lime pie, for that matter? Even my hair felt wrong. The dress I'd pulled from my closet was too fussy; I should never have allowed Mother to talk me into wearing it. And what was I thinking of when I bought the three-inch heels? The evening was going to be a disaster.

Another thought intruded—I'd made Dad's bouillabaisse for Andy and Dad had been a pilot and Andy was a pilot and maybe the whole thing was just too Freudian. I wanted to turn and run out of the airport before he could spot me. Then I had a better idea—my cell phone. I'd call one of the local restaurants.

Make a quick reservation.

But what about Mrs. Castelli's pie? She'd gone to so much trouble to make it. Oh, God, how did a simple dinner date get so complicated?

I paced the length of the lounge, taking deep breaths and ignoring the stares of a couple of pilots checking out their flight plans. It was just a dinner. It would be okay. Andy wasn't Dad and bouillabaisse was just fish stew.

By the time I returned to the window facing the runway, Andy had taxied the Cessna over to where several other small planes were aligned and climbed out of the cockpit. He had on a lightweight sports jacket with chinos and was wearing a tie. Suddenly I was glad I'd followed Mother's advice and worn the dress. The three-inch heels were a bit much, but maybe I'd be kicking them off later on.

I watched from the terminal as Andy circled his plane, checking it out. There was something comforting in his sureness, his solidity. His blond hair was cut short, almost military fashion. He was wearing dark glasses, but I knew that behind them sun crinkles outlined his clear blue eyes. The plane secured, he reached into the cockpit and pulled a bouquet of flowers and a small package. Then he was walking toward me, his expression expectant, but not yet aware that I was observing him behind the terminal's tinted windows.

We met in the waiting area and the formality of our clothing made for a certain restraint. The flowers and package were in the way as Andy gave me a "brush" kiss, one step removed from a handshake and well short of an all-out smooch. But after handing me the flowers, he placed his hand on my shoulders and held me off at a distance. "Your hair . . . it's different," he said. "Looks terrific. You look terrific."

Thank you, Giles! I breathed.

"Would you mind a change of plans?" I asked, as we climbed into my Jeep.

"The evening's yours. Whatever you've decided is fine with me."

CHAPTER 16

"You made this? I'm impressed." Andy's face lit with pleasure as he leaned over his bowl and drew in a deep breath of the combined odors.

His expression rendered all my efforts with the bouillabaisse worthwhile. In fact, by the time we sat down to dinner, I was blessing Rhonda for her suggestion. The flat package Andy had carried from the plane aroused my curiosity. "A gift for you," he said.

"If you don't mind, I'll wait to open it until we're having coffee and dessert so I can fully appreciate it."

Throughout dinner it was as if Andy and I had slipped back into the easy camaraderie of our fishing trip. It felt companionable, it felt good, it felt right. Even the glass of wine we shared before dinner seemed to take on a smoothness one might expect from the most expensive vintage.

At the table, conversation flowed, abetted by second glasses of the pinot grigio. By the time our soup bowls were empty, I knew for a certainty that the evening was not going to end with a simple kiss and a quick goodbye.

"I'll brew the coffee and we can have that along with Mrs. Castelli's pie," I said, then added, "She was going to make a cake for us, but she said the last two cakes she baked had come out thicker on one side than the other. She said the stove seemed to be tilting and that she was going to have Tuck put a little shim under the stove leg."

Andy rose. "I'll clear the table. Maybe take our dessert and your gift out on the porch?"

"Perfect."

That was the last time that evening the word 'perfect' passed my lips. I was just pouring the water into the coffeemaker when I heard a strangled noise from the living room and then Andy's hoarse cry of "Day!"

I ran back and saw that he was holding his hand to his throat and that his face had turned an unhealthy purplish shade. "Scallops," he croaked. "Were there scallops?"

*****

The Jeep's speedometer climbed well beyond the legal limit as we sped down the highway toward the hospital. Between gasps, Andy tried to apologize—sorry he'd ruined our evening . . . sorry he hadn't warned me he was allergic to scallops.

"Just breathe!" I yelled.

By then, I was also having difficulty breathing. *Oh, God— what if I'd killed him? Him, the father of two young children . . .*

I slammed to a stop behind the ambulance parked at the emergency entrance. An EMT who was replacing an empty gurney in the vehicle spotted me as I leaped out of the car and within seconds Andy was on the gurney being wheeled through the entrance with me racing behind. I gasped out an explanation, the intern on duty made a quick analysis and a needle with epinephrine was shoved into Andy's arm. It wasn't until his color faded from purple to red that the tight band around my chest eased a fraction.

"We'll keep him here for a couple of hours, just to make

sure everything's all right," the intern said, then left us alone in a small single room. Beyond the privacy curtain that separated us from the hallway a Saturday night spate of auto accidents and bar fights and one drug overdose kept up a constant bustle of hurrying feet and gurneys wheeling past.

"You won't be able to fly back tonight," I told Andy. "Shall I call your sister and let her know?"

Andy's grin was a little sheepish. "She's keeping the girls for the weekend," he said. "We arranged that before I left."

I looked at Andy . . . Andy looked at me. Right there in the hospital's emergency room, we burst out laughing. The harder we tried to stifle the gurgling sounds coming from us, the funnier it got. The nurse came running, sure her patient was having another attack.

Andy and I got back to my apartment well after midnight. The present he'd bought me was still lying unopened on the coffee table. We sat together on the sofa while I undid the ribbon and wrapping. Inside there was a small painting of the very cove in the Everglades where we'd had our fishing date. "It's beautiful," I breathed, overcome with delight. "Wherever did you find this?"

Andy grinned. "Not exactly found. I painted it for you."

"It's beautiful! You never told me you were an artist."

"Glad you like it. My work involves a lot of photography and that sort of led me into painting."

"This is so special. I don't know how to thank you."

His grin matched the twinkle in his eyes. "Maybe a slice of Mrs. Castelli's pie for starters? Wouldn't want her to think we didn't like it."

So at one in the morning, we sat on the porch drinking coffee and eating key lime pie. The breeze from the river had kicked up a bit and a half moon was skimming the wave tops. Somewhere off in the distance a night bird released a plaintive cry. We finished off our pie and both stood at the same time. Andy took my hand, and together we went inside.

Only a small bedside table lamp lighted my bedroom. Just enough to see Andy's smile as he took me in his arms and kissed me. My arms went around his neck and I pushed myself at him. We stood there for a long moment, anticipation rising like steam around us.

"I wanted to do this since you kissed me on our first date fishing in the Everglades," he murmured into my hair. "But I knew you'd think it was too soon and I was afraid you'd pull away from me, maybe permanently."

I drew my face a few inches away to meet his eyes. "It *was* too soon. I didn't know yet if I could trust you. I didn't know if I could trust myself."

We were already removing each other's clothes and moving toward the bed. Finally naked, Andy picked me up, tossed the covers aside and laid me down among the pillows. As urgently as we had begun, we both slowed down, intent on savoring each moment.

Murmurs and moans escaped into the quiet of the night. It was not like the frenzied passionate sex that I had with Derek and, later on, with Sam, but a more intimate exploring of each other, the giving of pleasure as fulfilling as the receiving of it. At one point, we both fell asleep, but as dawn's first pink and gold rays began to creep around the slats of my window blinds, we both woke up and made love again.

And so we passed the weekend. Ordering takeout food, walking on the beach in the morning sun, lunching at favorite outdoor restaurants where we could hear the pounding surf just beyond the dunes, and making love. Sunday afternoon we watched *Out of Africa* and I cried at the end when Robert Redford died in the crash of his plane, but with Andy's comforting arms around me I no longer felt the anguish that sometimes overcame me when watching it alone.

CHAPTER 17

Monday morning staff meeting. Voices flitted around me like gnats on a summer breeze, while my mind replayed the moments a little white Cessna taxied down the runway, picked up speed, then swooped skyward toward the southwest. It was late Sunday evening when Andy left, and the low-dropping sun had spread its apricot taffeta skirt across the horizon. A picture-perfect finale to our weekend.

Afterwards came the phone calls, the first from Rhonda. "What do you think now that you and Andy have had more . . . uh . . . *time* together?"

I fended off her obvious way of asking for a progress report. "Andy's really thoughtful. It was his idea that we invite Mrs. Castelli for lunch on Sunday. I think she's in love with him."

"Come on, Day, more details. Dish."

"All I'm saying is, yes, it went well."

"And?"

"On the Fourth he's going to bring his daughters to St. Augustine for a beach picnic."

"Now *that's* a major leap forward. Your idea or his?"

"Mutual, I suppose. Only now I'm not so sure—"

"It's almost July. No cold feet, Girl."

Polly's inquiry was more direct: "Did you follow my advice?" she wanted to know.

"Shut up," I told her.

The final call was from Mother. "Day, I kept dreaming all night that your friend Andy was swimming about in the ocean and these little sea creatures kept trying to devour him. It was all so *vivid*."

"Day. Day McKelvey. Earth to Day." Kyle's nudge snapped me back to the moment. I sat up straighter, suddenly aware of Carl Bailey's hasty entrance into the conference room, his round face a-glow with excitement. "Helluva turn down at Sand-Scapes." Carl reached for a doughnut before dropping into his chair. "Feds are in there auditing the books."

Puzzled glances all around the table. "Any tie-in to Valerie Kimmel's murder?" Shel wanted to know.

Carl shook his head. "Apparently it's Ballard's finances they're zooming in on. The Feds are close-mouthed and Ballard isn't talking, either, but he's hired Whitman, Grabel, and Weinblatt as his attorneys, so you know he's taking it seriously."

"How much of this is public knowledge?" Shel asked.

A bite of doughnut left a white swath of powdered sugar on Carl's upper lip. "Enough so that we can safely say that there's an ongoing investigation into his company's finances."

Shel still looked doubtful. "Let's hold off on reporting this until we get a tighter take on it. Meantime—" he turned to me, "your background piece on Ballard will give Carl a good starting point when we get the go-ahead on this story. In fact, you can work with Carl on this."

Carl and I both nodded approval.

Frank Burke interrupted. "If McKelvey's going to work on this Ballard thing, I suggest she dig a lot deeper. Her article on him in Sunday's Real Estate sounded like a press release from the man himself."

Wayne Sonderson intervened. "No blame to Day. She had to put that together in a hurry. Besides, it wasn't our intention to dig up dirt on Ballard, but to give him some ink so he wouldn't pull his ads."

I gave the sales director a thank you nod, but Frank's rebuke stung.

Back at my computer, Frank's crack that I hadn't looked carefully enough into Ballard's background grated like gravel in an open-toed shoe. I set to work, vowing to show the oh-so-professional Frank Burke that he wasn't the only one who knew how to research a story.

I went back to the bio I'd gotten from Cindy. Frank was right in one respect— Ballard's claims that he was born in a small north Carolina town whose name I didn't recognize, attended high school there, went on to Duke, then later served in Vietnam all sounded legitimate and, in the rush to finish the piece, I hadn't verified them. An hour later, a computer search had failed to confirm any of Ballard's claims.

At lunch I ran into Polly. To sidetrack her from asking more about my date with Andy, I told her about the difficulty I was having in tracing Compton Ballard's background.

She frowned. "His bio says he grew up in North Carolina? No way. I distinctly remember that when I was working at Sand-Scapes we all went out to lunch one day and I ordered a crab cake."

"So what has your crab cake to do with where Ballard—"

"Let me finish. When I gave the waiter my order, Ballard said—and I remember this clearly—'Never order crab cakes outside of Maryland. I grew up in Baltimore, and that's the only place on the continent where they make them the right way.'"

"But why would he lie and claim he was from somewhere else?"

"Don't know. If I were you, I'd be sure to check out that bit about Duke as well. Back in the day—the time when Ballard would have been there—Duke was mostly for rich white kids, students from old legacy families. The only exception would have been super-bright geeks. In my opinion, Ballard doesn't fit any of those categories."

My own impression of Ballard agreed with what Polly said. While he didn't come off as stupid, neither did he appear to be an intellectual. I judged his success to have sprung from his ability to promote himself, or to spot opportunities others might miss. It looked as if I had more searching to do.

Later, back at my desk, I was scouring the internet for more information on Ballard, when Skooky popped into my cubicle. "Miss Day, you got a minute?"

"Problem, Skook?"

"Kinda. Unc's got me scheduled to work next Friday and there's this big surfing contest down near Boca that weekend. I figure I can make some excuse and slip out a little early, but if Unc sees my board on top of the car . . ."

"Why can't you go home and get your board when you leave here?"

Skooky rolled his eyes. "You don't know my old man. I can't afford to have him spot me picking up the board, he'd be on the phone to Uncle Shel wanting to know why I was off work early."

"Skook, your plot continues to thicken, but I don't see what I—"

"If you'd let me stow the board in the back of your Jeep until I leave—"

Skooky, for all his nefarious ways, had an irresistible grin. I agreed, a little amused at my role in his scheme.

Skooky had no more than left when Everett came quietly into my cubicle and sat down.

"Uh, are you busy Day? I don't want to disturb you."

I closed the screen and turned to him. "Busy enough, but I could use a short break. How are you doing?"

Everett seemed pleased that I'd found time to talk, and he

relaxed, slumping somewhat in the seat. "I still like that house, and I think Maple would like it too. Someone else at SandScapes must be available to show it to us again."

Us? I'd had all I cared to see of number 23 Oleander Drive. Maple Brisby would hardly be keen on living in a house where her fiancé had found a dead body. "The thing is, Everett, if you moved in there with Maple, news that a woman had been killed in that very house would reach her before you unpacked the coffeepot. My friend Polly Ribideaux uses the word 'stigmatized' to describe a house where something undesirable has taken place. Many people are creeped out by being in those surroundings."

"I did like that house, though." Hopefulness still glimmered in his voice.

Unwilling to encourage him further in his mad quest, I offered as gently as possible, "Everett, you are going about this all wrong. Wouldn't it be better to tell Maple what you have in mind and see if there's any possibility she'd—"

He shook his head. "If I can find the right house, I'm sure that will persuade her." With that, the would-be Don Quixote left my cubicle, charging off toward the next windmill.

I was back on my web search when Kyle stopped by. "You know anything about this Alvaro Cardenas fellow Valerie Kimmel was hooked up with?" he said.

"Only that they rode horses together and that he gave her an expensive necklace. I met him briefly when I was at her condo."

"Any idea how seriously they were involved?"

I bit my lip. "Hard to say. He did insist that he loved her. Why do you ask?"

"Frank's got a bee in his bonnet that this is the guy the police ought to be focusing on as the killer. Disappointed lover . . . couldn't take rejection . . . that sort of thing."

"I can't see it," I said. "If he was the killer, why would he be making so much noise about wanting to reclaim his necklace?"

"Frank thinks that's a ploy to make himself look innocent. Or to make the killing look like a robbery."

"But the police checked his whereabouts the day of the murder. According to them, he was in New York that whole weekend."

"It appears they're not so sure of that. He can prove he was in New York and prove that he returned the following Monday, but there's no witness who can say that he was there the entire time."

After Kyle left, a nasty little thought slipped into my brain—let Frank chase after red herrings. My suspicion that the killer was someone closely connected with SandScapes was growing stronger by the minute. Any way I looked at it there was some financial connection—the shredded piece of a financial report in Valerie's pocket . . . the accountant's applying for another job, and now this financial audit. Alvaro Cardenas might be on Frank Burke's suspect let, but Harry Ports was at the top of mine.

CHAPTER 18

At six A.M. Tuesday morning the sun was still half hidden behind an orange-pink layer of clouds when I left my apartment and, yawning, climbed into the Jeep and headed for the Vilano Bridge.

In spite of my annoyance at Zelma Beauclaire's abruptness on the phone, the meeting place she'd ordained for our interview seemed a pleasant prospect—a leisurely stroll across the Vilano Bridge while we chatted about the golf ladies' plan to save the Coronado.

The view from the bridge, with its high curving arc and spectacular views of the Tolomato River, was always a treat when driving. Crossing it on foot was something I'd had on my to-do list ever since I moved back to St. Augustine, but had never gotten around to. When I left for college, an old one-lane drawbridge had been the only access to the pokey little seaside village of Vilano Beach. Since then much of the beachfront had been developed with expansive homes and even a few condos, a distinct contrast to the modest nature of the original cottages.

In the lot at Comachee Cove where I parked the Jeep, Zelma Beauclaire's short stocky figure stood out among the group of athletic types doing stretches next to the railing. Zelma spotted me and gave her watch a severe glance. "You'll want to do a few stretches," she called. "Then we'll need to get going. Busy day ahead, so you'll have to ask your questions as we go."

"I don't need to stretch," I assured her. "Ready whenever you are." I'd have to take it easy, of course—at seventy-two, Mrs. Beauclaire would hardly be up for walking the entire two miles across the bridge and back, especially with the daytime temperature already climbing.

Zelma set out at a brisk trot and I soon realized this wasn't going to be a leisurely stroll in the park, but I figured she'd soon slow down. Meanwhile, I was enjoying the endless vistas from the bridge. To the east, a white scarf of surf fringed Vilano Beach. The wide spread of the Tolomato River stretched away to the north and south. Down below the bridge, a gathering of wood storks was holding a solemn High Mass on a sandspit, while a nearby cluster of tiny shorebirds practiced their synchronized pecking.

A poke from Mrs. Beauclaire interrupted my contemplation. She gestured upriver toward the far bank. "Coronado's right there," she said. "Grandest spot God ever made for a golf course. Nothing fancy, mind you. Course has been there close to a hundred years, and it's become home to more birds and wildlife than any spot around."

"Do your ladies think there's a realistic chance to stop Southwind Enterprises from developing the Coronado?"

She shot me a scornful glance. "We do not merely *think* we will stop this travesty—we will go to whatever lengths are necessary to preserve the course. Why aren't you writing this down?"

I held up my cell phone. "I'm using the recorder app on here to take notes." I said, feeling a bit smug that I could one-up the assertive woman.

But my own assertiveness apparently upped her adrenaline rate, because she increased her pace. I lengthened my stride to match hers. "Can you describe for me how you plan to accomplish your goal?"

"First step of the operation, we'll put pressure on the commissioners. Halt the approval process. All my women will be on hand for every commission meeting, along with other supporters we've enlisted. Strength in numbers."

I visualized a platoon of ladies in little golfing outfits, five irons at the ready, marching into commission meetings, Generalissima Beauclaire leading the assault.

In my research on Ballard, I'd learned that he had attracted some serious financial backing for his Southwind Enterprises. While it was difficult to find out exactly who all the investors were since they tended to hide behind corporate names, it was pretty much a given that some of them wielded substantial political influence. Given the odds, I saw little chance that a few women golfers were going to deter such a juggernaut.

"Of course they'll try to shut us up," Zelma Beauclaire continued, "but we're prepared for that. Got some pretty effective ammunition on our side."

By this time, we'd reached the point where the bridge began its steepest incline, and I was puffing a bit. "And you think you can make the commissioners listen?"

"Can't divulge details. But I will say that Commissioner Pritkin in particular is in for a few surprises. Same for some of those who have contributed to his election campaigns. As for that slimy little garden slug of a Compton Ballard—" All this she said without drawing an extra breath.

"When I interviewed Mr. Ballard, I got the impression that he's quite a golfer. That makes it surprising that he'd want to destroy the Coronado."

Zelma snorted. "Ballard belongs to WestMill, a big fancy course up near Jacksonville. No carts, just caddies. Think they're Royal St. Andrews. His annual membership there would cover fees for a dozen and more golfers at the little old Coronado."

The brisk trot with which we'd started had become a full-out gallop. Apparently there was a big difference between jogging on flat ground and cantering one's way up a long, steep rise. I swiped at the trickle of sweat creeping down my forehead and gave a yearning glance back toward Camachee Cove's mast-steepled marina. "Pritkin's not the only . . ." I gulped in a lungful of air. "What about the other . . . other commissioners?"

"Backup plans," she said. "The Commission is just our starting place. Lots of environmental concerns. We'll enlist the Audubon Society, the Sierra Club, the Fish and Wildlife Commission, the Corps of Engineers, every environmental group in the country if we have to."

The picture came clear—old lock-and-load Beauclaire was going to wage this war on every front. I needed more details for my article, but my calves were burning, I was getting shin splints and we weren't even to the crest of the bridge. Zelma was still picking up speed.

"Oh, look," I gasped, and swung around to point out a trawler passing under the bridge, a lacy veil of wake spread behind. "Isn't this . . . isn't this just a gorgeous view? Why don't we stop here for a minute?"

"Not a good idea. Stop and you'll cramp up, better to keep moving. We're almost to the top, and after that it's a nice downhill stretch."

What made me think downhill was going to be easier? At the pace we were moving, it was just as hard to keep from pitching forward as it had been to haul myself upslope. The burn afflicting the fronts of my thighs would have made Jane Fonda proud.

I had a vague impression of other joggers passing us, people walking their dogs, a blue heron settling gracefully into the marsh grasses, but from there on it all became jumbled together in a sweat-dripping, muscle-screaming, lung gasping blur.

*****

By the time were back at Camachee Cove, it was obvious that Zelma Beauclaire was a tough, determined advocate for a cause she believed in passionately and that she relished the coming battle. If the other women in her group were anything like her, Compton Ballard and his partners in Southwind Enterprises were in for a bumpy ride.

The torture ended, all I wanted was to climb into my Jeep and head for home and a hot shower. But Zelma wasn't through with me yet. "Now, young lady," she said, not one bit out of breath, "I've given you plenty of good information. I hope the article you write won't be all fluff and feathers like the one you did on that snake Ballard."

"We had to . . . that is I didn't . . ."

"Of course you did. Whitewashed him. Made him look like Sir Galahad instead of the low life slime he actually is. You dig deeper and I'll wager you'll find Mr. Hoity-toity Compton Ballard crawled out of some cesspool."

Before I could reply, Zelma swung abruptly toward her car. Moments later she gunned the motor, jerked it into gear and wheeled it out of the lot, leaving me staring at the Lincoln's rear bumper plastered with "Save the Coronado" stickers.

Still steaming from her rebuke, I collapsed my screaming muscles into my Jeep. How dare that woman accuse me of not doing my job? I was a damned good investigative reporter, but Shel had made clear that my assignment wasn't to dig up dirt on Compton Ballard.

I shoved the Jeep into reverse and backed out of my spot. Zelma Beauclaire could take a flying leap, and Hell and the Tolomato River would both have to freeze solid before I'd ever again join "The Bridge Club" for their morning marathon.

CHAPTER 19

Shel must have intuited that I was determined to find out if there was anything in Ballard's background that would connect him with Valerie's murder because he piled on one assignment after another, including one that sent me back to Tallahassee for nearly a week. Before I could do any serious digging into Ballard's past, June had trailed off to July, the signal for the long, hot slide into autumn.

St. Augustine itself switched into summer mode. At the start of school vacations came the summer tourists. Vans and SUVs, their rooftops piled with beach gear, trundled along King Street or down San Marco, kids staring with hopeful eyes from rear windows, parents in the front seat, heads swiveling to take in St. Augustine's unique features—the giant steel cross on the Mission grounds, the ancient fort known as Castillo de San Marco, Flagler College's handsome architecture, a memento of the days of grand tourist hotels that lured northern visitors for the summer, and the unique Bridge of Lions with statues of the magnificent beasts standing guard.

Andy and I were tourists, too, in a sense, our relationship fresh territory to be explored. Most weeks he managed to fly to St. Augustine so we could spend an evening together—our "fly-in" dates as Polly dubbed them. He and I discovered more and more common interests and began to feel increasingly comfortable with each other. Comfortable, that was, until the conversation turned to his daughters, seven-year-old Lissa—short for Melissa—and Dana who was five. Unsure of my feelings about dating a man with children, I told myself that for the moment I'd just enjoy time spent with Andy and I'd deal with the kiddie issue later.

Meanwhile, the Fourth of July loomed on my calendar like a scheduled root canal. The plan Andy and I had concocted that he'd drive his daughters to St. Augustine—Lissa didn't like to fly—and we'd spend the holiday *en famille*—had seemed a good idea at the time. The closer the day approached, the steeper my panic escalated. "How do I entertain a seven-year-old and a five-year-old?" I moaned to Rhonda. "I've never even watched Sesame Street. They'll be judging me. Andy will be judging me."

"Relax." She gave my arm a reassuring pat. "It'll be fine—a nice picnic on the beach—kids that age don't need fancy fixings."

"But I'll have to feed them."

"Keep it simple—sandwiches, some fruit, cold drinks. Get your mother to make you some of her to-die-for potato salad."

I shook my head. "Don't go there. If I told Zanthia that Andy was bringing the girls to meet me, she'd drum up some excuse to hustle right over. Before Lissa and Dana were even out of the car, she'd be eyeing them as potential grandchildren."

On the Fourth, I set my alarm for seven, but by five-thirty I was too antsy to stay in bed. I got up, cleaned the refrigerator, beat the sofa pillows into shape a dozen times, re-arranged the porch furniture, then put everything back where it was originally. I switched Andy's painting of our Everglades cove to a different wall, then replaced it. I nearly tripped over the clutter on the inside stair landing trying to locate the box that held some of my children's books. I fished out *The Tale of Peter Rabbit* and *The Secret Garden*, then, afraid one was too juvenile and the other too advanced, put them back.

When I traipsed downstairs with some trash, Mrs. Castelli called to me from her kitchen, "Are you all right, Day?"

"Oh, sorry. I've probably been disturbing you."

"Don't worry. At my age, I don't do all that much sleeping. But I was concerned that something might be wrong."

"Nothing wrong. Nothing at all. I'm just worried about the weather and everything for today."

"Yes. The picnic with your young man and his daughters. But no need to worry—the weather girl on TV says it will be hot and sunny with no chance of showers until later in the week."

I pretended that made me feel better.

At nine-thirty the phone jangled and I jumped. "Hi," Andy's voice announced too brightly. "Almost there. We're on I-95, about ten miles from St. Augustine."

His voice told me he was as nervous, which bumped up my own jitters another notch. I waited for them on Mrs. Castelli's front porch while perspiration that had nothing to do with the "hot and sunny" forecast seeped down inside my t-shirt. Then, all too soon, Andy's Camry turned into the driveway, one young face peering from the passenger seat beside him and another staring out at me from the back window. My tentative wave brought no response.

Andy swung out of the car and greeted me with a cautious hug that clearly signaled "no unseemly displays of affection in front of the kids." The girls hung back until he turned and called to them, "Come on, Lissa and Dana. Come say hello to Ms. McKelvey."

Until that very minute, I hadn't given any thought to what the girls would call me. "Ms. McKelvey" sounded like a schoolteacher, "Day" was too familiar . . . and was I supposed to hug them or shake hands or what?

The smaller girl hopped out of the back seat without further urging.

"Hi, Dana," I said. "Your Dad's told me so much about you and I couldn't wait to meet you."

She looked around. "Where's the beach? My Daddy said you would take us to the beach so we could go swimming."

"Later, Dana. Now say hello to . . . uh . . . Ms. McKelvey." The name was a trap for him as well. He turned back to the car. "Lissa?"

The taller girl oozed her way from the front seat, her expression making it clear that, given her choice, she'd have stayed in the car until it was time to go home.

"And this is Lissa," Andy said, urging her forward with his hand on her back.

Lissa offered a reluctant hand. I'd had warmer handshakes from my grandfather's police dog. I repeated my inane little "couldn't wait to meet you" bit. She muttered what sounded like "hello," then looked away.

"Is that the beach?" Dana asked, pointing toward the river and clearly unimpressed.

I shook my head. "We'll drive over to the beach later. But if you'd like to walk out on the dock before we go, we can toss in some bread crumbs and see if the fish will come up to eat."

"I've seen fish before," Lissa muttered.

Andy, clearly embarrassed, suggested we get going. After a bathroom stop for the girls, we gathered the picnic supplies—I'd taken Rhonda's advice about the potato salad—and started back toward his car. Lissa headed for the front passenger seat. "Lissa, you'll need to get in back now," Andy reminded her.

She gave me a look that could have frozen molten lava into a glacier, then climbed into the back seat so slowly I was afraid we'd spend the rest of the morning in the driveway.

As we drove, my neck cricked from turning toward the pair in the back seat and pointing out sights along the way. My face felt about to crack from the pasted-on smile that brought little response. I breathed a prayer of thanks that I'd asked Rhonda, Rick and Kevin to meet us at the beach. Rhonda was a mother . . . she'd know how to talk to these kids.

Rhonda and her family were already there when we arrived, and Rick had set up their large cabana as a sunshade. Similar groups were gathering all up and down the beach, umbrellas, towels and bathing suits forming a bright kaleidoscope of colors against the background of sand and sky. From the ocean's blue-green depths, waves swept beach ward in a gentle swoosh. Little children made cautious approaches to the surf, while swimmers bobbed their way through the waves to deeper waters.

It should have been perfect.

How was I to know that offering potato salad to a seven-year-old would be taken as an insult? Or that Lissa's Daddy was the only one allowed to apply suntan lotion to her thin back? Or that she and Rhonda's son, Kevin, also seven, would take an instant dislike to each other? Or that getting knocked on her bottom by a wave would be a major trauma?

On her own, Dana would have made herself at home—she happily shared Kevin's skim board and helped him erect a moated castle in the sand. But Lissa, seeing that her sister was having too much fun, scowled her into submission. Andy and I tried to pretend we were enjoying ourselves, but Lissa's negative mood jerked us back each time with the force of a bungee cord. By three o'clock my head was pounding.

Even Rhonda, with all her parenting skills, couldn't pull Lissa out of her funk. Finally Rhonda announced that they had had enough sun. "The Sewards have invited us to view the fireworks from their cottage," she said. "We'll leave the cabana. I'll talk to you tomorrow."

As I watched the oh-so-normal Williams family pack up and leave, I felt abandoned and there was still the rest of the day to get through. I suggested that we go back to my apartment, shower, then head downtown for a bite of supper and the fireworks display.

Andy was the only one to greet my suggestion with enthusiasm. Dana wanted to stay and swim some more. Lissa, who had not uttered a complete sentence the entire day, shrugged a "whatever."

Andy apologized as we struggled to dismantle the cabana. "It takes Lissa a while to adjust to new people and strange situations."

"I'm sure she'll be fine once she gets used to me," I lied, certain in my heart that this kid would warm to me at about the same time palm trees grew in Antarctica.

We headed into town early, aware that parking spots would be at a premium by the time the fireworks started. I thought of suggesting a stroll up St. George Street, but there would be mother's shop to pass, not a good idea. Instead, I suggested we park in the city garage and walk over to tour the fort before having a quick snack at Harry's so we'd be close to the Bayfront.

At the restaurant, Andy explained the menu to the girls. Lissa muttered that it made no difference to her. We all had hamburgers, then crossed the street and grabbed a spot on the seawall perfect for fireworks viewing. Lissa whined that she was tired and why did they have to stay to see stupid old fireworks anyhow. My attempt to point out some of the more interesting boats anchored in the harbor met with indifference. I longed for darkness to fall and the display to begin.

As always, the fireworks were spectacular, as if something in the sharp gunpowder smell and the crisp spray of exploding stars set off a sort of patriotic awe and childlike wonder in the crowd. Even Lissa couldn't conceal her excitement as the sky over the Matanzas River bloomed with brilliant umbrellas of sparkling reds and golds and greens. She had planted herself at a spot on the seawall as far from me as possible, but Dana snuggled in between Andy and me. The warmth from her small body against mine felt surprisingly comfortable and a momentary feeling I couldn't quite identify passed through me. Andy, too, sensed the shift in the emotional climate and smiled at me over her head.

That moment didn't last. By the time we had the girls back in the car, even Andy's patience had worn thin. When he dropped me off at my apartment before driving the girls home, I invited them to come in, but I could scarcely contain my relief when he said it was getting late and everyone was pretty tired and that they had better get on back to Ocala and that he'd call me. Soon.

CHAPTER 20

Concerned as I was about my relationship with Andy and his daughters, the puzzle of Valerie Kimmel's unsolved murder was never far from my thoughts and no matter what else I was working on, I was constantly struggling to piece together the sparse evidence. The remains of a financial report I'd found in her jacket pocket could, of course, be coincidence . . . a scrap she'd picked up from the floor or fished out of the copier. But the more I thought about it, the more suspicious it seemed. What if Harry Ports was manipulating SandScapes's bookkeeping and she had caught on? What if she'd threatened to expose him and to keep her quiet, he killed her?

Carl Bailey said that the Feds had left after about a week, taking with them boxes of records. "My guess is it's something to do with the Coronado golf club business," Carl said, "but everyone over there from the top on down has clammed up, especially Ballard."

I tried without success to develop a scenario in which there was a connection between the Federal investigation and the murder and that Harry Ports was the key. Once, I even started to dial Sam's office number to see if he had any further information, but hung up before anyone answered. My suspicions would have to stay under wraps until I had definite proof. For a long moment, I sat staring at my screen-saver, a photo of the beach at sunrise with the crimson beauty of the clouds and water an omen of bad weather to come. That seemed an apt metaphor for the situation between Sam and me—what appeared most attractive could also threaten disaster.

At noon on Monday, I finished up a report on a local school band that had traveled to Washington to participate in the July Fourth parade. At one, the pangs of hunger persuaded me to make a quick trip back to my apartment to finish off one of the sandwiches left over from the ill-fated beach picnic.

On River Street I pulled to the curb up in front of Mrs. Castelli's house. Tucker Ford's battered pickup truck was in the drive, his utility trailer hitched behind loaded with his lawn-mower and garden tools. Parked behind Tuck's trailer was a van with a giant insect mounted on its roof. Tucker and a man wearing a dark green uniform were on the front porch talking to Mrs. Castelli. Judging by the way my landlady's hands were flying about in full Italian mode, she and the man in the uniform were arguing.

I left the Jeep parked by the curb and hurried toward them. "Ma'am, this is no gimmick," the man with a Bug-B-Gone logo on his shirt was assuring my landlady. "I'm not trying to sell you on anything. All I know is Tucker here asked me to come have a look and this is exactly what I saw." With that he held out a small glass jar the size baby food might come in. "You got termites, the dry wood kind."

In the bottom of the jar was what looked like a pile of tiny wings. Mrs. Castelli wheeled herself over for a better look. "You're telling me termites come in different varieties?" she snapped.

The man nodded. "Some we call subterranean because

they have underground colonies, but the ones that are chewing your house to pieces are airborne. Every so often the old colonies become crowded and they send out swarmers to start a new colony. That's where these wings come from, the swarmers. They leave the nest, but nymphs that are left behind continue to do their damage, thousands and thousands of 'em chewing away. Some of your basement beams are riddled with 'em. Some places they've gnawed away all the cellulose and the wood's so soft you can poke your finger right through it."

Tucker's dark face twisted the way he looked when an unexpected patch of dollar weed cropped up in the lawn. "Miz C," he said, "once I was down there in that crawl space, I knew was nothing a can of Raid could handle. Mr. Naylor here got rid of termites in another house where I mow, so I figured—"

Mrs. Castelli interrupted. "You did the right thing, Tuck. Not your fault if Mr. Naylor sees termites. That's his business." She turned to me. "Day, this man's saying he's got to tent the whole house and spray it with some kind of poison gas. Can you believe that?"

I grimaced, remembering the warning the plumber had given. "Are you sure it's all that bad?"

Mr. Naylor hitched up his belt and held out the jar. "If you care to come with me under that crawl space I can point out exactly—"

The idea of sticking so much as my arm into that dark, creepy, spider-webby space beneath the house was beyond repulsive. Mr. Naylor was a professional—if he said there were termites living down there, I'd take his word for it.

"Ladies, this is no joking matter," Mr. Naylor gave his belt another hitch. "The way that sill beam and a couple of joists been eaten away, I'm surprised the kitchen floor hasn't fallen through."

Mrs. Castelli's face paled. "My lopsided cakes," she gasped.

The men looked puzzled, but I caught her meaning—the floor underneath the kitchen had sagged causing her stove to tilt and her cake layers to come out uneven.

That, more than any other proof Mr. Naylor presented, finally convinced Mrs. Castelli that the situation was serious. And serious it was. Mr. Naylor informed us that while the fumigation was taking place, both of us would have to move out of the house for at least two days, along with the cats and any food, personal items or houseplants the gas might contaminate or kill.

There was more bad news "All shrubbery within a foot and a half of the foundation wall has to go," he said.

Mrs. Castelli gasped. "My azaleas and hydrangeas?"

He gave a grim nod. "Only way we can anchor the tarp to make sure it stays tight. Have to warn you, too, that some of your other yard plants might get burned."

As realization set in, Mrs. Castelli seemed to shrink in her wheelchair. "Dear God! This is as bad as a fire."

Mr. Naylor sighed sympathetically. "That's northern Florida for you. The little suckers like these older houses. Find 'em everywhere. Anyhow, when we're done, you'll still have your house. Just a bit of inconvenience along the way."

Considering the havoc we were about to endure, the man deserved a medal for understatement.

My usually chipper landlady appeared overwhelmed, and, considering all her kindnesses to me, I felt obligated to see her through the ordeal. While Mr. Naylor returned to his truck to prepare a contract, I called Shel and explained the situation. He said he'd try to get the Ballard interview postponed.

The next shock came when Mr. Naylor handed Mrs. Castelli his estimate of the cost for the extermination. "House this size, rough guess, I'd say you got about 900 cubic feet, give or take. At $50 a cubic foot that will run you close to $4,500 dollars, like I say, give or take. You being local and all, I'll cut that by $500."

Mr. Naylor handed me a long list of the preparations that had to be carried out before the extermination could begin. "Like it says here, the doors—room doors, cabinet doors, and the drawers as well—all will have to be left open. Any open containers or anything not sealed in glass or plastic has to be double bagged. I'll drop you by a supply of the special nylon polymer bags you'll use. You'll need plenty of them because everything—food, cosmetics, medicine—all of it has to either be bagged or moved out."

I watched the van with its giant bug on top back out of the driveway and wondered how I was going to clear not only my own apartment, but Mrs. Castelli's as well. Tucker, jewel that he was, tried to soothe Mrs. Castelli's concerns about her shrubbery. "Don't worry none about your plants. I'll dig 'em out careful and when those fellows are finished getting rid of the bugs, we'll just move 'em right back."

The first order of business was finding a place for Mrs. Castelli to stay while I cleared out any of her possessions that would be contaminated. For myself, I knew that I could always have Zanthia's spare bedroom. Sharing living quarters with my mother was far from an ideal arrangement, but at least it would only be for a couple of days, and how bad could that be?

For Mrs. Castelli, there were two problems, her cats and her wheelchair. My first suggestion was that she might move in with her sister, Madelina, who lived in an ocean-front condo near Ormond Beach, about 50 miles south of St. Augustine. That idea met immediate resistance. "Lina's place won't do, it's third floor," Mrs. Castelli objected.

"I thought you told me there was an elevator."

"Elevator? Oh, yes, but you can't depend on them. Come a fire and there I'd be trapped."

A little further probing brought out the true reason she didn't want to stay with her sister. "So fussy, Lina is. A little cat fur on her fancy carpets and I'd never hear the end of it."

The solution came when one of Mrs. Castelli's church friends called and learned of her predicament. Evelyn Stallings insisted that the cats would be no trouble, that her house was all one floor with scarcely any steps and that the bathroom doorway would easily accommodate a wheelchair. "You just bring her right over here, Day, and we'll have her set up in a jiffy."

The process of moving Mrs. Castelli, her medicines, her personal needs, along with her cats and their food and litter box was hardly accomplished in a jiffy, but with help from Rhonda and her husband it was done. The exterminators wouldn't be able to start until Friday, but Rhonda and I persuaded Mrs. Castelli to make the move immediately. At first she protested that it was unfair to leave all the work to me, but finally agreed that with only a couple of days to clear out and package all her possessions and mine, it would be easier if she and the cats were elsewhere.

*****

"Yes, Dear, I've already cleared space for you in the bathroom," Zanthia told me when I stopped by her shop to ask if I could occupy her spare bedroom from Wednesday night through the weekend. "And I moved my things from the closet in your bedroom."

"Mother, you didn't need to do that. I'm only going to be there for a couple of nights, five at the most."

She didn't answer, but I didn't like the gleam in her eyes as she stared off into space and murmured, "Not enough time to repaint, I suppose . . ."

*****

On Wednesday morning the bug-topped truck pulled into the drive before I'd finished dressing. Mr. Naylor came inside to inspect what I'd done so far and to give me further instructions. "Open that drawer under your oven," he reminded me. When he walked into the living room he noticed the door leading to the closed off stairwell was still shut. He opened it and peered inside. "Lotta stuff in here," he said.

"We don't use the stairs at all," I explained. "There's another door at the bottom that opens into Mrs. Castelli's foyer."

"Both of 'em gotta be left open," he said.

It turned out that Mrs. Castelli had hidden the key to the door at the bottom. I called her at Mrs. Stallings' house, but she couldn't remember where it might be. "Oh, dear, that door's not been opened in ages," she said. "Look in the bottom of that vase on the hall table, the one with those Chinese people around the edge."

My search was rewarded when I upended the vase Mrs. Castelli had described and the heavy, old fashioned key fell out with a clang. I used it to open the bottom door and then replaced it in the vase. Somewhere there was a similar key for the door at the top, but I had no idea where it might be as I never locked it.

The termites brought endless chaos into my life. Even with some help from Rhonda, Rick and Kyle Whitecloud, Tuesday and Wednesday nights were a blur of tedious hours spent sorting, packing and storing both my possessions and those of Mrs. Castelli. Spices, noodles, and cosmetics were double bagged. Refrigerators and freezers were emptied—the freezer-burned steaks I'd been hoarding for a special occasion were tossed along with all the frozen mystery packages. *Note to self: If freezing leftovers, must remember to label.*

Houseplants were removed and all doors and drawers were opened so the gas could circulate. Luckily, Mr. Naylor said it wasn't necessary to remove clothing.

I stayed in my own apartment for those two nights, even though it was depressing. By late Wednesday evening, the apartment looked as if a tornado had swept through, but the house was ready for the exterminators to begin their work.

I packed a light bag with the things I'd need while staying with Zanthia, then said goodbye to my apartment, closed the door behind me and headed down the stairs to my Jeep. I was glad Mrs. Castelli wasn't there to see how forlorn the exterior looked since Tucker had stripped away the shrubbery. I waved to the workmen who were already setting up ladders and scaffolding and drove away.

"All settled?" Shel asked when I arrived at the office.

I groaned. "It's a mess, but I guess we'll survive."

Several others offered condolences as we filed in for the staff meeting, but not Frank who pretended to be occupied with his cell phone. Not that I expected any sympathy from him.

Wednesday was a relatively quiet news day. At three-thirty, I was finally able to interview Compton Ballard about the golf course controversy. He adamantly defended his justification for rezoning the property with talk of an increased tax base for the city and soaring values for surrounding property owners. His mood was considerably more congenial than the last time I'd talked with him. Quite a bit of his self-importance reappeared when he informed me that later that evening he would be showing one of his company's prime residential listings to Cole Fanshaw, a name even I recognized as a famous golfer.

With Ballard's comments plus those from Zelma Beauclaire—hers of a decidedly different flavor—I had the makings of a good "he said . . . she said" interchange for my article.

"I'll have dinner ready when you get home," Zanthia told me when I called her during lunchtime.

"Please, Mother, don't go to any extra trouble for me."

"I could do the leg of lamb with a mustard coating. Or maybe the mint sauce . . ."

I pretended to lose the connection. Mr. Naylor had informed me that since the extermination was taking place on Friday, the earliest I'd be able to return to the house was Monday evening. It was going to be a long four nights. Still, by the time I left the office late that afternoon, I was looking forward to a nice relaxed evening, and, knowing Mother would ignore my protest, a good dinner.

Mother's living quarters were on the second floor of the old Spanish-style building on St. George Street that housed her shop. The rooms with their white plastered walls and dark beamed ceilings offered the perfect background for Zanthia's exotic taste for candles, incense, oriental art, hand-woven rugs and fabrics in ornate patterns and rich colors. A balcony furnished with comfortable teak chairs and garnished with a luxury of flowers extended over the street to provide an ever-changing view of the endless parade down below. Access to the second floor was from a side street entrance and there was also an interior stair leading up from her shop's storeroom.

Zanthia's intriguing little store, The Other Side, and Lee Hartshorn's Wild Wings Gallery shared space on the building's lower level with display windows facing on St. George Street. In spite of my doubts and trepidation when Mother bought the building, she had since managed to support herself with the income from her business plus the rent she collected from the gallery.

When I toted my suitcase upstairs to the second floor bedroom I'd be occupying, the appetite-taunting aroma of roasting lamb exuded from the kitchen at the apartment's rear. By the time I'd washed up, Mother called to say dinner was ready. The meal was delicious—she'd used the mustard rub on the lamb but also served a mint sauce on the side. "Just in case you prefer that," she said. She'd also concocted my favorite spinach salad and cauliflower au gratin.

The dinner ended with a Tarte Tatin from the nearby French bakery and I was beginning to think it might not be so bad to share quarters with Mother for a few days. That buoyancy was quickly punctured. While I was still savoring the delicious apple dessert—saving the very tip of the slice for last—Mother informed me, "This is perfect—Wednesday is séance night. The others arrive at eight. Claude will be so happy you've finally joined us."

Claude might be happy, but I was desperately fishing about for an excuse to leave. "There are some things at the office I didn't finish—"

I might as well have been whistling to the wind for all the attention she paid. "I do hope he can offer you some advice about the poor Kimmel girl's murder—I know her death has been heavy on your mind."

She was right about that part at least. With the police stumped and no new developments in the case, it felt as if everyone had given up and forgotten about Val. But I hadn't. Skeptical that spooky old Claude could supply any answer to the mystery, I reluctantly agreed to sit in. That reluctance increased when Mother informed me that, as she would be acting as the medium through which the spirits would communicate, it was important that I address her only as Zanthia. "Even in your thoughts I must be Zanthia; otherwise the communication will be broken."

As she spoke, she circled the room waving a bouquet of mint, sage and rosemary. "The cleansing," she said. I refrained from rolling my eyes, but the herbs along with the lingering roast lamb smell did leave a nice fragrance. That finished, she placed a large bowl in the center of the dining table, filled it with water and floated three chrysanthemum blossoms on top and centered them with a round copper vessel filled with burning incense.

Lee Hartshorn, the proprietor of Wild Wings, was first to arrive, closely followed by Sylvia Robard, whom I knew as the chairperson of St. Augustine's annual Menendez Ball. Next came Mother's chatty friend, Corinne Randall, and, to my surprise, my old fourth grade teacher, Miss Edna Strakes. Last to arrive was an even greater surprise, Boone Clemmons, the attorney who had defended my protégé Robbie Flynn in the case of the murdered college president. That Boone would participate in a séance was beyond belief.

When the drapes had been closed and the room lights lowered, Mother—Zanthia—began seating her guests in designated places around the oval dining table. "No you here, Miss Strakes," she ordered, "otherwise the psychic balance will be shifted."

As I was taking my seat between Miss Strakes and Sylvia Robard, my knee bumped the table causing the floating incense container to bob and rock. I felt as if I'd committed some psychic *faux pas*.

When all were seated, Zanthia took her place at the head of the table while Boone occupied the other end. She lit the single candle in front of her. The wick guttered for a moment then the flame became a straight column and its warm, waxy odor filled the darkness.

Zanthia, eyes closed, raised both hands for silence. With all voices stilled, flute music could be heard, the notes muted yet distinct as if wafting into the room from some place far away. The candle in front of Zanthia fluttered its light across the faces of Lee Hartshorn and Corinne Randall seated opposite me. It also picked up the structure of my mother's face in a way that made her truly seem to be Zanthia rather than the woman I knew as Mother.

"We welcome tonight the spirits who may choose to visit with us," Zanthia intoned in a voice scarcely above a whisper. "We are seven. A new communicant has joined us and we ask that you share with her your wisdom. In silence, we shall concentrate our efforts so that you may address us."

I had expected that we would be asked to hold hands, but instead we sat, each in our own space, for what seemed a very long time. I felt an overwhelming urge to yawn. This was all so ridiculous, hocus-pocus, an excursion into la-la land. A whiff of the incense blew my way and seemed to swirl through my brain. I fought to hold my eyes open, forced myself to think of something other than the candlelit faces and the floating chrysanthemums. I wondered what Sam—*no, Andy*—I wondered what Andy was doing at the moment. Probably reading his girls a bedtime story the way Dad used to read to me.

Rumpelstiltskin.

I started and stared across at Lee, sure he must have spoken that word aloud, but his face was calm and he was staring fixedly at the bowl, completely unaware of me.

No matter how many times I replayed the scene in my mind afterwards, I was never sure whether it was the wind that slapped the door open and swept the candle flame to one side just then, or if something else entered that room. All I knew was that in the near-darkness a voice began to speak, a voice like none I'd ever heard before, the words floating around me as distant and ethereal as the flute music. "There is a message for the daughter. She must pay closer attention to the dream," the voice intoned.

The daughter—that had to be me. And Zanthia's dream of the little boy. None of the others moved or spoke. I tried to look toward the end of the table where Zanthia sat, but could scarcely make out her still shape.

Once more the oddly distant voice emerged. "I see one who is about to take revenge for a great injustice. The daughter must not collide with that person's destiny, for unless the lock is secure the danger is very great."

In the silence that followed, a chill ran through me. Sure this was some sort of bizarre trick, I leaped to my feet, sending my chair crashing to the floor. "Mother, this is too much!" I snapped.

As the word Mother left my lips, a gust of wind swept through the room and the candle in front of Zanthia sputtered twice and then went dark.

CHAPTER 21

Thursday morning I showed up at the *Dispatch* frazzled and red-eyed. I'd spent the entire night tossing, turning and trying to decipher the meaning of those eerie words spinning through my mind. I set down my coffee and plunked into a seat at the conference table, glad that here a carton of doughnuts centered the table—no floating chrysanthemums or burning incense.

Kyle eased his tall frame into the chair next to mine and gave me a scrutinizing look. "You must have overdone it with the packing," he said. I could only answer with a weary shrug.

The usual buzz about weekend plans failed to distract me from the persistent memory of Claude's warning that the killer was ". . . someone seeking revenge for a great injustice," and that it would be ". . . dangerous to cross that person's path." And what was all that about a lock? What lock?

Kyle nudged me. "You really are spaced-out this morning. I asked if your landlady was settled in with her friend and you didn't even hear me."

"Sorry," I said. "Yes, Mrs. Castelli's okay, but her cats aren't. Seems Sniggles and Thomasina aren't at all happy in their new home. Sniggles mistook their hostess's closet for a litter box. Lots of trauma all around."

"Is that what's got you so preoccupied?"

I expelled a frustrated breath. "Zanthia roped me into a séance last night and Claude's prediction has me thinking about all sorts of possibilities in the murder case."

I repeated to Kyle what the voice had said. "I keep wondering if he was implying that Valerie Kimmel had been unjust to someone and that the person had killed her for revenge. And when he said that person was dangerous to me, did he mean it's someone I know? My common sense says the whole thing is just so much hocus-pocus. Besides, if Claude knows who the killer is, why didn't he come right out and say it?"

Kyle's serious frown reminded me that in Native American culture, messages from the spirits were taken seriously. "To reveal too much can alter the way the course of events has been structured," he said. "It's for us to perceive and interpret the messages we receive. Sometimes it can be a voice . . . sometimes it's as subtle as a falling leaf."

I took a sip of coffee and reached for a doughnut. Without thinking, I chose the kind I don't like with white icing and multi-colored sprinkles. "Okay, then," I said, "here's one possibility. Compton Ballard bought Valerie a horse and was paying the stable expenses. What if he became furious when she got involved with the Argentinean, Alvaro Cardenas?"

I almost mentioned the necklace Alvaro claimed to have given Val, then realized that information hadn't been made public.

Kyle tilted his head, thinking. "How could Ballard have killed her when he wasn't even in town? The cops seem to favor the vagrant angle—that Val took an intruder by surprise, so he killed her."

More coffee washed down the last bite of doughnut and I licked my finger to retrieve a couple of sprinkles from my napkin. "What if Val had done serious injury to someone she knew socially or someone she worked with?"

Further conjecture was cut off when Shel called everyone to attention, then, looking around realized Frank Burke's place was vacant. "We'll hold off a minute until Frank—"

Before he could finish the sentence, Frank Burke appeared in the open doorway, his features tautly drawn and his tie askew.

"Frank, we were waiting—" Shel started, then halted when he saw Frank's expression.

"Just got a call. Compton Ballard . . . he's dead." Frank's clipped phrases drew all eyes in his direction. "Killed while showing a house—"

Startled gasps rose from the people seated around the table and an exclamation exploded from me: "That can't be! I talked to Ballard just yesterday."

"Well, you won't be talking to him today," was Frank's terse reply. Then, noticing the others' shocked faces, he added in a less dismissive tone, "Was there anything in what Ballard said? . . . "

Still stunned by disbelief, I stammered, "Only that he had an evening appointment . . . was going to show the golfer Cole Fanshaw a property in Satsuma Shores. He seemed pleased with himself . . . as if it was a huge deal."

Frank nodded. "Satsuma Shores is where they found him. Security patrol checked the house this morning. Found it unlocked and there he was."

"But if he was meeting Cole Fanshaw—" Shel interjected.

Frank waved that away. "My source said it's pretty positive the whole Fanshaw thing was a ruse . . . merely a way to lure Ballard to the house. Fanshaw seems to know nothing about it. Said his agent never contacted Ballard."

"Wait a minute," Carl Bailey interrupted "This doesn't add up. If I know Satsuma Shores, that house was locked up like Fort Knox, all kinds of alarms and security systems."

Frank nodded. "That's right—gated community. The house

is vacant, but the security people check it morning and evening. Police aren't saying how anyone got in and no word yet on the M.O."

I felt a start and almost blurted out the word "flashlight," but the information Sam gave me had still not been made public.

Shel turned to me. "Day, you may have been one of the last people to talk with Ballard. I suspect that as soon as the police latch onto that, they'll want to interview you. Meanwhile, I want you to start working with Frank on this—the two of you scour through your interview notes from yesterday and the previous research you've done on him for anything that may be significant."

"My interview was about the Coronado business, so I doubt there's anything in my notes that will be helpful as far as the mur—" I began.

"Share what you have with Frank." Shel's voice left no room for further discussion.

Frank's scowl matched my glare, but he gestured toward his cubicle. I rose and followed him, determined not to let the great crime reporter Frank Burke throw me. I set up my laptop on his desk and pulled my notes from the previous day's interview with Ballard, then halted, hit by the realization that Compton Ballard, who just yesterday sat at his massive desk with the three photo images staring out behind him, was now dead. Murdered. "He was so proud to be showing a property to someone as famous as Cole Fanshaw," I said. "I could tell he was already seeing his name in the real estate headlines."

"Headlines of a different kind now, poor bastard," Frank murmured. His softer tone revealed a breach in Frank's usually grim attitude, like a sliver of light from a door barely cracked open. A moment later the door slammed shut—"I'll need to see more than just this Coronado stuff," he said with a disdainful wave toward my computer screen. "Where are the notes for the puff piece you did on him?"

Remembering Frank's sarcastic response when that article

came out, I felt my neck redden. "I've got those, but I've not had time to verify all the information he gave in his bio, his military service, his college and proof of where he was born."

"Okay. Send me what you've got. Then get busy tracking down any details you missed the first time."

Frank's condescending remark caused more than just my neck to turn red. Afraid that if I said anything I'd say too much, I snatched up my laptop and stomped off to my own cubicle. Kyle glanced up as I passed, seemed about to say something, then just gave me an inquisitive grimace.

"Don't ask," I snapped.

Still steaming—Frank Burke was an insufferable prick—I pulled out Ballard's printed bio and went over it again. I'd already run his name through the court records for Charlotte, North Carolina, but all I'd located was his first business license application there in 1984. Previous to that date, I'd found nothing except a driver's license application that same year. His name came up a number of times in newspaper archives, but all those were later than 1984. No high school or college records.

A phony, Zelma Beauclaire had called him. Suddenly I was aware of some little dust mote of memory hovering just out of reach. Then it hit me—Polly had said she was certain Ballard had grown up in Baltimore. I booted up my favorite search engine and ran the name Compton Ballard through official Baltimore court records. It showed up just once—in 1984, an application had been filed by a Lloyd Hostler to change his legal name to Compton Ballard. The appeal was granted. A little math told me that Ballard, who was born in 1950, would have been 34 at the time and that he'd first shown up in records for Charlotte, North Carolina that same year, 1984.

That connection raised my pulse a couple of beats. Excited as a hound who's caught first scent of a fox, I ran the name "Lloyd Hostler." It came up on a website for Baltimore's Forest Park School graduates, class of '68. Again a match with Ballard's age—18 when he graduated.

For a moment I became entranced with the realization that Ballard had attended the same school as Spiro Agnew and songstress Cass Elliott of the Mamas and the Papas. The yearbook headshot I located with help from a sweet-voiced woman in Baltimore's Pratt Library was grainy, but the face, although less puffy, seemed to fit with Compton Ballard's features.

Elation at the success of this search caused me to release my breath in a loud whistle. Kyle, eyebrows lifted questioningly, poked his head up over the partition that divided us. I gave a thumbs-up gesture to let him know I was onto something important, and he sank back out of sight.

My excitement was quelled a bit when nothing more appeared in any Baltimore records under Lloyd Hostler that would account for the years between the time he graduated from high school and sixteen years later when he moved to North Carolina.

My groan of aggravation when the search dead-ended brought Kyle to peer over my shoulder. When I explained my dilemma, he suggested, "Try running just the last name. Hostler seems unusual enough that if there's anything there it ought to show up."

He watched as I keyed in the name and we both breathed "ah-ha!" when the screen filled with references to a Milton Hostler. The name appeared as the defendant in a number of civil suits that had been filed against Hostler as the proprietor of businesses operating under several different names—"Easy Pay Loans," "Quik N Easy Loans," and "Cash Today Loans."

Milton Hostler's birth date was given as 1928. "Maybe Ballard's father?" Kyle said.

"I'll try birth records for the year Ballard was born."

I went back to 1950 and there it was—a baby boy, 7 pounds 12 ounces, born 4:19 A.M. on July 12, 1950 to Milton and Hannah Hostler at Maryland General Hospital. The child's name was Lloyd Wydell Hostler.

With a congratulatory grin, Kyle returned to his cubicle while I immersed myself in rounding out the story on Ballard's father. What I found was a picture of a man engaged in financial dealings that skirted the edges of the law and took advantage of people in desperate straits. Exorbitant interest rates meant that many of Hostler's victims ended up owing double and triple the amount they had originally borrowed. When Hostler sued to recover the loans, he almost always won. In cases where he was being charged with fraud, he was occasionally fined, but mostly the charges were dismissed.

More important to my research, Lloyd Hostler, whom I now knew to be Compton Ballard, was mentioned a number of times as a partner in his father's various shady businesses, although it seemed he was never charged in any of the civil cases.

Another gleeful chirp brought Kyle back to my side. "I think I've hit on the reason for Ballard's name change." I pointed to an article on my screen from newspaper archives dated November 1983. The name Milton Hostler splashed across the front page. This time it was no mere civil suit that Hostler could buy his way out of, but charges of arson and manslaughter. Hostler senior, operating as "Easy Home Loans," had foreclosed on a property, then, when he was unable to sell the unoccupied dwelling, it conveniently caught fire late one night.

"They call that 'selling it to the insurance company,'" Kyle commented wryly.

We read on. Before any alarm could be sounded, the fire had spread to an adjoining home of an elderly couple, both of whom perished in the fire. A passerby reported having seen a man carrying a gas can flee from the premises moments before the fire started. "In seconds the whole place went up in flames," he stated.

In later newspaper accounts, it was reported that, as the building's owner, Milton Hostler immediately came under suspicion. Apparently he had not realized there was a witness and he failed to dispose of the gasoline-splashed shoes he was wearing when he set the fire. While the passerby could not offer a positive identification, the details he gave police closely fit Hostler's height and build. Hostler was arrested and held for trial. Later is-sues of the newspaper reported that he had been found guilty of arson and involuntary manslaughter and was sentenced to thirty years in prison. Ten years later a small obituary notice reported Milton Hostler's death.

The puzzle began to come together. Stained by his father's notoriety, at age 34, Lloyd Hostler had remade himself, first with a name change to Compton Ballard and then with a move to Charlotte, North Carolina where he began a new life. The mil-itary service and the Duke education he listed in his bio were as fake as the new name—he'd been in Baltimore all that time, active in his father's loan shark business.

From there, his trail was easier to follow. He'd started out in Charlotte running a business similar to that he'd been involved with in Baltimore, but soon progressed to the more legitimate environs of real estate. Although he had managed to assume the trappings of a successful entrepreneur, it seemed he had inher-ited his father's lack of ethics. After several dubious real estate transactions, he moved to Atlanta, Georgia where, as I'd pre-viously learned, he'd nearly been caught out by the Moreland Hotel deal. That seemed to provide a logical reason why he had transferred his dealings to St. Augustine.

My hunt was complete and I'd double- and triple-checked each of my sources. Frank Burke was out of the office, so my information would have to wait until he returned, but this time he'd have no basis for a complaint.

Absorbed in finalizing my notes, I'd forgotten Shel's re-mark that the police would want to talk to me about my inter-view with Ballard until I looked up to find Sam Stansfield and Corporal Tim Robb approaching my cubicle.

The solemnity of Sam's expression indicated this was po-lice business, not personal, but a certain gleam in his eye gave him away. Sam was gloating just a bit at this legitimate excuse to see me. The redness at the tip of Tim Robb's ears revealed that he knew enough about Sam's and my relationship to be embarrassed.

Determined to prove to Sam that I could be totally businesslike, I said, "I assume you want to know about my interview yesterday with Compton Ballard."

"The late Compton Ballard," Sam confirmed.

I picked up my laptop and indicated they should follow me. "We can talk more privately in the conference room," I said.

I determined that I'd tell the officers any details they wished to know about my interview with Ballard concerning the Coronado, but for the time being I'd keep to myself the rest of what I'd just uncovered.

Had Ballard seemed at all nervous or uneasy, Sam wanted to know. "More like excited," I said. "He obviously saw a sale to Cole Fanshaw as a feather in his cap."

"At eight million, it would give him enough feathers to fly," Tim cracked.

"So any idea how . . ." I started.

"Don't go there, Day," Sam warned. "You know we can't give out details."

"I was just wondering about a weapon," I shot back, giving Sam a meaningful look.

The change in his coloring revealed that he'd caught my message. "Soon as we can release that I'll let you know."

"Frank Burke's the one who'll be writing the story. He's the one you'll be talking with."

One-upping Sam gave me a little glow of triumph, quickly followed by the realization that a man had been murdered and the two of us were playing childish games. Sam must have sensed that, too, because the rest of our interview was strictly business. I did not, however, tell him I'd discovered Compton Ballard's true identity.

I'd later regret that decision, but at the time I felt smug in the knowledge that I had information Sam did not.

As the two officers were about to leave, Sam halted and said to Tim, "Didn't you mention some phone call from Day?"

I quickly interjected, "That was when you were out of town. I just wanted to know if you had some information about—" I stopped short, not wanting to make it obvious in front of Tim that I might be prying privileged information from Sam.

Luckily for me, Sam relented. "Go ahead out to the car," he told Tim. "I'll catch up with you in just a minute." Then he turned to me. "So what was the call about?"

"It was just some little detail—I was wondering about the whereabouts of the SandScapes' people the morning of Val's murder."

"Someone in particular?"

Not wanting Sam to know I was focusing on Harry Ports, I improvised. "I keep thinking it would take a man to strike such a deadly blow and was wondering about the men in the Sand-Scapes office, like, uh, that Rodman fellow and there's Nick Petroski and Harry Ports, the company comptroller or accountant and I believe there are a couple of men who work there part time."

Sam stared down at me for a long pause then his eyes lit with recognition. "So, the Ports guy," he said. "Well you can put your little heart at ease about him. Ports lives on his boat in Victory Cove marina. He says he sailed up to Fernandina Beach that weekend. The dockmaster up there confirms that he was moored at their marina from four o'clock Saturday night until noon on Sunday."

I thought about that. "What if he was up there but rented a car and—"

"We checked. No car rental records. So don't go jumping off the deep end with your Ports theory."

As he turned again to leave he added, "But if you *did* have some actual information, you know who you can always come to for help."

I thought of a thousand smart-assed responses after he'd gone. But as always with Sam and me, it was too late.

CHAPTER 22

As I passed Zanthia's bedroom door Friday morning, I heard chanting and felt grateful for a few minutes alone before she appeared. I was still toweling off from my morning shower as I hurried to the kitchen and switched on the TV.

All the local news channels displayed versions of the same trailer, *Prominent St. Augustine Realtor Murdered.* On a Jacksonville station, the anchors, male on the left, female on the right, volleyed details of the crime back and forth.

"St. Augustine residents were shocked to learn yesterday that Compton Ballard, one of the town's most successful realtors, has been murdered," trilled the perky blond wearing an orange V-neck blouse. A headshot of Ballard lurked on the screen behind her right shoulder, a copy of the photo in his office in which he was staring thoughtfully at the camera, his hand cupping his chin.

"Yes, Andrea," replied her blow-dried co-anchor whose tie was patterned in an orange shade that matched the color of his cohort's blouse, "police report that security guards discovered

Ballard's body in the media room of a Satsuma Shores mansion."

A photo filled the screen, the exterior of the oceanfront mansion where the killing took place, a multi-storied, multi-windowed, multi-balconied wedding cake of a house, now lashed behind strands of yellow police tape. The camera panned to where a plastic-gloved crime scene tech was reaching into the shrubbery to collect a cigarette butt that was more than likely to yield a DNA match to some hapless lawn service employee.

"Satsuma Shores is an exclusive ocean-front community several miles north of St. Augustine," Andrea supplied.

"Yes, Andrea, and residents there are very concerned. This is an area in which violent crimes seldom occur."

A few more such exchanges and they cut to a commercial for an underarm deodorant "with a manly scent she will love." After six or seven more commercials, huge glowing letters flashed on the screen—*BREAKING NEWS*.

The two reappeared, looking freshly energized by this latest development. "We have just learned," Mike announced, "that preliminary findings indicate Ballard's death occurred as a result of trauma from repeated blows."

I paused in my toweling. *Repeated blows with what?* I wondered. *A flashlight, perhaps?*

"This is the second murder involving a staff member of SandScapes Realty," Mike intoned solemnly. "Warnings have been issued to all real estate offices in the area."

None of this was news in the sense of being previously unknown—the *Dispatch* was an afternoon paper, and Thursday's edition had carried virtually the same information, thanks to our staff's diligent work. The irony of it was that while salaries at the *Dispatch* were embarrassingly low, the two TV anchors were paid mega-bucks to disseminate mere snippets of the same news.

A journalism professor had once warned our class that we should ". . . aim for careers in the electronic media because newspapers are mastodons with the ice age closing in on their feeding grounds. Books and magazines won't fare any better," had been his dire and all-too-accurate prediction.

I switched off the TV and returned to my room—mother's guest room, more accurately—to finish dressing. When I returned to the kitchen, the blender was whirring out the crisp fragrance of strawberries and fresh pineapple. Mother, busy concocting the fruit smoothie with which she started her day, gave me an anxious smile. "I was worried all night," she said. "I know you tend to discount Claude, but—"

"Mother, I've got a lot more on my mind just now than mumbo-jumbo from the beyond."

From the way her neck stiffened, I knew I'd offended her and I hurried across the room to give her a hug. "Sorry, Mums," I said, unconsciously reverting to my childhood name for her. "Yesterday was wicked, what with another murder."

She looked up from adding blueberries to the blender jar. "That's it—I feel certain the warning Claude gave you is tied directly to that man's death."

"That's absurd. If Claude has the inside scoop on this, why doesn't he just come right out and say who the killer is?"

Mother selected a banana from the fruit bowl and began peeling back the skin. "Foreknowledge of events is extremely dangerous. To alter the framework can have disastrous results."

The similarity of her response to Kyle's silenced me. I gathered my bag and keys, kissed her goodbye and left her to commune with Claude while I departed for another day in a newsroom that rocked in the wake of the second murder.

At the office, I passed on to Frank the background I'd collected on Ballard, including the Baltimore connection, his re-inventing himself in North Carolina, and his history of less-than-ethical dealings. I'd no more than clicked "Send" when a message came back—*Did you trace any of these other lawsuits against the father, this Milton Hostler?*

Is that relevant? I shot back.

Perhaps not, but we'll never know until your research is complete.

The sound of my teeth gnashing should have been heard across the room—the man was impossible. Sure, I could go off in a dozen different directions, search the background on the old couple who'd died in the fire, or check what kind of car Milton Hostler drove when he went around collecting usurious payments from those desperate enough to borrow from him. I'd done a good research job, but Frank was too mule-headed to acknowledge it.

Still, if he wanted more information, then more information I'd give him. First, though, I needed to check with Shel about my piece on the Coronado controversy. "Let's hold that for the moment until we see how Ballard's murder settles out," he said, then assigned me to cover the city council meeting later that morning.

That gave me time to fire up my favorite search engine and do some deeper research on Ballard's father. I hit pay dirt rather easily on that score. A bit of schmoozing persuaded a clerk at the tax office to compile for me a complete list of any real estate transactions involving Milton Hostler. "We've got it all digital now, a lot easier than when we had to go through the records manually," she said. "I should have this back to you in an hour or so."

She was as good as her word and as I was getting ready to leave the office for the council meeting, the file she'd promised arrived on my computer. With no time to look it over, I forwarded it to Frank.

The council meeting dragged on as usual. After a preliminary discussion in which various opinions were given about Compton Ballard's murder, the commission proceeded with mundane affairs such as repair of a broken sewer line on Ponce de Leon Boulevard and the need for a traffic signal at the entrance to a new development. Both issues were tabled for further discussion. I returned to the office and completed my piece about the meeting before lunchtime.

Carl Bailey stopped by my desk and I asked him what was going on at SandScapes now that Ballard was gone. "I suppose they'll be closed for a while?"

"You would think," Carl said, "but practically before Ballard was hauled off to the morgue his wife stepped in and took charge. So I guess you could say they're open for business as usual. The staff over there area is calling Mrs. B. the Little General. She told them that their clients are depending on them to continue work as usual, and she lit into Cindy the receptionist. Told her that if she showed up for work again with her boobs half exposed she could look for another job."

"She actually said 'boobs?'" I felt my jaw drop, remembering the rather innocuous woman I'd interviewed for the puff piece on Ballard's career. "Oh, dear, I'm afraid you'll have to ask my husband about that," had been her stock answer to most of my questions.

At noon, I left the *Dispatch* building, intending to walk downtown to the Bean for a sandwich and coffee. Puffy white clouds overhead were being rapidly shoved aside by more ominous layers of pewter gray ones moving in from the west, predictable weather for north Florida in mid-July, one minute a downpour, next minute the sun baking through. Rather than risk a drenching, I decided to drive to the Bean, a good decision as the first drops came whirling in on a windy gust as I ducked and ran for the spot where my Jeep was parked. I was groping for the driver's side door when Skooky Mandell popped up from behind the vehicle.

"Can I talk to you Miss Day?" Skooky's usually unperturbed face wore an anxious expression.

I stopped still, frowning. "Why out here? I could have listened just as well in the office."

"It's a problem, something I don't know what to do with."

"Don't let Everett catch you ending a sentence with a preposition," I joked as I pulled out my keys.

"It's not something funny, Miss Day. It could be—"

I looked closer. Skooky's usual happy-go-lucky expression was nowhere in evidence—he looked scared."

I sighed, figuring it was one of two things—he'd either screwed up badly on some assignment or his fondness for marijuana had gotten him in trouble. "Okay. Let's sit in the Jeep while you tell me what's bugging you."

We climbed into the front seat just as a gust of wind swept raindrops crackling across the windshield. I waited for Skooky to begin. He chewed at his lower lip, seeming undecided. "Come on, Skook, let's have it," I said, "My lunch awaits."

"I found something," he said, "and it might be valuable. But I don't know who to give it to. Or maybe it would be better if I just got rid of it. I don't know."

"And what is the mysterious 'it' you found? If it's drugs—"

He shook his head then pushed back the blond forelock that had fallen down over his eyes. "Nothing like that." He hesitated. "Well, maybe drugs did have something to do with my finding it."

He reached into his pants pocket and drew out a gold chain to which was attached a cameo pendant, a woman's elegant profile carved in ivory mounted against a rose background and surrounded by a gold filigree border. It could only have been the necklace Alvaro Cardenas had described, the one he said he'd given to Valerie.

A rumble of thunder nearly drowned out my gasp. "How did you—"

Seeing my shocked expression, Skooky sagged. "I was right, wasn't I? This could be worth a lot of bucks even though the chain's broke?"

I decided to hold off telling him that the necklace's monetary value wasn't the issue, that it could be directly connected to a murder.

While rain pounded against the Jeep's roof like little demons demanding to be let in, Skooky's story came out in disjointed spurts, and it took some time for me to piece together the sequence of the events he was relating. He began with the marijuana part of his story, after assuring me repeatedly that his

own marijuana use was only on weekends and only recreation-
al—"No more than if I was to have a couple of beers," as he put
it.

"Okay, I get that, but what's that got to do with the necklace?"

"Thing is, you can't buy weed out in the open here," he said.
"Same with anybody selling, they've gotta be extra careful."

Skooky revealed that he had a "regular guy" from whom
he made his purchases. "So nobody gets caught, my guy gets the
money up front and then tells me where to meet him to pick up
the weed. That cuts down the risk. If the cops catch on, nobody
can swear they saw money being exchanged for weed."

That, at least, made sense and showed better planning that
he generally displayed. The previous weekend, Skooky said,
he'd paid for the weed and was waiting underneath the Route
312 Bridge for his guy to show up. "Like usual, he was late. He's
careful, likes to check things out first. So I'm hanging out there
under the bridge and I see something shiny sticking in the mud
right at the water's edge. A piece of copper wire, I thought, but
when I stooped down and looked closer I could tell it looked
more like gold. Sometimes teen-aged kids make out down there
under the bridge, and I figured it was probably just a piece of
junk jewelry some girl might have lost."

He explained that he'd found a stick lying nearby and used
it to dig down into the mud. "That's when I saw it."

Any hope of lunch was forgotten. I filled Skooky in on the
necklace's possible connection to Valerie's murder and Alvaro's
claim to ownership. "So far, the police have kept any mention of
the necklace from the papers," I told him.

"Yeah, I've seen on *Law and Order* how cops hold back
on a clue. Then when they catch the guy he gives himself away
'cause he's the only one knows—" Skooky halted, his eyes wid-
ening as he realized his own situation. "I swear, Miss Day," he
blurted, "I didn't know anything about this necklace 'til I found
it down there in the mud. I wish now I'd never dug it up or I'd just

thrown it in the river."

I turned the ignition key and started the wipers for a minute to clear the windshield. "This could be important evidence," I said. "There's no choice but to hand it over to the police."

Skooky clapped both hands to his head. "Oh, Christ, Miss Day, how will I ever explain to the cops about why I was there? My old man's gonna kill me. And Uncle Shel will fire me for sure."

In silence, we watched the squall roll off into the distance, but the turmoil inside my brain was still growing. Skooky had trusted me enough to show me the necklace, and he was right in that he could have thrown it away. But why should I get pulled into what could turn out to be a messy business? Best just to send him off to the police station with the necklace and let him take the consequences.

But then I looked at the pleading in the guileless blue eyes staring back at me. "Sit tight," I said. "I need to talk to someone."

CHAPTER 23

If I had remembered to call Zanthia and tell her I wouldn't be home for dinner, I would have saved myself a lot of hassle, but Skooky's astonishing find drove everything else from my mind.

First, it took quite some time to contact Sam as he was in court until late that afternoon. Then came the difficulty of persuading him that it was critical he meet with Skooky and me.

"What do you mean, 'on an unofficial basis'?" he grumbled.

"I can't say. I think it's better you hear this first-hand."

"Damn it, Day, I'm in no mood for games. I've just been grilled for three hours in a case that should have taken fifteen minutes to settle."

"I promise this is no game."

Even after I convinced him the issue was serious, we still faced the logistical problem of where to meet. My apartment was unavailable, Sam's office and the newsroom were too public, Zanthia's place would never do—the very thought of Sam and my mother colliding gave me the vapors. At last Skooky provided the answer. "Me and a couple of my buds got this place," he suggested.

So it was that Sam, Skooky and I met in an Airstream trailer parked on a wooded lot off a country road several miles from town. "We call it The Bubble," Skooky told me as we were approaching the vehicle. "It's got kind of a double meaning, like the trailer's shaped that way and then there's this place over in the Canaries called The Bubble where the surfing—"

He stopped short, seeing the police cruiser already parked by the Airstream and Sam standing beside it. I pulled up next to the cruiser just as another squall hit. Skooky and I exited my vehicle, both aware that facing the downpour was a less daunting prospect than what lay ahead. Sam gave only a brief nod as all three of us dove, heads down, for the trailer entrance.

Sam and I waited while Skooky unlocked the metal door, his trembling fingers barely able to manipulate the multiple locks. We started to enter, but Sam waved the two of us back. We hunched against the rain while he went inside alone. We could hear his footsteps going through the trailer, cabinet doors opening and closing until finally he reappeared in the entrance and waved us aboard.

I glared at Sam as I shook the rain from my hair and mopped my face with tissues. Skooky didn't make any effort to dry off except to swipe with his arm at the drops running down his cheeks. Sam's uniform was a bit water-spotted, but otherwise showed little evidence of the drenching.

While drying off, I checked on my surroundings. The trailer's inside wasn't too bad, considering it was the hangout for a bunch of post-teens, mostly Skooky's surfing crowd. It smelled of pizza and beer and marijuana and male sweat. Someone had made an effort at décor with fishnet curtains and prints on the walls of surfers sliding down the curl. Skooky had mentioned on the way over that vandals had once broken into the trailer. "Messed the place up and stole some of our stuff," he said. "After that we bolted all the windows shut and made sure the door had a lock they couldn't break."

Sam motioned for the two of us to take the sofa. He seated himself opposite in one of the two unmatched armchairs, probably scrounged from some parent's attic to replace what was once the trailer's dinette. It felt as if Skooky and I were facing an inquisition, and Sam's expression did nothing to dispel that notion.

"You do realize, Day, what a position you're putting me in?" were Sam's first words to me. The suspicious glare he sent Skooky must have felt to the frightened kid like a jail door slamming shut.

My voice raised to compete against the pounding of rain on the trailer's aluminum roof, I started to explain how Skooky had come into possession of the necklace, but Sam's raised hand stopped me. "Let me hear this from him," he demanded.

Skooky, his lanky body drawn together as if he were trying to minimize himself, told his story of finding the necklace. When he finished, Sam swung toward me. "So how come this guy reported his find to you rather than to the authorities? Right off, that makes it look suspicious."

I glanced over at Skooky and shrugged to indicate he had no choice but to tell about the marijuana buy under the bridge. Skooky's shoulders sagged as he accepted the inevitable. He stumbled though his explanation, reiterating at every opportunity that the amount of weed Denny sold him was minimal. "A lot less than 20 grams. It's not like he's some big dealer," he assured Sam.

When Skooky finished, Sam jumped to his feet and paced the length of the trailer and back. "Jesus, Day! Bad enough this kid having in his possession an important piece of evidence in a murder case. On top of that, you're asking me, a police officer, to cover for him in what is a clear-cut violation of the law."

I had no response to that. Skooky, with Sam towering over him, was scarcely breathing, let alone speaking, and his face seemed to have lost all traces of his surfer tan. Finally Sam reseated himself, but his grim expression offered little hope. "First off," he said, "I want to meet this guy, your supplier."

"Hey, Man—" Skooky started to protest.

"Do not 'Hey, Man' me," Sam snapped. "I want the guy's name and I want it now, otherwise you and I are taking a little trip back to town and you won't be riding with your friend here." Sam gestured toward me, but his eyes drilled straight into Skooky's terrified face.

"And," Sam continued, "this guy better confirm everything you've told me and then I want to know his supplier."

"It's just he's got a coupla plants—" Skooky started, then cringed, aware he was saying too much.

Skooky supplied the name, and I started when I heard it—Denny Descuto. Descuto wasn't a common name around St. Augustine, and it sounded as if this might be Elaine Descuto's Denny, the kid who hadn't found himself, or who maybe had found himself, but in the wrong place. I stowed my assumption in the back of my mind as Sam continued drilling Skooky.

"So when this guy, this Denny Descuto, got there with the weed, did you show him the necklace you'd found?" Sam demanded.

"No . . . no, Sir. There wasn't time. Denny was late like I said. By then I'd rinsed the mud off the necklace and put it in my pocket. Denny was kinda jumpy that day, said he'd spotted a cop . . . I mean a police officer . . . spotted one on the way over that seemed to be looking at him funny. He just handed me the bag with the stuff and took off."

"You say he took off. What kind of vehicle was he driving?"

"No vehicle. Just his bike."

Sam released a huge sigh. "This is the kind of garbage I wish I didn't have to deal with—a punk growing pot and delivering it on his bike. Takes as much time and costs as much to prosecute a case like this as it does to go after some creep riding around in a stretch Lincoln with a trunk full of cocaine and an armory of AK-47s."

Neither Skooky nor I had a response for that. Sam also wanted to know how it was I'd recognized the necklace when Skooky showed it to me. "I know Frank Burke is good at ferreting out information that's being held back from the public," he said, "but I always thought he was a straight up guy who knew how to protect what was told to him in confidence."

I shook my head. "I didn't hear about the necklace from Frank."

I went on to explain how, when I was at the scene of Valerie's murder, the medical examiner had noticed a scrape on her neck. "The ME surmised that the killer might have grabbed her necklace. Then later when I was at Valerie's condo—"

"You were in the woman's condo after she was killed?"

That forced me to go into a lengthy explanation of Val's sister's request that I get the dress in which Valerie was to be buried. "While I was there this Alvaro fellow came looking for a necklace he claimed he had given her. He even wanted to search through her condo for it, but I told him he needed police permission to do that."

Sam's mouth drew back in a grimace. "That Cardenas guy keeps bugging us to find his necklace. At first we thought he might have something to do with the murder, you know, had a fight with her, wanted his necklace back, but he was in New York when she was killed, plenty of witnesses to testify to that. So far as we can tell, he's clear."

"None of which explains how the necklace ended up in the mud under the bridge," I said.

Sam sat silent for a moment, his upper lip clasped in his teeth. "Not all that far from the murder scene, either. Almost as if the killer just took it to make it look like his motive was robbery, but wanted to get rid of it in a hurry. We've never located her watch or cell phone, either, so it's possible he threw those away, too."

"If he tossed them off the bridge, they could easily have landed in the river," I pointed out.

Sam nodded. "I'll send in our dive team to have a look, but chances are slim they'll come up with anything. It's been some time and the current runs fast through that bridge."

It was a small thing, but I felt relieved that for those couple of minutes Sam and I had been able to share our thoughts without that wall of disappointed hopes between us. But after that, the gate clanged shut. I didn't know if I should feel relieved or sorry.

Skooky's interrogation wasn't finished, and it went on until evening darkened the trailer's murky windows. In the end, Sam took possession of the necklace as evidence in the murder case, and said he would write up the report of how Skooky had found it, leaving out the marijuana part. "Provided, this Descuto guy confirms it exactly as you've told it to me," Sam warned as we were leaving the trailer.

While Sam and I stood waiting, Skooky locked the trailer door behind us. If I'd expected Sam to say anything more to me, I was disappointed. His scowl said it all.

CHAPTER 24

By the time I arrived back at Mother's apartment, twilight had merged into a deceptively clear evening sky. Zanthia was sitting outside on the second floor balcony, wearing a silk caftan in watery shades of green and an expression that told me my phone call on the way back to town wasn't good enough. I bent to give her a hug. "Sorry, Mother, it's been one of those crazy days when the sky's come crashing down all around me."

Zanthia, for all her mystical powers, is a mother at heart—she gave me a kiss and a forgiving smile. She'd already eaten, she said, but offered to reheat the casserole she'd prepared for our dinner. It was only then I realized I'd totally forgotten lunch, and gratefully accepted.

Added to the day's stress, I'd driven by River Street on my way home. In the darkness, Mrs. Castelli's house loomed under its massive blue plastic tent like a huge ugly blob descended from an alien and not-too-friendly planet. The *Danger—Keep Out* signs posted in the yard gave it an even more menacing aspect. When I thought of the job I'd have putting everything in the house back in order, the idea of returning to my apartment held less appeal.

That made me even more appreciative of Mother's hospitality. After she went tripping off to the kitchen, I wandered over to the railing where I could look down on the flow of tourists and locals parading along St. George Street. Some were no doubt on their way to or from one of the town's many restaurants, others off perhaps to a performance or maybe indulging in a bit of late shopping. Most, I surmised, were simply enjoying a leisurely stroll in the fresh air the afternoon storms had bestowed like a hostess gift on the town. The lively chatter that drifted up to me, the sight of a little boy stooping to pat a tiny Yorkshire terrier, and a whiff of the salty air sweeping in off the bay front shifted my anxiety gauge a degree or so toward normal.

Normalcy didn't last long. Mother had just carried the tray she'd prepared for me out onto the balcony when my cell phone rang. Kyle was calling. "Just got home and when you never came back to the office after lunch I was . . . well, with all that's going on—"

"Kyle, I'm not a real estate agent. No reason anyone would—"

"I know, I know. It's just that you sometimes have a tendency to—"

"Stick my nose in where it doesn't belong?"

"It's just that with you digging into Ballard's background I was afraid you might have stumbled on something that would put the killer on guard."

"I promise I'll be doubly careful. So any more word on the case?"

"Just that the cops are still puzzling over how the killer got into the Satsuma Shores house. Absolutely no sign of any entry except through the front and the only code that showed up when they checked the keypad was Ballard's. But get this—the weird thing is, his code was used twice, the first time an hour earlier than Ballard's scheduled appointment."

"Maybe Ballard got there early for some reason and then left and came back."

"That would explain it, except it doesn't agree with the time Ballard left the office."

"Are the police thinking the killer somehow managed to duplicate Ballard's code?"

"Or maybe knew how to tamper with the device that records who comes and goes. That, along with the security cameras and motion sensors all being put out of commission makes it seem like our killer can walk through walls."

After Kyle hung up, I sat thinking about what he'd said and a shudder ran down my spine as I visualized a spectral figure lurking in wait to murder Ballard. But that was nonsense and there had to be a more logical answer.

The dinner Mother had prepared for me—a delicious-smelling mushroom lasagna accompanied by my favorite spinach-with-bacon salad and a slice of key lime cheesecake—grew cold as I phoned Polly. I knew that the keys to vacant houses for sale were secured inside lockboxes attached to a door's handle, but I wasn't sure exactly how the codes Kyle referred to operated.

"Back when I first started in the real estate business," Polly told me, "agents had to carry special keys to open the lockboxes. Nowadays it's a lot simpler—an agent can either buy a key ring fob that's actually an electronic device designed to open lockboxes or there's a phone app that will do the same thing. Most agents prefer the app as they always have their cellphones with them and don't have to carry an extra device."

"So when an agent uses either the device or the cellphone app to open a lockbox, it leaves a record?"

"Most definitely—the box records the code used to open it and the time of entry and departure. Does this have something to do with Compton Ballard's murder?"

"Maybe everything. Is it possible someone could duplicate someone else's code?"

"Now you're beyond me technologically. I've never heard

of that happening, but possibly a total computer geek or someone who knows a lot about security procedures."

I was still talking with Polly when Mother returned, saw that my dinner was growing cold and whisked the tray away, saying she'd give the lasagna a quick zap in the microwave. I signaled that wasn't necessary, but she ignored that. For once, it felt good to let her take charge.

I was just finishing the last bite of key lime pie—I ate mine like Dad always did, starting with the crust and saving the tip for a last delicious bite—when my phone's ring alerted me that Mrs. Castelli was calling. "Day, I don't know how much longer I can stay here," she began. "Evelyn has been lovely, but her husband can't stand cats. The man thinks nothing of swatting Winkles off the kitchen counter. Today the poor thing went flying halfway across the room."

My feelings about cats being somewhat similar to Mr. Stallings', I had to force a tone of sympathy. "Oh, dear, I'm sorry, Mrs. C., but it's only for a couple days more."

"And Evelyn won't let me turn a hand, treats me like an invalid. I'm not used to that sort of thing . . . I need to be up and doing."

"It will all be over in a day or so," I assured her.

"That's the trouble," she said. "Mr. Naylor called to tell me an inspector came to check out the house before they started fumigating and said that the sill and several beams under the kitchen will have to be replaced. Even worse, he found the termites have eaten away the stringers that support the interior stairs and even weakened some of the treads. We won't be allowed back in until they're repaired."

"But we don't even use—"

"I know, but try reasoning with an inspector."

I felt my hopes for a speedy return home sinking like a punctured rubber raft, but was relieved when she added, "I've already called Jake Somers to come fix the stairs and the beams. He said it shouldn't take more than a couple of days once the bug people are gone."

With a silken rustle, Mother rejoined me on the balcony and settled into the chair next to mine. When I told her Mrs. Castelli's bad news, she murmured the proper commiseration, but she didn't fool me—underneath she was smiling as if Claude had just whispered to her that I was moving in with her for good. We were still sitting there when my cellphone buzzed again. I was pleasantly surprised to hear Andy's voice, and also pleased when Zanthia diplomatically withdrew, her devious way of demonstrating that she'd be the last to interfere in my personal life.

I told Andy about Skooky's discovery of the necklace and we puzzled over the mystery of how the killer might have gained access to the Satsuma house. Andy talked about his recent trip to the panhandle where the marshes were still suffering the effects of a Gulf oil spill. "Stuff comes in like thick tar," he said, "the birds get that on their feathers and they don't stand a chance unless our rescue volunteers get to them right away."

It felt good to be talking over normal, everyday concerns with Andy, and I realized once again how comfortable I felt with him. Maybe his daughters and I had gotten off to a rocky start, but Dana and Lissa were actually sweet little girls. Their Fourth of July visit had been rather disastrous and Lissa had resisted every attempt I'd made to get close to her, but, after all, she was only seven. A child that age couldn't be expected take to a stranger the first go-round.

On an impulse, I said, "I'm looking forward to seeing Dana and Lissa again. Do you think they'd enjoy a trip to the Alligator Farm? It's really very educational as well as fun."

Andy's voice brightened at my suggestion and, after a bit more discussion, he said, "Should we set a date then?"

"How would a Saturday work?" I suggested, figuring that by the end of next week the repairs to Mrs. Castelli's house would be finished and I'd be back in my apartment and there'd be no need to meet at Mother's place.

Andy agreed that Saturday was fine, but before we finalized our arrangements, I could hear a child's voice calling him. "Oops," he said, "Dana can't find Mr. Teddy, so I've got to go. About nine o'clock be okay?"

"Sounds good," I assured him as he hurriedly signed off.

It wasn't until I closed my phone that I realized we'd been talking for nearly half an hour. I also realized that Mother had remained discreetly indoors, even though it was a safe bet that she'd been eavesdropping—probably gloating that things were going well with Andy and me. But then, she was a mother, and entitled to an occasional gloat.

Before heading for bed, I flipped on the late night news. The TV announcers were still expounding with orgasmic intensity on Ballard's murder.

I was brushing my teeth and had no more than swished out the sink when my cellphone summoned me again. I checked the caller ID hoping it was some telemarketer I could ignore, but it was Sam. "I checked out the Descuto kid," he announced without preamble.

"And?"

"He pretty much confirmed what Skooky told me. Thing is, if I bring this kid in for selling a small amount of pot, there's no way I can avoid involving Skooky for buying the stuff. Even if I charged them both, I'd be going through the whole effort for nothing—the Descuto kid has no priors nor does Skooky, so the most either of them gets is a slap on the wrist and maybe a few hours of community service. Meanwhile, our department would have wasted hours and hours of time better spent finding this murderer before he or she strikes again."

"Skooky's not a bad kid," I said. "A little immature, but a sweet kind of guy. I hope there's some way you can avoid . . . well, you know. Even if he gets off with a slap as you say, I'm afraid it would cost him his job, not to mention a ton of grief from his parents."

"Denny Descuto isn't all that bad either, just a kid who got a bit off the track when his parents split. Gave his Mom quite a shock when I showed up at their house last night."

"Is her name Elaine?"

"That's the one. Like too many mothers—dads, too, I suppose, although they're inclined to be more suspicious of their kids' activities—she had no idea that her Denny was involved in anything illegal like growing pot and selling it to his friends. She got all teary and defensive and that's not what her kid needs, which is a little strong-arming to throw the fear of God into him."

"I've met Elaine Descuto a couple of times. She's a nice woman, very devoted to her kids."

"Nice or not, unless she puts the clamps on her son's illegal enterprise and gets him straightened out right quick, he's going to go down and take Skooky with him. I'm afraid she saw me as the big, bad policeman out to persecute her boy. If you know her well enough, you might do her a favor by having a heart-to-heart."

"I'm not sure we're that close—not close at all, actually. And I'm pretty busy right now with—"

He cut me off. "Let's put it this way—once again you've dragged my sorry ass into a situation where, if I do as you ask, I'll be compromised up the wazoo. So if you want to save Skooky's hide, you better buddy up to Mrs. Descuto and convince her that her son's got to straighten out." He paused, then added, "Of course if you're too busy with fly boy—"

It hurt that Sam's tone was not that of a former lover, not even that of a friend. Unwilling to leave it like that, I decided to share with him what I learned in my research on Ballard. "Sam," I said, "I've been looking into Compton Ballard's background. Did you know that Ballard's original name was Lloyd Hostler and that he grew up in Baltimore?"

Silence on the other end told me the police department hadn't yet unearthed that fact. I went on, hoping that my information would buy back a little of Sam's goodwill. "Ballard—he was Lloyd Hostler then—was in business with his father, Milton Hostler. They ran a loan shark operation, charged exorbitant interest rates, repossessed property when borrowers couldn't pay, that sort of thing. When Ballard was in his mid-thirties, his father got sent to prison on an arson and manslaughter charge. That's when Ballard changed his name."

I went over with Sam how I'd learned of Ballard's Baltimore background and how he'd managed to start a new life in Charlotte, North Carolina, and became successful in the real estate business.

"Anything else you turned up?" Sam's tone a little less grudging.

"Frank still has me working on the Baltimore angle, although after 30 years I suspect that's a waste of time insofar as the murders here are concerned."

"We'll follow up on all that. And Day?—"

"Yes?"

"Thanks. We're still checking out all of SandScapes's staff and if anything turns up I'll let you know before . . . well, before you-know-who. And I'll do my best on the Skooky business."

*****

TGIF, I thought as I sank wearily into bed. The week ahead loomed with all sorts of obligations—my promise to Sam that I'd talk with Elaine Descuto, finishing research on Ballard's background, repairs on Mrs. Castelli's house to be completed, the move back to my apartment. At least I'd have the entire week before Andy and girls arrived next Saturday. The talk with Elaine Descuto was urgent, but except for that, I'd give myself a Saturday break, take a book, head for the beach, and do absolutely nothing for the whole day. Satisfied with that plan, I turned off my phone and headed for dreamland.

CHAPTER 25

The voice brought me bolt upright in bed. I squinted through half-closed lids and could have sworn I saw something—a shadow . . . a wisp of vapor –pass through the closed door. The words, too distinct for me to have mistaken them, shimmered in my bemused brain—"Follow the dirty money. . . Follow the dirty money." Twice came that same phrase, and then nothing. I looked wildly about, trying to make out the room's shapes through the dim filter of light from the smoke detector's tiny red LED bulb. Was it my imagination or was there a peculiar odor, something that suggested curry or dead flowers or cigar smoke?

Stiff with fright, I clutched the coverlet close to my body. Follow what dirty money? Whose dirty money? Follow it where? Finally, my pulse slowed and sanity returned. Only a dream— there'd been no ghostly figure, no sinuous whispers, nothing but my too-vivid imagination. Like that business at the séance, it had been pure illusion. I had to get back to my own apartment. And soon. A few more days in this place and I'd be as whacky as Zanthia herself.

By the time I woke again, a wedge of sunlight commanded the space between the blind and the windowsill and my mysterious nighttime visit seemed all the more ludicrous. Dirty money—parents always warned their kids not to put money in their mouths, that it was loaded with germs. Filthy lucre, money was sometimes referred to, as if misuse contaminated the bills and coins, when actually it was the humans misusing them who were tainted. Banks concealed dye packets in bundles of money handed over to thieves, so that might be dirty money as well.

I lay for a few more minutes, glad it was Saturday and there was no urgency to get out of bed. After a run and breakfast, I'd call Elaine Descuto and ask her to meet me.

*****

By nine o'clock, the Essential Bean was crowded, so I was pleased to see that Elaine had commandeered a booth near the rear. Her eagerness to meet with me when I phoned left me no time to change, so I was still in my running gear and probably smelling a bit gamy.

Elaine raised a cup to show she'd already gotten her coffee and I signaled to her that I'd grab mine and then join her. While waiting, I reached for my cell phone, then realized I'd left it on my nightstand. Any calls would have to go to voice mail. Zanthia wouldn't hear it as she was already in the store, ready to cope with another busy Saturday of runes and Ouija boards and books about how to concoct magic potions.

With cup in hand, I approached the booth. Up close it was obvious that Elaine's eyes were red-rimmed and her usually neatly styled gray-streaked hair hung in wisps about her face. I slid into the seat opposite. "Glad we could get together," I said.

"I should apologize to Lieutenant Stansfield for being so abrupt last night," she said. "But that was just too—"

"I know. That's why Sa— that is the lieutenant—why he asked me to talk with you."

"He's not really bad, you know."

For a moment I thought she was referring to Sam, then realized she meant Denny. "Neither is Skooky," I said, "I'm sure you don't have any more desire to see Denny get in trouble with the law than Skooky's parents do for him."

"Denny's been so lost since the divorce. He used to play sports, he had nice friends, a girlfriend, even. Now, it's as if he's lost his center. Refuses to go back to college. Says there are no jobs that interest him. Lies around the house all day and then is out until all hours of the night."

I sensed she needed to vent about Denny's troubles and I let her go on for some time before asking, "Do you think Denny realizes the seriousness of his situation?"

She gave a despairing sigh. "Denny tried to brazen it out while Lieutenant Stansfield was there, but I could tell he was terrified he'd be arrested. After the lieutenant left, Denny and I had a long talk . . . a very long talk. Probably the most honest talk since . . ."

Her voice broke and I stayed quiet while she collected herself enough to add, "It broke my heart when he said he'd been struggling to find something that would make life seem worthwhile again."

The pain in Elaine's voice reminded me what an obligation parents took on when they decided to have children. She started again telling me of all Denny's good qualities, or perhaps reassuring herself that he was still the decent kid he had once been. At one point she mentioned that one of the things Denny had enjoyed with his father was fishing. "That was before Patrick and his child bride moved to San Diego," she added, the bitterness in her voice reflected in her eyes.

At her reference to fishing, a preposterous plan began to form in my mind. My grandfather, MacKenzie Richards—Mac to everyone—had once before taken an obstreperous boy and turned him into a man. Mac's firm guidance and hard work on the charter boat had turned Robbie Flynn from a rebellious 13-year-old into a man anyone would be proud of. But Denny Descuto was already a grown man, probably twenty or twenty-one. Still, he was in many ways a lost child, and there was always the possibility that Mac could use a crew hand on the *Jancey Day*.

Excited at that possibility, I started to ask Elaine if I could borrow her cell phone, then thought better of it. Probably better, too, not to get Elaine's hopes too high before I got Mac's reaction to my plan. Instead, I told her I had something in mind that might interest Denny and get him out of temptation's way.

When we parted, her face appeared a lot more optimistic than it had been earlier. I only hoped I could follow through.

*****

It was nearly ten when I left the coffee shop, and the heat was already building toward its midday crescendo. Just the short jog down St. George Street to Mother's shop had me sweating all over again. I rounded the building to the side entrance and once upstairs headed immediately for the shower. Long minutes under lukewarm water left me feeling renewed and ready for the relaxed day I'd planned at the beach. Maybe for lunch I'd try the fish tacos from the new stand everyone raved about.

I was toweling off my hair when I remembered my phone. The one voice mail was from Andy. I listened and heard his cheerful voice say, "Hi, Day, we're on our way."

"Way?" I stammered aloud. "On the way where?"

"See you in about forty minutes," the voice went on.

An OMG moment hit and I slumped onto the bed. I'd said Saturday and Andy had thought I meant *this* Saturday. And now he'd driven all the way from Ocala and could be arriving any moment. I checked the phone and saw that the call had been made at nine fifty, which meant they could be arriving any second.

A dread realization hit—if I didn't manage to get them in and out without Zanthia knowing, she'd be playing the doting grandmother to Dana and Lissa and sizing up Andy as son-in-law material. My best hope was that she'd be occupied in the store. If I rushed, I could get dressed and be waiting outside to whisk them away when they arrived. I'd call Mother later and explain about the mix-up in dates and how I hadn't wanted to bother her when she was busy with customers.

Throwing on the first thing I could grab—denim capris, a patterned tee and sandals—I dashed down the stairs to the apartment's side-street entrance. Andy's car was parked at the curb. No one was inside.

With an ominous feeling in my throat, I rounded the corner into St. George Street, entered the store and was immediately immersed in the smell of incense, the tinkle of wind chimes and the music of flutes and panpipes. Caroline, Mother's shop assistant, was waiting on a pair of women who were trying on the brightly-colored scarves Mother had just imported from India.

I searched about and saw Andy and Dana at the far side of the shop next to the tiered display of fountains. Dana had one of her hands in Andy's, tentatively reaching with the other to feel the splash of water from the beaks of tiny birds atop one of the fountains. At a table on the opposite side, Lissa and Zanthia were bent over a Ouija board. "Just rest your fingertips ever so lightly on the planchette and let it go where it wants," Zanthia was telling the wide-eyed Lissa.

"It moved!" Lissa exclaimed. "There's an "R" and now an "E.""

"Mother!" I screeched. "What do you think?—"

Zanthia swung around. "I think this little girl may have a true knack. Her aura—"

"Lissa's seven," I yelped, "She doesn't *have* an aura."

Andy came to join me. I started to stammer out introductions, but he and Zanthia both smiled and said they'd already introduced themselves. I didn't like the smugness in Mother's smile, that cat-who's-found-the-cream look of hers.

I was forced to explain to Andy about the mix-up in dates and we were both embarrassed. "Hope we didn't upset everyone's schedule," Andy apologized, nodding toward both Zanthia and me.

"Not at all," Zanthia assured him with way too much enthusiasm. "My horoscope said that today those I've been anxious to meet would enter my sphere. Day, I can't believe you've delayed in introducing me to this handsome young man. Such an interesting profession, too—a pilot, for the Fish and Wildlife Commission. And how could you keep these two lovely little girls a secret?"

I released my breath in a half-disguised groan. "We'd better be going," I told Andy. "I'm sure the girls are anxious to see the alligators."

"Do we have to?" Lissa whined. "I like this magic place. Can't I stay with Miss Zanthia while you go look at ugly old alligators?"

I could just visualize how much nonsense Zanthia would stuff into the child's head if she was allowed to stay. I looked to Andy for support and he caught my message. "Girls," he announced. "Time to get going. The alligators await."

Dana tugged at Andy's hand, eager to go, but Lissa still held back. "Do we have to?" Wistfully, she reached to touch a bamboo wind chime and released its soft hollow music.

With some persuasion and a little bit of sternness Andy managed to induce Lissa to say goodbye to Zanthia and we headed for his car. I slid into the front passenger seat with a grateful sigh even though I could feel Lissa's resentment rising from the back seat like juice from an apple pie dripping over into a hot oven.

Andy had no more than ordered, "Seat belts, everyone," when his cellphone jangled. With an apologetic shrug he pulled it from his pocket, checked the number and put it to his ear. "Thompson," he said in a brisk tone that told me the call was official business. He listened for a moment, then asked, "How far out?" He listened again then said, "Any idea how many on board?" Moments later, his tone crisp, he said, "Of course I will. Give me—" he looked at his watch, "say twenty minutes."

He snapped the phone shut and turned to face me. "A call has come in that a shrimp boat's taking on water about 20 miles off the coast, due east of here. She started foundering late last night, but before the Coast Guard could pick up the exact coordinates they lost communication. My division chief has arranged for me to pick up a charter plane at the airport here and help in the search."

"Of course. You've got to go."

"But the girls—I don't know how long it'll take and—"

"Go," I told him. "I'll take care of the girls."

CHAPTER 26

Andy gave a final wave as his car rounded the corner and disappeared from sight. The girls and I stood on the sidewalk under the sign reading "The Other Side." Mother's shop had never seemed more appropriately named. Lissa's stony little face was set in that don't-even-try-to-make-me-like-you stiffness and Dana looked as if the tears were about to burst through at any moment. The mission for which I'd volunteered dawned on me. Moments before, my voice had sounded so gallant—the young bride sending her valiant trooper off to war while she stands guard over the home front—but now, if I dared open my mouth, all that would come out was a timid quaver. Suppose Andy didn't come back right away? Suppose I was left to take care of the two girls for days and days? How would I know what to feed them or what time they had to be in bed?

A gulped-down sob from Dana reminded me that I should be reassuring the girls instead of indulging my own fears. "Okay," I said, with more bravado than I was feeling, "we'll just hop right in my Jeep and off we'll go to see the alligators."

"I'm not going," Lissa planted herself, arms folded. "Daddy's not here and I hate alligators."

"But there are all kinds of other wildlife besides the gators," I said. "They have snakes and birds and—" I halted, Lissa's expression making it clear she rejected any and all forms of wildlife. If only I'd taken some course in how to deal with kids instead of all those journalism classes.

Lissa's resistance to our plans seemed to bring out an opposite reaction in her sister. "I want to go," Dana insisted. "Daddy promised we would see birds and snakes and alligators."

Lissa glared down at her shoes. "Daddy's not here," she said. "I want to go home."

"But think of all the interesting things you'll have to tell your Dad when he gets back," I cajoled, fighting to keep the desperation out of my voice.

"Don't care. If I can't go home, I want to stay right here with Miss Zanthia."

Mother—no doubt at the command of her spirit advisor, Claude—came swirling out onto the sidewalk just in time to overhear Lissa's demand. "But of course," Mother gloated, "Lissa will stay here and be my assistant. We'll have a wonderful time. Day, you and Dana go right ahead."

Blindsided, I considered the alternatives. One, I could insist that Lissa come look at alligators, in which case I'd be stuck with hours and hours of straight-out whining. Or two, I could take Dana to the Alligator Farm and allow Lissa to stay with Zanthia who would no doubt fill the girl's head with all sorts of occult nonsense.

Mother confirmed my misgivings—"Lissa and I are going to have an absolutely marvelous time," she bubbled. "I've so many exciting things to show her. Don't worry about lunch, you and Dana take all the time you need."

"Mother, please remember she's seven. No palm reading or crystal balls and none of that C-l-a-u-d-e business."

"What's a Claude?" Lissa asked, turning to Zanthia for the

answer.

I took the coward's way out. With Dana in hand, I headed for the Jeep, gratified to know that Lissa was good at spelling but wondering what other words she'd learn before the day was over.

Now that I didn't have to listen to Lissa whine, I actually looked forward to sharing with Dana an experience that was an important part of my history. A picture in the family album recorded my first trip to the Alligator Farm, me in a stroller and Mother and Dad with that glow young couples have when showing off their brand new offspring. In the years that followed, I'd come back many times, sometimes on school trips, other times on my own or to show off the exhibits to visiting friends. Over time, both the Alligator Farm and I had changed and grown up. Once a tourist attraction, the Farm had developed into a nature study center that attracted scientists from all over the world.

Luckily, Dana proved to be as intrigued by the alligators and other wildlife as I'd always been. At the pit where the albino gators were on display, Dana let go of my hand and ran to the barrier to peer closer. "White ones," she breathed. At the macaw exhibit she talked back to the birds and skipped across the marsh walkway, eager for an up-close look at the egret rookery.

After viewing various habitats filled with gators and crocodiles and other wildlife native to the area, we seated ourselves in the large pavilion where a naturalist was giving a lecture on snakes. The woman reached into a cage and extracted a snake whose belly was bright red and held it up for display. "This is a red-bellied snake and it's one of our many harmless Florida snakes," she said. "Would anyone like come up and touch it?"

Before I could react, Dana slipped out of her seat and ran to where the ranger was holding the snake. I half rose, then reseated myself when I saw that Dana, without the least sign of fear, was stroking her hand along the snake's sinuous body.

It was mid-afternoon when Dana and I returned to the shop, she cuddling her plush alligator from the gift shop. I felt some trepidation when I entered The Other Side, but to my surprise,

Lissa came running to me to show off the picture she'd created of a gold-colored pony decorated in spangles and crystals and with pink and blue feathers for a mane and tail.

Shortly after that, Andy returned and reported that the sinking shrimper had been located and that the crew had been safely taken aboard another vessel. "So, how did my girls manage while I was gone?" he asked with a look that included me in the "my girls." A little less comforting was that his glance seemed to take in Zanthia as well.

Because the girls were tired, Andy and I decided we'd have an early supper before they headed back to Ocala. "We should ask your mother to join us, to thank her for looking after Lissa," he reminded me.

I was forced to agree, knowing Zanthia would gladly have paid for the privilege of spending time with the girls. We settled on a nearby restaurant that served mac and cheese and hamburgers and shakes as well as more adult food for Andy, Zanthia and me. Dana was beginning to droop by the time our food arrived, but Lissa chattered all through the meal, still full of her day in what she now called "Miss Zanthia's magic store."

I was drooping, too, by the time Andy and the girls left, but I still had some business to take care of. While Mother returned to help her assistant close the shop, I got on the phone to my grandfather. The conversation was a long one and Mac said he couldn't commit himself in any way, but he did need a hand since a local kid he'd hired was leaving to go on vacation with his parents, and that he'd be willing to meet the young man.

Then I called Elaine Descuto and told her what I had in mind. We arranged that she, Denny and I would drive up to Mayport the following day. So much for a weekend in which I'd planned to do nothing but relax.

CHAPTER 27

Sam's phone call came at an opportune time. I was still on my Sunday morning run, nearing the Mission de Nombre de Dios, safely away from Mother's apartment, so no chance of her eavesdropping. On the negative side, Sam's tone was the same officially caustic one on which we'd parted after the Skooky episode on Friday. "I hope you're sleeping well," he said, "because I sure as hell haven't. If Chief Oberholt gets wind of the business with your boy Skooky and his pot-pushing pal, I'm in it up to my ass."

"Sam, I've got a plan—"

"And where have I heard that before?"

"Just listen. What if I can find a way to get Denny Descuto out of town and into a situation where he won't have the time, the energy or the opportunity to continue with . . . with the thing he's been doing."

"So you've got some private jail where you can lock him up until he achieves some common sense?"

I slowed my pace in order to talk. "It's no joke, Sam. If what

I have in mind works, I can almost guarantee he'll get straight-ened out. Can't you just pretend you never heard the marijuana part of the story, that Skooky just came to you with the necklace and—"

"Came to *you* with it, if I remember correctly."

I didn't have a rebuttal for that, so I stayed silent. Sam knew as well as I did that involving Skooky and Denny Descuto with the legal system wasn't the best answer. It was obvious too, that he wanted to give me a hard time, but knowing Sam as I do, I was betting that once he got his digs in, he'd soften.

My guess proved right. After a bit more hassling, Sam al-lowed me to explain what I had in mind for Denny Descuto, then grudgingly said, "This better work."

"Sam, I owe you for this."

"Don't worry—I've marked it down in my book. You real-ize, though, there's still a big question remaining—how the hell did the necklace end up down there on the river bank?"

"The divers find anything, like Valerie's watch or cell phone?"

"They did a sweep of the river in that area, but that was pretty much hopeless from the git-go considering the current and how much time has passed."

I made a right turn into the Mission grounds. "At least you've got the necklace. What about that Argentinian guy who claims it's his?"

"We've double checked Alvaro Cardenas, and his alibi is airtight. Besides, the fuss he's made about the necklace doesn't fit with his being the perpetrator."

"Have you told him the necklace has been recovered?"

"Told him, yes. I wish you could have heard him yelling 'Give me back my necklace!' in six different languages when he found out we're holding it as evidence until this case is solved."

"Poor guy. Looks like he got caught in the middle."

"Don't waste too much pity. The guy's a real smoothie with the ladies. By the time he left the office he was hitting on Sergeant Jessie Randall."

"The one with the big . . ."

"That's the one."

I was pleased that Sam's tone had undergone a transformation as we talked, but that also left me in an awkward position as far as ending the conversation. Too many times Sam had lured me—or had I lured myself?—back into our relationship, so I hastily improvised—"Oh, gosh, I'm here on the Mission grounds and a kid has just fallen off his bike. Better go see if he needs help. Catch you later."

I pretended not to hear Sam's "Hold on!" and clicked the phone shut. Somewhere there probably *was* a kid who'd fallen off his bike.

*****

Elaine and I occupied the front seat of my Jeep with Denny in the back, folded into himself like a kid being hauled off to the principal's office. Elaine kept turning around to assure her son that nothing had been settled yet, that the trip up to Mayport was just to see if he would like working on my grandfather's charter boat.

"You know how much you've always enjoyed fishing," she reminded him.

Denny's grunted "Yeah" was hardly responsive.

Their conversation continued like that all the way up the coast, Denny brushing off every attempt his mother made to cajole him out of his self-inflicted misery. By the time we made the turn for Mayport I'd had enough. We were knocking ourselves out to keep him out of jail—"aiding and abetting" in legal terms—and I didn't appreciate his attitude one bit.

After a few more such interchanges between the two, I swerved the Jeep off onto the shoulder, braked to an abrupt halt and swung to face the rear. "Look here, young man," I snapped. "I can turn this car around right now and haul you back to St. Augustine. We'll go straight to Lieutenant Stansfield and let him file charges on you for your illegal pot enterprise. Is that what you want?"

I caught his startled look. "No . . ."

"'No' what?" I demanded. "And sit up straight."

He actually straightened at my command. "No, ma'am," he stammered. "I mean yes, ma'am."

"Now do we keep on or turn back? Your decision. But if we go on, you're going to behave respectfully to your mother, to me, and to my grandfather when you meet him. So which will it be?"

Elaine's mouth gaped as her glance swiveled from Denny to me and back. She started to say something, but seemed to think better of it.

Apparently my tirade surprised Denny almost as much as it surprised me. To my relief, he apologized and said he appreciated all we were doing for him. It wasn't until I'd pulled the car back on the roadway and we were again heading for Mayport that I had time to wonder where my challenge to the sulky young man had come from. I also wondered if, had Elaine been firmer with Denny early on, the results might have been different for them. Above all, the episode set me to wondering if I might have the makings of a parent after all.

*****

If I was feeling a bit smug about my success with Denny when we pulled into my grandfather's cottage at Mayport, that soon evaporated. Mac suggested we first go on board the *Jancey Day* so he could explain to Denny what his duties would be if he took him on as crew. While Denny seemed fairly knowledgeable, neither did he show any enthusiasm. He didn't return to his sulk, but his closed expression throughout was that of someone being forced into agreement against his will.

Corporal, Mac's retired police dog, followed us around the boat, obviously taking stock of the newcomers. He gave Elaine a nudge of approval as soon as she bent to scratch behind his ears. Denny he was not so quick to accept, and continued to keep his distance as if checking him out.

Mac glanced at me as we stepped back onto the dock, and

I could read in his eyes that he was dubious this was going to work. Elaine had interjected hopeful little comments as we made our tour, but I could sense that she, too, was less than hopeful.

Back at the cottage, Mac suggested Elaine and Denny seat themselves on the deck while he and I prepared a pitcher of lemonade. As usual, Mac's deck, which I referred to as his workshop, was strewn with various boat parts and fishing gear in need of repair. Denny picked up a snarled reel from one of the chairs before seating himself. Again, Corporal was watchful, taking a position some distance from Denny but with his eyes on the young man's every move.

As I expected, once inside the cottage, Mac voiced his concern that unless Denny showed more enthusiasm for the job, it wouldn't work out. "The boy seems to know quite a bit about boats, so I'm not concerned from that angle," Mac said as he reamed the juice from a lemon, "but I have to consider the folks who pay good money to charter my boat. I don't think a surly crew member will bring me much repeat business."

After the pitcher was filled with lemonade, I arranged glasses on a tray and we returned to the deck. I don't know which of us, Mac or I, was more surprised to see Denny rewinding the now unsnarled reel with Corporal's muzzle snuggled into his lap.

*****

The ride back to St. Augustine was made in a happier mood than the one in which we'd approached Mayport. As it turned out, Mac had an early charter the following morning and he and Denny agreed that it would be a good opportunity for Denny to try out as a crewmember on the *Jancey Day*. He would spend the night at the cottage and Elaine would arrange to collect him when they returned the following evening. When we left, Denny was taking Corporal for a walk and my grandfather was looking, if not convinced, at least more optimistic.

I was glad of the time alone with Elaine because I'd been hoping for an opportunity to find out more about Harry Ports. Without revealing my suspicions of the man, I tried to bring the conversation around to him. I must have done so rather awkwardly because Elaine looked at me for a long moment without speaking. "If you're thinking that Harry might have killed Mr. Ballard, that can't be right," she said.

I gave her a quizzical look.

"No one is supposed to know this, but Mr. Ballard's father met Harry Ports when they were both in prison. Kathy, who does all our personnel work, told me and if she knew . . ."

"I promise anything you tell me will go no further," I assured her.

"Well, it was up in Maryland. Ballard's father was in prison for setting a fire that killed someone. That's all I know about that. Anyhow, Harry Ports was an accountant who had been convicted of embezzlement. He nearly died in that same prison, according to Kathy—was attacked by a gang and that's where he got that deep dent in his head. Anyhow, Ballard's father saw how smart Harry is and when Harry was released he advised his son to hire him as his accountant."

"Wait. Why would he want an embezzler as his . . ." I halted, getting the picture.

Elaine nodded. "That's another thing. Besides the regular home and property sales, I'm pretty sure Mr. Ballard had other business transactions that nobody in the company was supposed to know about. Under the table business. Maybe with Harry being indebted to him, Mr. Ballard . . ."

"Hire an embezzler so he can help you embezzle—" I mused on a take-off of the old 'hire a thief to catch a thief.'

"Please keep this very, very secret. It could cost me—"

"Not a word," I assured her, then asked, "Do you think anyone else in SandScapes knows about this?"

She thought for a minute. "Possibly Nick Petroski. He's the only one Harry ever socializes with, if you can call talking about baseball all the time socializing. They're both big fans of the Baltimore Orioles. I think Nick can recite the names of every pitcher since the club began."

I recalled what I knew about Nick Petroski, the one with the built-up shoe—polio as a child Elaine had once mentioned. She'd also said Nick was the only one in the office with whom Harry Ports socialized. During my interview with Nick, there'd been that phone call right after Harry Ports freaked out over the copier being broken. Suppose Nick knew about Ports' role in Ballard's financial operations. Suppose Ports had killed Valerie on Sunday and then came in on Monday and discovered those papers jammed in the copier, papers that might expose him. It was possible that Ports would call Nick when he realized his plan was in jeopardy.

A lot of supposes and maybes. No real proof of anything. Before I reported my suspicions of Harry Ports to Sam, I needed dead-on evidence. Still, what Elaine told me was enough to make me want to talk with Nick Petroski.

CHAPTER 28

Eager as I was to find out if Nick Petroski was aware of what was going on with SandScapes' accountant, work came first. At the Monday staff meeting I was handed two immediate assignments, one the commission hearing on whether Segways should be subject to the same restrictions in the historic area as the rental carts and mopeds. The other was a court hearing on the dispute between a developer and an adjoining property owner who claimed that run-off from the new development was flooding his lawn each time it rained.

Both items required some preliminary research. My nose was buried in the computer screen and my fingers were flying over the keyboard when the phone jangled on my desk. Annoyed at the interruption, I picked it up with a very curt "yes?"

"I'm looking for a Miss Day McKelvey," said a soft voice that identified the person at the other end as an older woman.

Chagrined that my voice may have held some animosity for this stranger, I answered, "I'm Day McKelvey. I'm sorry, the phone surprised me."

"Maple Brisby here. Everett has told me so much about you, I figured you'd be the person to talk to."

My immediate reaction was that Everett's ladylove had no doubt learned about our finding a dead person in the house and freaked out. "Talk to me about what, Mrs. Brisby?"

"Maple, if you please. It's that lovely house on Oleander Drive, such a pretty name, oleander, although if I'm not mistaken that plant's leaves can be very poisonous. Someone once told me about a cat that ate—"

I interrupted. "About that house, Maple, I'm surprised you're interested in it after . . ."

"Oh, no," she assured me. "Everett's told me all about that poor girl being killed right there in the bedroom. I said, 'Gracious, why should that make me think any less of the house?' I mean, people die in all sorts of places—like hospitals and nursing homes. They don't seal off the room and never use it again because someone died there, do they?"

I responded with "Uh, I guess not," intrigued to see where this conversation was leading.

"What I'm calling about—" she was interrupted by a raucous shriek in the background, *Demasiados telephono! Hable conmigo!* repeated several times.

Even with my rudimentary Spanish I could translate that as "Too much telephone! Talk to me!"

"Now you hush," Maple said, hopefully not to me but to the parrot. "I'm looking to find you a nueva casa."

The parrot quieted, Maple prattled on, "About the listing picture of 23 Oleander, I need to know which direction the house faces, so I'll be sure there's a good view from the living room's bay for McDuff. He tends to shout obscenities when he can't see what's going on outside."

I gulped. "So he needs a nice clear view to keep him from using foul language."

Maple failed to catch my intended pun and went cheerily on. "It helps that I'm teaching him Shakespeare. Already he's mastered several sentences. I started with 'to be or not to be', since those are short words. He's stuck on the word 'whether'. I guess his tongue can't handle some diphthongs. Maybe I should move on to 'out, out, damned spot,' but I don't really want him learning any more curse words."

Afraid that she'd go on forever with her favorite Shakespearean phrases, I told a white lie. "Maple, I'll be happy to find out which way the house faces, and if it has a view, but right now, I have to go into a meeting with my boss. Should I report back to Everett?" Let him tell her and get the update on the soliloquies.

"Oh, no," Maple insisted. "If Everett knows I've asked you to do this for me, he'll assume I'm ready to move and I'm not . . . at least not yet. So, if you don't mind, can we just keep my request our little secret?"

Unable to think of an out, I agreed to check out the house for Maple . . . or rather for McDuff. She asked if I would take my cellphone inside the house on Oleander Drive and snap pictures of the view from the window. I said I'd arrange with SandScapes Realty to get inside the house, and that I'd take pictures from every angle so that McDuff could be assured of his view.

Maple's request, although a bit bizarre, gave me exactly the opportunity I needed to follow up on Elaine's hint that Nick Petroski might have key information about Harry Ports. Nick knew I was a reporter, so he might suspect my motive if I focused only on the house at 23 Oleander Drive. I pulled up the Sunday real estate section and selected two SandScapes listings of similar houses. Seeing all three would take a while and somewhere along our route, I'd attempt to steer the conversation to Harry Ports.

Before I could call SandScapes to make the appointment, Skooky approached my cubicle. "Thanks Miss D," he said. "I heard about the job you got for Denny."

"It's only a try-out," I said. "He'll have to prove himself. I just hope your finding the necklace will take the focus off your other . . . activity. "

"That Lieutenant Stansfield must really like you to go to so much . . . you know what I mean."

I felt my mouth twist in a wry grimace. "Don't count on that. I strongly suggest you play it straight with him. Otherwise, you and Denny could both end up in very deep doo-doo."

"You bet, Miss D." Skooky's translucent blue eyes shone with the gratitude of someone who was seeing the sunlight after a narrow escape. "Anyhow, I just wanted to say thanks."

Skooky turned to leave then snapped his fingers. "Shoot!" He spun back around. "Almost forgot to tell you that before Mr. Burke left this morning, he asked me to tell you he found something interesting in that stuff you forwarded to him. You know, about that business up in Baltimore."

"And?"

"Said he needed to check a couple of things and he'd talk to you about it later."

Just then Shel emerged from his office door and motioned to Skooky. "That's all he said," Skooky called over his shoulder as he hurried away.

From what Skooky had told me, it was a safe assumption that Frank had picked up on some niggling detail I'd overlooked in the court records and tax records and newspaper clippings I'd forwarded to him. All the information I'd pulled up on Ballard and Ballard's father, Milton Hostler, would have taken hours to scour though, even with the computer's "Search" function. Frank was probably eager to point out any ineptness on my part, but to be on the safe side, I'd go over those documents again before I talked to him. Meanwhile, there was the appointment to arrange with Nick Petroski. If the results were what I was hoping for, I'd have some information a lot more relevant to the murders than anything Frank might have come across.

*****

Receptionist Cindy Kaufman's voice grew cautious when I announced my name. "Mrs. Ballard says we are not—"

"This isn't about my newspaper work," I told her. "I'm calling to check out several homes for an out-of-town friend who plans to move to St. Augustine."

"Just a minute and I'll see which agent—"

"I'd prefer to speak with Mr. Petroski," I told her.

"He's not in this morning. I can have him call you when he gets back. But in the meantime, I'll have to register you as one of his clients. We do that for all prospects."

Did I feel a little twinge of guilt over pretending to buy a house, even if it was for a "friend"? Well, I supposed I could consider Maple Brisby as a newfound friend, and I *was* going to take some photos for her. I'd take shots of the other houses as well to make it look legitimate.

I gave Cindy the required info – namely my address, phone number and the desired area plus the price range my friend was considering. As in the H&GTV show, *Love it or List It*, I chose one less expensive than 23 Oleander Lane and one at a higher price, a sort of Goldilocks and the three bears scenario. Cindy said she'd forward the info to Nick. About an hour later my phone rang. In his somewhat stilted phrases, Nick Petroski agreed that he would be glad to show me any the properties I'd chosen, but would not be available to do so until late afternoon. That fit my schedule as the court hearing on the homeowner's flood case was scheduled for 3 P.M. We arranged to meet at the *Dispatch* office at 5 P.M.

As I feared, the case preceding the one I was assigned to cover dragged on well past 3 P.M. When the homeowner's case was called, it appeared he planned to call numerous witnesses on his behalf. Adjacent property owners and a very long-winded landscaper testified at excruciating length and with photographs as to the damage flood waters had done to the man's property. The developer had a phalanx of lawyers on his side for rebuttal. Meanwhile outside there was the ominous rumble of thunder and one nearby lightning strike that caused the courtroom's lights to flicker.

At 5:15 I dashed out of the courtroom and stopped in the

hallway to turn on my cellphone. There were two messages from Shel and two more from Kyle, not a good sign. I tried first to connect with Shel's line, but got a busy signal. Kyle answered immediately. "Need you here right away," he said. "Zelma Beauclaire's been arrested."

CHAPTER 29

"I swear it's no joke—they've got her in the pokey."

I stared at Kyle in disbelief. "For what?"

"Far as I can make out, she tried to run down Compton Ballard's widow with a golf cart."

"Deliberately?"

The way Kyle rolled his eyes heavenward confirmed my guess. "Since Ballard's murder, some of the backers have gotten antsy and withdrawn from Southwind Enterprises. Mrs. Ballard is trying to bring in other potential investors. Today she took several of them out to the course, was showing them around, trying to persuade them that the project still has great potential. Zelma Beauclaire spotted them and went ballistic. Hit the gas and ran them down in the middle of the 16th fairway."

An involuntary snort escaped me, the sort that comes when something is both appalling and hilarious. "Was anyone hurt?"

"Mostly a case of injured dignity and wounded egos. Nothing serious except for a sizable bruise on Mrs. Ballard's derriere and a few scrapes on one fellow's leg. But they're both pressing charges."

Shel's order to me was abrupt. "Get down there and grab her soon as she's bailed out. She talked to you before, so you've got the best chance of getting her version of the story."

*****

In the jail's waiting area, I phoned Nick Petroski, apologizing that I had to cancel our appointment, and promising to arrange another time after I knew when I'd be free to meet with him. I didn't reveal the reason for breaking our meeting, and he mentioned nothing about Mrs. Ballard, so I assumed he'd not yet gotten the word.

That done, I spent some time thinking of Mother's dream about Zelma Beauclaire wearing prison garb and came dangerously close to believing that there was some mysterious force behind her revelations.

The minute hand on the big round clock hanging on the opposite wall clicked from mark to mark with maddening slowness. After hours on the hard bench, my derriere, in contrast to Mrs. Ballard's injured one, had no feeling whatsoever. At one point the desk officer answered a phone call, then hung up laughing aloud. He called to another officer, "Her old man says he's not in any hurry to arrange bail. Said it's best to let her sit for a while in the cooler because when she's steamed up she's too hot for anybody to handle."

It was mid-afternoon before Mrs. Beauclaire's husband's attorney arrived to post bond. The lawyer was not in the least happy to see me there, but allowed me to accompany him to the small interview room where he would meet with his client. "Just don't say anything you'll regret later," he warned her when the three of us were seated around the scarred wooden table. "No need to add libel on top of this personal injury business."

Luckily for me, Zelma Beauclaire was not at all subdued by her imprisonment and ignored her lawyer's advice. Her square jaw set in steel, she informed him, "Clive, I am quite capable of controlling my tongue."

I smothered a grin—*Just like she controlled that golf cart*, I thought.

After a few more warnings from Clive, she dismissed him with a wave. "Go on back to your office. This young lady can drive me home."

Trailing a worried look, the lawyer left the room.

I rose, expecting Mrs. Beauclaire would be anxious to get out of there, but her gesture demanded I reseat myself. "We'll talk right here," she said. "No snooping ears around."

"Would you care to recount for me exactly how this . . .ah . . . incident came about?"

"Why else would you be here?"

After getting her permission, I touched the recorder app on my cellphone. For the next twenty minutes I listened as she vented non-stop about the criminality of what she referred to as "the on-going dastardly scheme to destroy the finest old golf course in the county, if not all of North Florida," all of which I'd heard before, although not in quite so vehement a fashion.

It was only after she'd expelled this tirade that she added something that grabbed my attention. "If those fool government men had listened to me and done their job, they could have put an end to the whole scheme, and Compton Ballard would be behind bars where he belonged instead of lying dead in the morgue."

"I don't understand how the government would consider an attempt to buy a golf course as a criminal action—"

"It's nothing to do with that," she snapped, then paused, mouth twisted to one side as if trying to reach a decision. Finally, she straightened and gave her chin an upward jerk. "My husband said he would kill me if I involved him in any way, so this has got to be strictly off the record. Turn off that machine." She gestured toward my cellphone and I demonstrated that I was turning off the recorder app.

"Some time ago," she began, "Henry let slip that he'd heard a rumor that Compton Ballard kept two sets of books, one for the IRS, the other that showed a true accounting of his company profits. I didn't think anything of it at the time, but when Ballard's group started threatening to take over our course, I decided to do a little investigating."

She went on to describe how she'd hired a private detective to look into Ballard's company finances. "He didn't have a lot of luck at first. There was no money trail he could follow, and it seemed as if everyone over there at SandScapes was either awfully close-mouthed or else unaware of what was going on. A couple of agents who'd left SandScapes told my man they'd suspected there was something fishy about the company's finances, but couldn't offer any definite proof."

Zelma paused to take a sip of water. "It seemed we'd hit a dead end, but then my detective came across one fellow at Sand-Scapes—I can't say who, you understand—but this man detested Ballard even more than I did, hated him with a vengeance, and he said that Ballard deserved to burn in hell. Wouldn't say why he loathed Ballard so, but that didn't matter so long as he was willing to help us."

My instinct meter went off the scale. My guess had been right—Harry Ports . . . the bookkeeper. Who better to know the company's financial secrets? Everything pointed to him. I leaned forward, eager to hear the rest of the story.

Mrs. Beauclaire went on, "This fellow we found was able to get us some information, but it was risky business. He nearly got caught and he clammed up, refused to hand over anything else. But by then we had enough information about Ballard's financial manipulations to turn it over to the Internal Revenue Service and let them take it from there."

"What did you expect to gain from reporting Ballard to the Feds?"

She gave me her Generalissimo stare. "Bring him down, of course. If he went under, so would the golf course deal, the whole Southwind Enterprises thing. Only trouble is, the Feds bungled it. Said they didn't have enough evidence to file charges. Ballard even tried to shift any blame to his bookkeeper. Now, with

Ballard dead and his wife taking the helm, I'm afraid it's only a matter of time until the bulldozers move in."

Barely able to restrain my jubilation, I drove Zelma Beauclaire home and dropped her off at a mansion-like riverfront dwelling that would have dwarfed most hotels in town. She gave me a brief wave of thanks before disappearing through the doorway, and I took a moment to mentally send condolences to her poor husband who would no doubt pay for his tardiness in bailing her out of jail.

The Zelma story was hot news and Shel would be waiting for my article, so I headed back to the office. All the while my fingers were keying in my note, my mind was busy adding up the evidence against Harry Ports. It all made sense now—the scene that day at the copy machine. Ports had been copying information from the financial records to hand over to Zelma's detective and wasn't aware that some of the papers had become stuck in the machine. That was why he was so distraught when he saw the pieces of paper the repairman had scattered across the floor.

Even the scrap of paper I'd found in Valerie's pocket fit the picture. She'd picked it up or maybe found it in the copier that Saturday afternoon and realized something fishy was going on. She tried to call Ballard and tell him about it and Ports must have overheard that conversation. That part was a little iffy—I had no way of knowing if the bookkeeper was in the office when Val made that call, but it was pretty safe to assume that was what had happened.

He must have panicked, knowing he was doomed if Ballard caught on that he was feeding information to Zelma Beauclaire's detective. It would have been easy enough for him to find out that Val was showing the Oleander Lane house the following morning. He must have secreted himself in the house ahead of time and attacked her when she showed up. Then he took her necklace and watch to make it look like a burglary and threw them away when he crossed back over the bridge so they could never be traced to him.

That he would have killed Valerie to keep from being exposed didn't seem too far-fetched. After all, the man had been in prison and nearly been killed there. Murder might seem a small price to pay to avoid going back. And didn't Zelma say the man absolutely detested Ballard? When Ballard tried to shift the blame to him for any irregularities in the company finances, Ports must have snapped and decided to kill Ballard as well.

The scenario I'd concocted for both murders filled me with a strange mixture of elation and fear. If I was right—and what other explanation could there be?—the man was extremely dangerous. He'd killed Val without hesitation and would no doubt do the same to anyone else who came close to exposing his secret.

One part of me wanted to rush right to Sam and lay the whole thing in front of him. But the saner part prevailed. So far I had plenty of supposition, but would that be enough? Thanks to Maple Brisby, my appointment with Nick Petroski gave me an opportunity to find out more—maybe even confirm my suspicions of Harry Ports—without raising any red flags.

CHAPTER 30

Zelma Beauclaire's golf cart attack on Ballard's widow had repercussions even the redoubtable Zelma couldn't have foreseen. The aggressive act forced police to take a closer look at her activities at the time of Compton Ballard's death and consider as well her possible involvement in Valerie Kimmel's murder. Far-fetched as it seemed that the banker's wife had committed those crimes, the *Dispatch* could not ignore the newsworthiness of this latest development. As a result, that story consumed my next several days.

In the end, Mrs. Beauclaire proved to have impeccable evidence of her whereabouts on both occasions—on the Sunday Valerie was killed, she was on the golf course with her usual foursome, having teed off at 8:15 A.M. and completed the round at 11:45. At the time of Ballard's murder, she and her husband were aboard a ship cruising the Caribbean with ample witnesses to testify to her presence.

"So the Beauclaire/Ballard confrontation once again becomes more comedy than tragedy," Kyle remarked.

"Thankfully so. I was afraid it would drag on through the weekend and I'd have to cancel with Rhonda and Polly."

"Ah, yes, the big weekend getaway. Do I suspect a bit of bar-hopping might be on the agenda?"

I shrugged and grinned. "What's a little black dress for?"

Wednesday, when it seemed as if I might finally have some free time, I rescheduled my appointment with Nick Petroski for Thursday afternoon. Had it not been for my hunch that Nick might confirm my theory of Harry Ports as the murderer, I would have squirmed my way out of inspecting the houses I'd chosen. It had been a hectic week. I still couldn't move back into my apartment and was increasingly tired of dodging Zanthia's constant questions about when Andy was going to come back and "bring those darling children."

"Are you packed for our trip yet?" Rhonda wanted to know when we met Wednesday noon for lunch.

"Not really. My suitcase and some of the clothes I'll need for the weekend are still in my apartment. The exterminators have finally finished, but the building inspector won't let us move back in until the repairs are completed and approved."

"Poor Mrs. Castelli."

"She's in a tizzy. Especially when the inspector told her that the repairs to the interior stairway had to be completed before we could occupy the house. She fussed and fumed that we never used those stairs, but he refuses to budge."

Rhonda gave me a sly look. "Don't forget your underwear and your bathing suit this time. I remember when we were in Acapulco, you had to go buy a lot of stuff."

I shrugged. "Great excuse to go shopping wasn't it? I got that to-die-for bathing suit, and some great bikini panties."

"Who needs an excuse to go shopping?" Rhonda countered. "Isn't that what vacations are all about? I'm excited just talking about it."

"Me too, but I'd better remember all the important stuff this time. My bank account isn't too happy about the prospect of unnecessary purchases, or *any* purchases for that matter."

"I'll call Polly as soon as I get back to the office. Make sure nothing has crept up on her that could delay our leaving. So it's no later than 7:30 on Saturday morning, right?"

"Not a problem. I'll pick up my stuff at the apartment to-morrow evening after I'm done looking at houses for Maple."

"The parrot-view quest?—that takes the silly prize if you ask me."

For a moment I was tempted to confide in Rhonda the plan behind my house-hunt and tell her my suspicions of Harry Ports. But better to wait—if I could get Nick Petroski to open up, by the following day I might have not just suspicions but a way to verify them.

Like the best-laid plans of mice and men, that one hit a snag later that afternoon when Shel assigned me to go to Tallahassee the following day. I'd be covering the story of a local firefighter the governor was going to recognize for having rescued a family from their burning home. That meant another postponement of the house tour.

I got back to St. Augustine too late on Thursday to call Nick Petroski and reset our appointment. On Friday morning, I again called SandScapes to let him know I was finally available. Considering that I'd probably blown his schedule twice before, he was reasonably polite if not particularly enthusiastic. "I am afraid that I have that entire day booked," he told me. "Could we perhaps arrange it for sometime this weekend?"

"Not possible. I'll be out of town."

"Perhaps then another agent—"

"No, no. After disrupting your schedule so many times, I'd feel guilty if another agent got credit for the sale."

In a tone that told me he did not wish to lose a potential cus-tomer, even an iffy one, he offered, "The closing I have sched-uled for Friday afternoon should not present any difficulties. Perhaps if you are available around 5:30—"

I squinted my eyes, trying to visualize how much time it

might take to tour the three homes I'd selected, none of which was in the same area. If we were through no later than 7 or 7:30, I'd still have time to retrieve my things from the apartment and finish packing for the trip. I agreed to the 5:30 appointment.

"Very good. I will meet you at the *Dispatch* building."

Promptly at 5:28, our receptionist, Misti-with-an-i phoned my cubicle to inform me that a man was waiting for me in the lobby. Nick was checking out a display of paintings by a local artist when I arrived, and I had a chance to observe him before he was aware of me. He was taller than I'd at first thought, six feet at least, possibly an inch or so more. His frame was slender and more sinewy than muscular. When he heard me approach, he turned in a movement that would have been smooth except for the rigidness of his right leg. He greeted me with a firm hand-shake and a restrained smile that seemed more professional than personal. It gave me an odd feeling that attached to the pocket of his burgundy blazer-style jacket was a pin with his name and SandScapes Realty on it, exactly like the one Valerie had been wearing.

We left the building and Nick ushered me toward his car, a late model Volvo of a non-descript brownish-gray color. If cars defined a man's personality, Nick's vehicle would identify him as safety-conscious, reserved and unimaginative. As we walked across the parking lot, I noted that while he held himself ex-tremely erect, the built-up shoe couldn't quite compensate for his irregular gait.

"I have checked over the list of properties you wish to see and all are vacant and available," he said in the same clipped tones I remembered from our previous meeting. "But are you sure about this 23 Oleander Lane? Sometimes clients—"

"My friend knows all about what happened there," I as-sured him. "She says she's not the least superstitious."

I sensed he wanted to say something more, but instead continued toward his car. The Volvo's interior proved to be as bland and impersonal as its exterior. Once buckled in, we set out toward North City where the first house I'd chosen was located. I didn't approach the subject of Harry Ports immediately but inquired in a general way about Nick's work at SandScapes. His brief, non-committal replies dampened my hopes of prying information from him, and it seemed likely the whole ridiculous errand was a waste of time.

We turned off US 1 into the narrower streets of North City, an area where a stucco-clad Spanish bungalow might sit next to a New England salt box, a Tudor or a flat-roofed neo-modern. The mixture gave the area a certain charm that contrasted with the bland sameness of planned developments. The house I'd picked from the ads was a tin-roofed Key West style with exterior Bahama shutters perched like half-open eyelids over each window. It didn't take long to realize it offered no parrot-worthy views and after a brief inspection, we returned to the car. Again, conversation, at least on Nick's part, was minimal.

The second house was located west of town off Route 207. Houses flanked it closely on either side but a bay window at the rear of the living room offered a nice view of a landscaped lawn. I pretended as if it might be a possibility for "my friend," even though I knew that only 23 Oleander had the potential Maple wanted. To verify my interest, I went about taking photos inside and out with my cell phone.

Nick, apparently convinced by my faked enthusiasm, glanced at his watch. "If you think this house is suitable for your friend, perhaps you wish to skip the other as it is getting late."

Given my druthers, I'd have done exactly that. I'd tried to bring up the issue of Harry Ports, but hadn't gotten so much as a dribble of information from close-mouthed Nick. I was tired, it was getting late and I still had to get to the apartment, collect my things, go back to Mother's and complete my packing. Besides, returning to 23 Oleander wasn't a pleasant prospect. If it weren't for my promise to Maple, I'd have been more than happy to call it a day. Instead, I said I had plenty of time and that the lateness made no difference.

Nick's nod of agreement didn't quite conceal his reluctance as he shifted into drive and we set off for 23 Oleander Drive.

CHAPTER 31

It was nearly seven when we passed through town and headed toward Anastasia Island and 23 Oleander. Still plenty of time, I thought, but then I realized that the double line of cars in front of us was at a dead stop. At the crest of the 312 bridge, red and blue lights were flashing and a lumber truck lay on its side, its load splayed across both lanes. Traffic piled up behind us, and we were stuck with no way forward or back.

Nick maintained his polite demeanor, but the set of his jaw and the way he leaned forward over the wheel told me he was anxious to be finished with me. If he was angry, I couldn't blame him—I'd taken him from one end of town to the other on what by then he must suspect was little more than a pretense of checking out houses for a friend.

To reassure him that my search was in earnest, I chattered on about how the listing for this next house made it seem exactly what my friend had in mind. "If this one's as good as it sounds, I'm practically certain she'll be making an offer on it after I report back to her."

After I said that, it came to me that Nick must surely know I had been at that house the very day Valerie was killed, yet there I was, acting as if I hadn't ever seen it. To cover, I quickly added, "I was with a friend who was looking at that house the day of the . . . you know, the day your fellow staff member was killed. But the situation was so hectic that I really don't remember much about the house itself."

His response was a noncommittal nod. I concluded his steely quiet must be due to his reluctance to enter a house where a colleague had met her death. That feeling I shared—my work had often exposed me to crime scenes, some far more gory that Valerie's murder, but finding her dead like that had struck me in a much more personal way. The image of her dead body was etched on my memory, and the thought of returning to that scene set my stomach roiling.

After about twenty long minutes, the officers on the scene managed to open one traffic lane. Our line of cars crawled past the spilled boards and overturned truck, then accelerated like released rabbits once the jam-up was behind. Ten minutes later, Nick pulled the Volvo to the curb in front of number twenty-three.

A glance skyward as I waited for him to unlock the door showed that the light was beginning to go, so while he extracted the key from the lockbox, I stepped around the corner of the house to get several exterior shots. When I returned, I expected that Nick would have gone inside, but he still stood waiting by the open door.

We entered and I paused just inside, peering from the small entry hall into the living room. Its drawn draperies created an air of gloom, in contrast to the previous time when Valerie had already prepared the house for showing. Glancing in the other direction, a feeling gripped me that if I went down the hall to that bedroom, Valerie's undiscovered corpse would still be sprawled on the floor, her blood spilled onto the beige carpet. I wanted to turn and run. What sort of game was I playing—it wasn't out of concern for Valerie's death I'd been trying to outdo Frank Burke in solving the murders—at least not entirely. It was an ego trip—my determination to prove to my nemesis that he wasn't the *Dispatch's* only competent reporter.

Like the shudder that comes when someone steps on your grave, all those emotions flashed through me in a nano-second. Nick had gone ahead to draw back the living room drapes, releasing a swarm of dust motes that spun off into the slanting rays of the late afternoon sun. By the time he turned to face me, I had reined in my too-vivid imagination, even though it took an effort to steady my cell phone enough to take several shots of the view from the wide bay window. I took angled shots as well, not knowing what McDuff's perspective would be, but confident that Maple would appreciate the effort.

Perhaps noticing my tremor, he looked at me strangely. "Are you all right, Miss McKelvey? Perhaps the heat—"

Unable to help myself, I blurted, "Doesn't it give you a strange feeling, coming here where one of your fellow agents was . . . you know—".

Nick's expression didn't change, but I noticed his cheek muscle stiffen. His terse answer curiously echoed the view Maple Brisby had expressed—"Death happens in many places."

"But don't you ever speculate as to who might have done that to her? And then a second murder within the same agency . . ."

"I believe that is the job of the law officers. I am not given to speculation."

The wooden manner in which he spoke put me off a bit, and I got the definite impression that this was someone who closely guarded his feelings, or perhaps someone able to compartmentalize himself. "As a reporter, I can't help speculating," I said, "or at least looking at the possibilities."

Instead of responding he led the way into the dining room and drew back the draperies from the front window which looked out on a lawn shaded by one of the great oaks.

I concentrated on focusing my camera on the view.

Nick stood by as I got my shots. "I'll just do a quick tour of the other rooms," I said. "I know you must be in a hurry."

"Please take your time. If you will excuse me, I will make some phone calls while you look about."

Ah-ha! I thought. Maybe the stolid Nick Petroski has some feeling after all. Otherwise, why would he avoid looking through the rest of the house?

Guilt pushed me to make a cursory inspection of the other rooms. At the room where we'd found Val's body, I only opened the door far enough to release a slight chemical odor that told me the carpet had been replaced. The rest of the house held nothing of particular interest. Nick nodded when I returned to the living room, closed his phone and ushered me out the door.

Back in the car, the light had faded to the extent that headlights were necessary. With nothing to lose, I made one last try at getting Nick to open up. "I understand from Mrs. Descuto that you and Mr. Ports are both big baseball fans—the Baltimore Orioles, I believe she said."

"Mr. Ports. Yes. We do sometimes discuss the games."

"Why the Orioles? I mean, baseball's not the big sport here."

"Football." He ejected the word with disdain. "It is too bad that the only exposure people here have to professional baseball is the television. Only from the grandstand seats can one appreciate the game's unique atmosphere."

The refrain "Buy me some peanuts and Cracker Jacks" popped into my mind. "How interesting that both you and Mr. Ports are fans of the same team. Did you both grow up in Baltimore?"

Again I noticed him stiffen, as if I'd touched a sensitive nerve. "I gave the Orioles merely as an example," he said. "And now would you care to share with me your impression of the three houses we've inspected?" The finality in his tone told me he was finished discussing Harry Ports.

It was obvious my questions were prodding him past his comfort level. But in for a penny in for a pound as my grandmother used to say. "If you had to guess, would you say that someone who works in the SandScapes office is most likely the killer?" I asked. "Possibly someone working as an agent . . . or in some other capacity?" I phrased it that way deliberately, hoping he'd give some sign that he was aware of Harry Ports' involvement.

I never found out what his reply would have been, because my cell phone rang just then. It was Kyle. "Just wanted to alert you that Frank thinks he's spotted something in the research you gave him you may have overlooked."

"So he wants to crow again. Why doesn't he tell me himself?"

"He had to leave to cover a shoot-out during a domestic over in Lincolnville, but the way he said it, it sounded important so I wanted you to be on the alert."

"Didn't he give you any hint as to what it was about?"

"He did say it had to do with that business of why Ballard changed his name."

"You mean that Hostler thing?"

"Guess so. Anyhow, thought you ought to be prepared. Maybe do a little further checking through your notes."

"I can't do anything at the moment. It's getting dark, and soon as I get to my car I've got to head over to my apartment and pick up clothes for the trip."

"Thought you couldn't get back in there."

"I can get in. We just can't move back in yet."

"Okay. Don't let Frank spoil your weekend. Whatever it was I'm sure can wait until Monday."

"Thanks for the heads-up."

"Okay. Behave yourself and have a great time."

"That forces me to choose Door Number One or Door Number Two. Anyhow, we're back at the parking lot, so gotta go."

I closed my phone and pointed out to Nick where my Jeep was parked at the side of the building. As Nick braked to a stop. I turned and looked across at him, but he merely sat staring through the windshield, making it clear he was waiting for me to exit. As I hopped out, I thanked him for taking the time to show me the houses. His only reply was, "Yes—I will wait to hear your friend's decision."

CHAPTER 32

At the apartment, I opened the stairwell door to retrieve my suitcases and was greeted with a lingering whiff of the termite fumigant. Once again, I fretted at the lack of light—next time Tuck came to mow I'd remember to ask him to replace the ceiling bulb for sure. I groped my way toward the second step from the top to where I'd stored the suitcase. Lacking visibility, I clumsily knocked over the old coffee pot I'd intended for Goodwill after I'd indulged in a new cappuccino machine. The pot went bouncing from step to step, clanging and clattering on its way down. I didn't attempt to retrieve it—the stairway's weakened wooden treads were another of the hazards the inspector had warned of.

Suitcase in hand, I retreated to my bedroom and began selecting the clothes I intended to take with me. As always, I meant to pack light, taking only the items I'd actually need, but, as usual, I ended up with a heap of just-in-case items. When I was done, closing the suitcase took some effort. Only after the latch was secured did I remember that the skanky 4-inch heels that went with the black dress were in the guestroom closet.

That room was also my home office, and after digging out the pumps, I sat down at my computer for a quick email check. Several were Saves, the ads and political entreaties went direct to Trash, and none of the personal ones required immediate attention. I started to close the screen when Kyle's message from Frank nagged at me—something he'd said about Ballard's name change to Hostler.

I pulled up the files I'd collected and ran a search on the name Hostler. Five or six pages came up, most of them either about business transactions of *Hostler and Son*, the company Ballard and his father ran, or news items about the father's arrest and imprisonment. Then, on the fifth page, I ran into a human interest story that had been published in the *Baltimore Star* headlined "A Family Tragedy."

When Jozef Petroski's wife, Crystyna, became ill with cancer, the Polish immigrant had no alternative but to mortgage their modest East Baltimore row house in order to meet the mounting expenses for her treatment.

Then a second disaster struck the Petroski family—Jozef was laid off from his job at a local meat packinghouse. He went from bank to bank attempting to obtain a mortgage, but with no steady source of income, none would lend to him.

In desperation, his wife increasingly ill and a young son to take care of, Jozef turned to a company that promised he and his family could remain in the house and he would receive a regular monthly stipend to cover his expenses. The only condition was that he sign over the deed to his home as security. He was assured that that once he was able to repay the loan he could reclaim the deed to his home.

Only seven months later, Jozef and his family were served with an eviction notice. His appeals to Hostler and Son went unanswered and when a lawyer friend checked the note Jozef had signed, it appeared he had no recourse—the house belonged to the Hostlers and the Petroskis faced eviction.

Driven to the edge of despair by his wife's suffering and the inability to provide for his family, Jozef Petroski sent his young son to a neighbor's house. Then he carried his wife into the kitchen. After closing all the doors and windows, he turned on the gas jets to the oven. The couple's bodies were discovered clasped in each other's arms in the armchair Jozef had placed in front of the stove.

"Calls by this reporter to reach Hostler and Son have gone unanswered," the article continued. "The City Solicitor's office has responded that, while the actions of the Hostlers were reprehensible, they possessed a legal deed to the property.

"The Petroski's five-year-old son, Nicholas, has since been placed in St. Mary's Home for Orphaned Children."

I stopped reading at that point, so overcome by the story of evil and injustice that it was hard to breathe. How could I have been so stupid that I missed it? Why had I focused all my attention on proving Harry Ports was the killer, when here was someone with a far more powerful motive to want Compton Ballard dead?

I jumped up from the desk without bothering to turn off the computer. Packing for the trip would have to wait—this was too important to ignore. *Sam . . . I'll call Sam, let him take it from there.*

My phone was in my bag in the bedroom, but before I could get to it, I heard a sound as if someone were on the outside stairs. I turned off the light and listened. The noise halted for a moment, then I heard it again, an irregular clumping of someone climbing step by step up the stairs.

I peered from the bedroom window, craning my neck to glimpse around the corner. A shadowy figure appeared at the top of the outside stairway. Even if those uneven footsteps hadn't alerted me, and even if the darkness hadn't hidden all but the man's dim silhouette, I knew instinctively that it was Nick Petroski.

Too frozen to think, I watched him move across the porch

toward the French doors that led into my living room. There came a rattling noise, as he tried the door handle. This was no social call, no polite knock or calling out to ask if anyone was home. Seconds later, the sound of glass smashing told me he was breaking in.

CHAPTER 33

The usual exit from the apartment was cut off, so I made a mad dash for the inner stairwell. Clutching the door closed behind me, I waited in almost complete darkness, only the faintest brush of light coming through the open door at the bottom of the stairs. I cursed that I'd failed to grab the bag with my phone before fleeing. My only chance for escape was to make my way down to Mrs. Castelli's foyer and outside. In the near total darkness, finding my way was hazardous and I could only creep downward step by step.

"Dear God" I prayed, *"let me get to the bottom before he knows where I've gone!"* My prayer came out as a strangled gasp as I crept cautiously downward, one stair tread at a time. Above me I could hear his off-beat gait hurrying through the rooms. Any minute he would check the stairwell door.

Halfway to the bottom, the tread I stepped on almost gave way, and I grabbed the railing to avoid breaking through the soft wood. Breath held, I edged another step downward, but instead of the next tread my foot landed on something round and metallic that went crashing all the way to the bottom. My grip on the railing kept me from falling, but my left ankle skidded sideways and made a popping sound. The clamor from the falling object combined with my howl of pain, was destined to alert my pursuer. Before I could move, the door above was flung open.

Scarcely able to bear the pain I scrambled my way downward. In the scant light from above, I could barely make out the bottom door, still some five or six steps below. I expected Nick to call out to me to stop or to say something but there was just the ominous thud of his built-up shoe as he started down the stairs.

Grimacing against the pain, I used the banister as a crutch to work my way onto the next tread. Behind me I could hear Nick's panting breath and a moment later his hand grabbed my hair, pulling me backward. My desperate jerk to break free was futile and I knew at that moment I was going to die right there in that dark stairwell. "Don't!" I screamed, but his hold tightened.

Then, as I was about to lose my balance, without warning, Nick let out a startled yelp and released his grip on my hair. Next came the sound of wood splintering. I didn't look back, but threw myself at the dim outline of the open door at the bottom. I landed on all fours and scrambled out into Mrs. Castelli's foyer. Only then did I turn enough to see that Nick's right leg had broken entirely through the tread he was standing on. He hung there, his right leg trapped up to his groin, his left leg twisted outward at an abnormal angle.

The foyer was nearly as dark as the stairwell except for feeble glow leaking through the front door's glass panels. Nick was still struggling to free himself as I slammed the stairwell door shut. Through the closed door I could hear Nick's furious screams and curses as I hobbled to the Chinese bowl on Mrs. Castelli's foyer table and retrieved her key.

My phone, still in my bag upstairs was my only hope of summoning help before he escaped. To get to it, I'd have to circle the house, and climb the outside stairs. But could I make it with my badly sprained ankle and what if before I got there he managed to free himself? I had to chance that—this was the man who'd killed my friend. I'd lock the top door and once he was securely trapped, I'd phone for help.

Not sure where I'd left the key to the top door, I snatched Mrs. Castelli's from the keyhole, hoping it would fit. After a struggle to release Mrs. Castelli's front door locks, I ignored the excruciating pain in my ankle as I bolted out onto the veranda and headlong down the front steps. Limping around the side of the house in a sorry simulation of warp speed, in the dark I failed to see the slabs of termite-damaged lumber the contractor had removed from under the house. A board caught my foot and I went plunging headfirst. There was no mistaking the crunching sound from my left wrist as I hit the ground.

The key flew from my fingers and for a moment, I could only lie moaning in agony. On hands and knees and using only my good hand, I searched frantically through the damp grass. Thanks to the old-fashioned key's size and bulk, my fingers finally closed on it. With great difficulty, I pulled myself upright and, half limping, half crawling, made my way to the rear stairway. Using the railing I hauled myself up step by agonizing step, nearly passing out as I neared the top. On the opposite side of the porch, my smashed front door gaped open. It took the last of my breath and my last bit of courage, to crunch my way through the broken glass and enter the apartment.

Across the living room, the stairwell door stood open. Loud keening wails came from the stairwell, along with the crash of objects being flung about. Not knowing if Nick had already freed himself, I was afraid to approach it directly. Instead, I flattened myself against the adjoining wall and gradually slid over until I could peer down inside.

In the dim light I could just make out Nick's form. He was still trying to jerk his trapped leg free from the broken tread while pinwheeling his arms to keep from falling. Great moans of pain and anger issued from his throat and I felt a moment of pity, but when he twisted about and raised his head, staring directly up at me, the murderous expression on his face blasted away my uncertainties. I slammed the door shut and shoved the key into the lock, barely managing to turn it before, overcome by pain and fear, I collapsed against the locked door.

From below, the screams ceased as abruptly as sound dies when a switch is turned off. Then there was complete and utter silence. I wondered if it was some ruse or if he'd passed out from pain. I put my ear to the door and was able to make out a faint mewling sound such as a small animal might make with its leg in a trap. Then came a repeated wail, the voice as terrified and plaintive as a child's—"Don't! Please don't! Not the dark!"

*****

I suppose I ought to have eliminated Sam's number from the speed dial on my phone, but for once the sight of him brought more comfort than I was willing to admit. He let his fellow officers take care of extracting Nick from the stairwell while he supported me to the sofa, then went to the kitchen and found the bottle of brandy I'd once bought thinking I'd make Cherries Jubilee for him—another story that. He came back with a generously filled wine glass.

The paramedics arrived and had two patients to attend to. Nick's femur was broken as was my wrist, although my ankle was only sprained. They transported us to the hospital in separate ambulances, for which I was grateful. In those long minutes before help arrived, it was not my wrist or my ankle that tortured me, it was the repeated cries and sobs coming from the stairwell—"Please! Please!—not the dark!"

CHAPTER 34

On an early November day, Judge Samuelson's courtroom was packed to the walls with spectators and media. Outside, the air had grown clear and crisp; inside, the jam-packed bodies produced the dense solemnity a murder trial always seemed to generate. The spectators' clothing—funereal grays and browns and blacks—further confirmed the seriousness of the occasion.

I should have felt good. Frank Burke had suggested to Shel that I be allowed to report on the trial and actually praised my research as having been crucial in identifying Nick Petroski as the killer. But this was Murder One, too grave to offer any personal gratification; the likely outcome too grim.

Kyle and I, in our adjoining seats, had listened for four days as the state presented witnesses and forensic evidence against Nick Petroski. Photographs of Ballard's bloody beaten corpse, his face pounded beyond recognition, sent gasps of horror throughout the room, despite the judge's warning against emotional outbursts. A police officer testified that a heavy flashlight had been identified as the weapon and that a broken piece of its lens had been recovered and traced to Nick through DNA testing of a blood spot.

That Valerie had been bludgeoned from the rear and the necklace ripped from her dead body was offered as additional proof of callous and inhuman behavior. I rubbed the lump on my left wrist. Like Valerie, I had crossed Nick's path at the wrong time.

Throughout that gruesome display, Nick sat erect and expressionless next to his attorney, never glancing about. His months in jail had left him paler and his gray suit hung loosely from his shoulders as if his once vigorous body had deflated.

Even though my suspicions had focused on the wrong person, some of what I had assumed about the murders was confirmed when Harry Ports took the stand. Before he began questioning Ports, the prosecutor reported to the court that in return for his cooperation in the current case, the witness had been granted immunity from any criminal charges arising from information he might offer.

No doubt to forestall Nick's lawyer from offering evidence that would discount the witness's testimony, the prosecutor asked Ports to explain how he came to be employed by Compton Ballard. In a tremulous voice that was at times barely audible, Ports admitted to having been imprisoned in Maryland for embezzlement and was nearly killed when a prison gang attacked him. It was there, he said, that he met Ballard's father, Milton Hostler, a fellow prisoner. "He knew I was eligible for parole and recommended to his son that he hire me."

Again forestalling the inevitable questions Ports would face on cross examination, the prosecutor asked, "Were you aware at that time, Mr. Ports, that you were involving yourself with a man who would be using you to help him commit fraud?"

Ports' answer was startling in its directness, "No one else was going to hire me."

Ports then testified how the discovery of certain financial records jammed in the copier machine had alerted him that someone was stealing the company's financial records. "When I recalled some of the questions Nick Petroski had been asking me, it didn't take long to figure it was him."

"Are you saying that you left the company's financial reports where anyone might get them?"

Ports shook his head. "Not anyone. But Nick had worked as a security guard before he came to SandScapes and he knew a lot about locks. Once when Miss Kimmel forgot her keys I saw him unlock her office door."

In response to the attorney's question, "Why, at that point, Mr. Ports, didn't you reveal to your employer that Mr. Petroski was in possession of those documents?" Ports replied that Nick threatened to expose to the authorities Ports' involvement in Ballard's illegal financial manipulations. "I could not afford to chance going back to prison," he said. The overhead courtroom lights gave cruel exposure to the deep crease in his sweaty forehead, and I could well believe the terror Nick's threat must have instilled.

Under further questioning, Ports declared vehemently that he did not know that Nick had murdered Valerie Kimmel. I turned to give Kyle a look and saw in his expression that he also doubted Ports' word on that.

On the fourth day of the trial, the prosecutor rested his case. The jurors' failure to look at Nick as they filed from the room did not bode well for the defendant. Now, on the fifth day, Nick's attorney needed to mitigate the damage if his client was to avoid a death sentence.

A rustle of curiosity ran through the audience as Attorney Rawlings called as his first defense witness, a Mrs. Elsie Bates from Nick's old neighborhood in East Baltimore. The elderly woman told how, when Nick's mother was dying of cancer, the Hostlers had defrauded the Petroski family of their home. "He said—Mr. Petroski said—that while he was alive he would not see his wife put out on the street. That's when he did . . . what he did."

She was followed by a man approximately Nick's age—mid to late thirties—who had also been an inmate of the orphanage where Nick had been confined until age eighteen. The man described severe punishments the orphanage children had endured, including being routinely beaten and forced to endure long hours locked in dark, lightless cubicles. "Take an extra slice of bread at mealtime and you were in for it," he said.

Perhaps sensing that this Dickensian tale might seem overdone, Rawlings asked the man if there had been any more positive aspects to orphanage life. Nick's fascination with baseball was explained when the witness told how the orphanage was located next to the old Baltimore stadium where the Orioles then played. "Some of us boys would sneak up to the roof on game nights and even though we couldn't see much of the field we could hear the announcements. Once a year, the team gave us free tickets so the attendants marched us over there and we got to see a real game from high up in the grandstand."

Rawling's next witness was the doctor who had treated Nick at the time he had polio. "From the records it appears," Doctor Wakefield said, "that the child, Nicolas Petroski, had not attended school prior to being admitted to the orphanage and had not been vaccinated against the poliomyelitis virus. For some reason, reports from the orphanage stated in error that he had received the vaccine."

The doctor raised his head from his notes and then, as if realizing his audience might not be familiar with polio, added, "Remember, this was in the late 1970s. By then polio had virtually been wiped out in the United States and Canada."

"How then," Attorney Rawlings asked, "was Mr. Petroski exposed to the disease?"

"Unfortunately a recently immigrated child from El Salvador was admitted to the institution and was carrying the active virus. Also unfortunately, he was assigned to the same dormitory as Nicolas Petroski."

The doctor went on to explain that Nick had been fortunate

in that the paralysis associated with the disease had affected only the right side of his body, resulting in the shortening of his right calf and forcing him to rely on his left hand for most activities.

When Dr. Wakefield finished, Mr. Rawlings announced that he would call only one other witness—the defendant. The judge called a short recess at that point.

Kyle and I wandered out into the hall to discuss what had transpired so far. "Rawlings is doing a good job of building sympathy for his client," Kyle said, "but it will take a miracle to erase from the juror's minds those pictures of how brutally Ballard's body was beaten."

I nodded agreement. "That and the deliberate planning that went into Ballard's murder—arranging the fake showing of the Satsuma house to Cole Fanshaw, the fact that his experience as a security guard gave him the ability to bypass the house's alarm systems. I don't see how Rawlings can refute all that."

"Even though the murder may have been committed in anger, it was clearly premeditated. That limits the judge's options when it comes to sentencing."

What had been announced as a short recess was unexpectedly extended, and the bailiff announced that the judge was meeting with both attorneys and the defendant in his chambers. When court reconvened, there was increased tension and a sense of expectancy in the air. Attorney Rawlings, seated at the defense table, looked perturbed and Judge Samuelson entered wearing a serious frown. He tapped his gavel and announced, "Because of a new development, court is adjourned for the day. Bailiff, please escort the jurors from the room." A buzz as if a wasp's nest had been disturbed spread through the room and the television people made a dash for the door. No one appeared to have any clue as to what the new development might be—plea bargain was the prevailing speculation.

The following morning, tensions were at a feverish peak in the courtroom and before all else the judge announced that he would tolerate no disturbances. Then he went on to state, "The defendant, Mr. Petroski, has requested that for the remainder of this trial he wishes to act as his own attorney. Both Mr. Rawlings and I have thoroughly instructed him of the possible consequences. Mr. Petroski insists that it is his wish to serve as his own counsel."

Despite the judge's stern warning, a murmur of astonished gasps rose from the seats behind me. "Crazy!" Kyle whispered. "He could be signing his own death sentence."

The judge's gavel came down hard and an uneasy order was restored. "Mr. Petroski will take the stand and present his testimony," the judge announced. I noted that Attorney Rawlings' expression was still distraught and he remained at the defendant's table preparing to take notes. The prosecutor failed to reveal any emotion either pro or con this latest development.

Nick took the stand and recited the oath in an expressionless voice. Once seated, he began without preamble, "Throughout my years at the orphanage, I had but one goal in mind—to find Milton and Lloyd Hostler, and make them suffer as my family had suffered."

Not a whisper was heard from behind me as he went on to say that by the time he was released from the orphanage and free to carry out his intention, he found that Milton Hostler, Ballard's father, was deceased. "His son, Lloyd Hostler, seemed to have disappeared. "I was 18 and had no money. I found work as a security guard."

The judge stopped Nick at that point to ask, "Was there some particular reason you chose that line of work?"

Nick looked taken aback at the question and hesitated before replying, "I wanted to work where I could feel I was helping to keep people safe."

That statement, both ironic and pathetic, brought another gasp, but its effect was nullified by Nick's next statement. "I worked hard at my job, but I spent my every spare moment trying to find Lloyd Hostler."

Nick's quest, he said, was made even more difficult because he did not know that Lloyd Hostler had changed his name to Compton Ballard and had moved several times. It was only after years of searching that he found his quarry, and then it was almost by chance. "On my night shift I was glancing through a copy of the *Wall Street Journal* someone had left at my station. I saw the story about a big real estate deal in Atlanta. There was a picture. Even though the name was different, I recognized the man immediately—he looked exactly like his father."

That revelation sent another stir throughout the courtroom and the judge called a short recess.

"Everything he's said about Ballard so far makes it look like premeditated murder," Kyle said as we compared notes.

I shook my head. "It wouldn't surprise me if this is what Nick wants. I think he intends to reveal the decision he made to avenge his parents' deaths with no apologies."

"That would take a lot of guts, considering that he might be reserving a seat for himself in the electric chair."

The reconvened courtroom was breathlessly silent as Nick told how he set out immediately for Atlanta and began carefully scouting out Ballard's habits and whereabouts. Before he could carry out his plan, Ballard sold his Atlanta business and moved to St. Augustine. "I told myself that I would not hurry. It had taken years to come this far and I would wait until the time was right. I obtained a real estate license then applied to SandScapes and was accepted. That put me in a position to carry out my goal to ruin Ballard financially."

At the next adjournment, Kyle and I left the building. He asked, "Did you get the impression that Nick's original intention wasn't to kill Ballard but to see him jailed and left penniless?"

I halted to let a television crew crowd past me. "In a way, I can believe that's what Nick originally intended. I think what sent him over the edge was after he'd turned over evidence to the Feds that Ballard was involved in shady tax dodges and that plan failed."

Kyle nodded agreement. "Just imagine, all those years of

hunting Ballard down, waiting for his chance, and then to see it all gone for nothing. At that point, he must have felt driven to kill Ballard."

"And even Valerie when she got in his way," I said. "I'll always wonder how much she'd figured out from that scrap of paper in her pocket."

"Doesn't matter," Kyle said. "Once Nick knew she had it and it could incriminate him, she was doomed." A chill ran down my spine as I recalled how close I had come to being victim number three.

In the rebuttal segment of the trial, the state attempted to mitigate any sympathy Nick's story had roused. So far as I could judge, a few of the jurors' faces reflected conflicted feelings.

Then began days of jury deliberation during which those of us assigned to the story dared not be out of touch for a moment. The sequestered jury's deliberations often continued into the night, and, had they reached a decision during that time, the court would be recalled to session. Kyle and I spelled each other, and took turns ducking out to a nearby sub shop for our evening meal.

"Indigestion, the reporter's hazard," Kyle quipped when I complained of having to hurry through my dinner.

Finally, the jurors having agreed upon a verdict, we all filed back into the courtroom. I studied each face as the panel returned to their seats, and knew in my heart what the verdict would be. In a vacuum-silent courtroom, the jury foreman announced that they had found Nicolas Petroski guilty of first degree murder in the case of Compton Ballard. At a previous hearing, Nick had pled guilty to second degree murder in the case of Valerie Kimmel. Sentencing for that had been deferred until the Ballard trial was complete.

That left it to Judge Samuelson to determine Nick's sentence. In mid-December, on a blustery day when a northeaster was pounding the Florida coast, we were back in court to hear the decision. Sam was in the courtroom that day, too. He spotted me as I entered. He congratulated me on the part I'd played in Nick's capture, and we chatted for a couple of minutes.

"Did that Alvaro fellow ever get his necklace back?" I asked him.

Sam nodded. "The sister was Valerie's executor and she said he was welcome to it. Guy was royally pissed off when he had to sign a couple of papers to reclaim it from our property room. Said he was heading back to Argentina where such things didn't happen."

We both laughed and I was glad for that brief moment of irony in the midst of the grim business that would decide the remainder of a man's life.

The bailiff's "All rise," brought immediate order. Every eye was on Judge Samuelson's face as he emerged from chambers. The rustle of the spectators reseating themselves was followed by a delicately balanced stillness, a communal withholding of all coughs and sniffles, a straining of senses toward where Nick sat at the defendant's table, flanked by two uniformed guards. At the judge's order he rose, still erect, to stand before the bench.

Judge Samuelson sentenced Nick to life in prison with no possibility of parole.

CHAPTER 35

The cloud of Nick's trial and sentencing still darkened my mood as I began planning for Christmas. In recent years, there'd been just Mother and me, and whatever similarly unattached friends and acquaintances we might gather. The previous year, Christmas dinner had included Polly and Giles, Lee Hartshorn, proprietor of Wild Wings Gallery next door to Mother's shop, and Kyle who brought his companion, Eric Morgan, owner of a local radio station.

Despite that the feast was sumptuous, the company convivial and conversation sparked like the several bottles of champagne we consumed, I was unable to put aside the sense of vacancy that came from being unattached during that most family of holidays. Even Mother had Lee Hartshorn who was, if not a romantic involvement, at least a reliable date for social occasions. I put on my happy mask and made every effort to join in, but always in the back of my mind, there lurked the image of Sam—either alone or with Diana, depending upon the status of their marriage.

Christmas this year would be different. Andy and I had become closer in the weeks following Nick's capture when I was hobbling around my apartment on one crutch, my other arm ensconced in a cast practically to my elbow. We'd watched old movies together, played Scrabble with Mrs. Castelli and, yes, made love despite the obstacles of the cast and my gimpy ankle.

If my deeper involvement with Andy solved the problem of my single status, it also raised the question of how to weave him and his daughters into the holiday celebration, especially as the only day they could come was Christmas Eve, since he and the girls were to spend Christmas Day with his sister's family, and the day following Christmas, Polly, Rhonda and I were scheduled to leave on a cruise to Cozumel, making up for the all-girls' weekend we'd missed.

Even though Christmas day was out, I was determined to make their visit special. Not sure what presents were suitable for girls their age, I called Rhonda. "I can meet you at the mall on Saturday around three," she said, "but I won't be able to stay long. And remember, Kevin's school concert is that night."

I had forgotten, but knew my penance for dragging Rhonda on the shopping trip would be two hours on a hard metal folding chair listening to Kevin and his classmates perform off-key renditions of "Jingle Bells" and "Frosty the Snowman."

"I was thinking maybe dolls or stuffed animals," I said as we started out.

Rhonda shook her head. "The girls are already bound to have plenty of those. Besides they'd know right off that you took the easy way out. I'd skip clothes, too, if you want to make a good impression."

"Then what can I get them?"

"Stocking stuffer gifts are easy to find and kids enjoy unwrapping them. Then you'll want one special gift for each."

The stocking stuffers proved easy—for Lissa the popular Rainbow Loom used for making bracelets, for Dana a CD of the humorous children's book, *Flat Stanley*, little pink notebooks with matching pens, puzzles, a set of colored pencils for Lissa, crayons for Dana. To peek from the very top of each stocking, I ignored Rhonda's no-stuffed-animals-rule and chose a miniature panda for Lissa and a cute little raccoon for Dana.

Since Lissa was in second grade and already computer wise, for her special present we found her a Password Journal that would open only when a secret word was spoken. It included a pen that wrote with invisible ink that could only be seen under the included glow light. For Dana, we spotted a Fairy Dome Terrarium with tiny fairytale figures inside the glass. Packets of seeds came with it, and the display model showed the wee mythical figures placed among tiny plants that formed a miniature forest.

"Gotta run now," Rhonda announced as the cashier rang up the terrarium.

We hugged. "Many, many thanks," I said. "See you tonight."

"Have you finished packing for our trip?"

"Sort of," I said. "Maybe while I'm here I'll look for a bathing suit. What with too many holiday goodies at work and my not being able to run for so long, the old one feels a trifle snug."

Rhonda left, and I was crossing the food court when I spotted Everett Peabody and his Maple seated at one of the tables. The pair was holding hands across the table as they shared a single slice of apple pie. Everett had purchased the house at 23 Oleander Drive, Maple had moved to St. Augustine, and the two seemed to be making up for the years spent apart. Everett repeatedly thanked me for my help in bringing that about, but that didn't stop him from pouncing on any grammatical errors in my copy.

I went over to say hello. We chatted a bit—McDuff was delighted with his new home, Maple informed me, although he hated the blue jays that kept stealing all the sunflower seeds from the feeder outside his window. "Shakespeare may have been a mistake," Maple said. "He keeps yelling at them 'Out,

out, damned spot!'"

Before I left, I asked if there would soon be a wedding announcement in the *Dispatch*. Maple blinked up at me through her bifocals. "No point in that," she said. "We're just going to live together the way you young folks do."

Judging by Everett's besotted expression, that arrangement suited him as well. Shaking my head in disbelief, I headed for the Sun 'n' Surf Shop. I was checking out the bathing suits in the window display when a masculine voice behind me said, "The blue with the low-cut back. Definitely you."

I didn't want to turn around. I turned around.

Sam was standing there and the first thing I noticed was that he was carrying a bag from the lingerie shop Sheer Delights. He saw me glance down at the bag's logo and his face reddened. "Little last minute shopping," he mumbled.

"Good," I said. "I hope Diana likes what you've bought her."

The blush went deeper. "Guess you haven't heard. She's filed for divorce."

The effect of Sam's words was as if I'd unwittingly stuck my finger into an electric socket. I froze, then finally managed to stammer, "I-I'm sorry. I didn't know . . ."

There seemed nothing more to say. Through stiffened lips, I wished him a merry Christmas, made an awkward turn, and hurried into the shop.

*****

If Christmas Eve found me nervous and jittery, that had nothing whatsoever to do with Sam's startling announcement. He was out of my life. Whoever he was buying lingerie for was none of my business. I had Andy, a man my friends and family approved of, a man with whom there was no need to sneak around and hide in dark corners.

For once, I was glad of Mother's offer to help, even though to her "help" meant taking control of the affair. "I'll close the shop early and fix lunch for all of us and bring it to your apartment," she said. "Oh, and I've found the cleverest little gifts for each of the girls."

I gratefully accepted her offer of lunch, but was firm about the plans Andy and I had made for the day. "The college is having a performance of the *Nutcracker* that afternoon and the girls will love that. Dana and Lissa can open their presents before we leave for the play. After the show we'll walk around downtown and see the Christmas decorations and still have time for a snack before they have to leave."

Mother arrived at my apartment Christmas Eve morning at 7:00, well before I'd rubbed the sleep out of my eyes. She appeared at the door carrying a huge basket in either hand.

"Mother, what? . ."

"The lunch ingredients. The rest are in my car," she waved in the direction of the driveway below. "And the presents. But they can wait until we get things in order."

"But I'm not even dressed yet."

"Yes, I see. I'll just get started on tidying up while you bring the rest of the food. Your tree looks lovely, but I think we need to move that . . ."

I made a hasty exit to my bedroom before she could finish giving her orders. One thing at least for which I was grateful—her hair was an ash blond color, arranged in a neat pageboy and was almost normal-looking except for having been spritzed with silvery sprinkles.

Andy and the girls arrived just before noon. The luncheon Mother prepared—tiny sandwiches cut into star shapes, individual Jell-O salads molded like Santas, fruit punch, and a plateful of Christmas cookies—was a big hit. So were the stocking gifts, even the little stuffed animals I'd chosen. Then it was time for each of them to open their special gift, but Dana insisted I open the present she'd brought me first. "I picked it out all by myself," she said, then added, "Daddy paid for it."

Her gift was a beautifully illustrated book about butterflies.

Lissa then presented me with a bottle of lavender-scented

hand lotion. "I paid for it with my own money," she announced with a little toss of her head.

I thanked both girls and smoothed on some of Lissa's lotion and let everyone smell it on my hands. I told Dana her book was going to have a place of honor on the coffee table where I could share it with visitors.

"And for Miss Zanthia," Andy said, "the girls and I went together for her gift."

"But I picked it out," Lissa said.

Mother carefully unwrapped the box. Inside was a filmy silk scarf in translucent shades of green and aqua. She stood and wrapped it around her shoulders with her special flair and it was truly spectacular. She swooped both girls into her arms to thank them and then planted a kiss on Andy's cheek as well.

When it was time for the girls to open their special gifts I held my breath, hoping I'd made good choices. Dana squealed with delight when the terrarium became visible beneath the wrappings. She stared through the glass at the tiny fairy figures arranged on the mossy base. I pointed out the seed packets. "You plant these and when they grow they'll create a tiny forest," I said.

"Can I plant them now?"

"Probably better to wait until you're home and can put the terrarium where you want it to be. Then you can plant the seeds, add a little water and watch them grow," I said.

"Just what I wanted!" She flung herself at me and gave me a huge hug.

Lissa approached her gift more cautiously and when the pink Password Journal was exposed she stared at it for a few seconds before saying anything.

My heart dropped. It was wrong, all wrong. I should have looked for something different, something more exciting.

Then her face lit and my heart resumed its beat. "Look, Daddy!" she exclaimed. "I saw these in a catalog and you have to say a magic word to get it to open."

Andy grinned. "Well, let's hear your magic word, Sweetie."
Lissa gave him a look. "If I told you it wouldn't be a secret."
"Aren't you going to thank Miss Day for your present?"
Andy asked.

"Thank you," Lissa said. "It's very nice."

I figured that was all I was going to get from her, but a little later after the girls had opened their presents from Mother and Andy and I exchanged gifts, Lissa slipped up beside my chair. "The journal is really nice. I thought you'd probably get us dolls like everybody else does."

*****

The *Nutcracker* was magical. St. Augustine's sparkling Christmas lights, woven through all trees in the square and outlining the town's historic buildings, prolonged the performance's fairy tale atmosphere. When we were all tired of walking, we went to Mother's shop on St. George Street where she had prepared a festive, but child centered, dinner of macaroni and cheese, apple salad and more Christmas cookies.

At the end of the day, we all returned to my apartment. After we'd piled the girls and their gifts into car, Andy had kissed me goodbye and the car had pulled away, Mother and I stood together on the sidewalk, waving them out of sight.

"Such sweet little girls," Mother murmured. "I do think everything went well."

"And much of the thanks for that goes to you," I said. "I truly don't know what I'd have done without your help."

As I said that, I realized three things—First, I'd actually enjoyed this visit with the girls. Secondly, my mother, for all the angst she sometimes caused me, was a remarkable woman and an important part of my life. The third thing?—I hadn't given a single thought to Sam Stansfield the entire day.

Mother, as if she'd sensed that final thought, added, "How lucky you are to have such a kind, stable man as Andy. And wait until you hear the plans I have for the girls on their spring break."

"Moth-er!" I started, then laughed. "Come on," I said,

grabbing her arm, "let's go inside. Mrs. Castelli will be waiting for us to come sample her famous Christmas egg nog."

CHAPTER 36

The re-dedication of the old Coronado Golf Club—now the New Coronado Golf Club—took place on an April Saturday. A gay breeze carried the smell of new-mown grass as it skittered through the invited guests seated on the lawn, demanding attention as it flirted with ladies' hat brims and lifted the skirts of light spring dresses.

Outside the pro shop, purple and yellow balloons attached to the line-up of golf carts tugged at the ribbons holding them in place as if impatient to be part of the action. Even the television crew gathered to record the historic moment seemed to catch the spirit, although the gin-and-tonics surreptitiously passed to the techs may have had something to do with it.

As the reporter who'd followed the story of the Coronado ladies' struggle to save their course, I was assigned to cover the dedication. Miles Arkin was also on hand to photograph the occasion. I was able to catch a few minutes of interview time with Zelma Beauclaire before the ceremonies began. It was evident that her arrest and subsequent court appearance had done nothing to curtail her brusque manner. Still I'd come to admire her—when the judge ordered her to perform 100 hours of community service, she immediately set up a free golf clinic for girls and continued it even after her punishment had expired.

The threat of Southwind Enterprises or other would-be developers taking over the property had died when soil tests revealed that in years past the club's greens keepers had used arsenic for insect control. The deadly chemical had leeched deep into the soil, and any attempts at excavation would have required total removal by HazMat specialists at enormous cost. I reflected how easy it was to underestimate the power of the little creatures that live beneath the soil. Insects—termites—had nearly eaten Mrs. Castelli and me out of our home, yet the damage they inflicted to the stairwell had led to Nick's capture. Now the same insects that posed a threat to greens and fairways had played a role in saving the Coronado.

When it was determined that the property was still safe as a golf course so long as its soil remained undisturbed, Zelma and her ladies coerced local investors—including many of their own and their friends' husbands—to buy the property. Under its new ownership, the course had been freshly landscaped, the greens and fairways trimmed to nail-scissor perfection, and the old ball washers replaced with shiny new ones. The clubhouse, too, had been revamped and the once utilitarian women's locker room now glistened like an expensive spa.

After the final speech, Zelma Beauclaire rose from her seat, broke a bottle of champagne on the veranda's new railing and the pro declared the new Coronado course ready for play. Immediately, the golfing ladies piled into the balloon-bedecked carts and took off for the first tee, waving golf towels and whooping loudly. Zelma Beauclaire was in the lead cart, but she was not driving. At her hearing she'd also been sentenced to a one year ban on golf cart driving.

*****

At home after the ceremony, for once I found myself with a

free Saturday afternoon. I could clean my apartment, take a long run, head for the beach or pull out one of the books I'd put aside for just such an occasion. Instead, I put on shorts, a t-top and sandals, poured a tall glass of iced tea and sank into the porch's wicker settee. A reflective mood took over as I watched a small sailboat out on the river tacking against both the current and a head wind, its boom shifting each time the sails began to luff.

The past months had been like that for me, with little smooth sailing. The trial, of course. Nick had received his just punishment, if life in prison without parole was justice for having taken two lives. Yet there were moments when the image of that small boy who had lost everything in the world that mattered to him haunted me. As did that terrifying moment when he nearly captured me in the stairwell. My injuries from that night had long since healed except for a pain in my wrist when the weather changes, but the memory of that night has left a permanent scar.

A swoop of gulls heading downriver diverted me from that disturbing picture. Unlike the sailboat, they had the advantage of a following wind, and glided swiftly with that inexplicable ability birds have to maintain their flight pattern. During our long days covering the trial, Kyle and I had developed a pattern of our own, sharing information, comparing notes and debating the outcome.

I was lucky to have Kyle, both as a colleague and as a friend. When I'd been forced to move from my apartment, he'd been there, pitching in along with Rhonda and others to help get the house ready for the exterminators. Then, when it was time to move back in and I was hardly able to walk around, much less unpack crates and rearrange furniture, he was there again without my asking.

I was lucky to have friends like Kyle and Rhonda and Polly, but Mother is the person who's always come through when I needed her. Seeing the relief in her eyes when she learned I was safe made me forgive her attempts to interfere in my life. Maybe that was the role a mother was destined to play, to set a protective force field around her child early on and never quite turn it off no matter how grown they become.

If Mother's predictions and her use of the occult to control my life were annoying, there was also comfort in knowing that to one person in the world I would always be at the center of her concerns.

Something about that observation niggled at the back of my mind—perhaps I took too much for granted that Mother's concern extended to me, but had I been negligent in my concern for her? After Dad's death she'd made a new life for herself as Zanthia, but how easy could that have been for her? While I was carping about those changes, had I ever given thought to the fact that it had to have been a difficult and scary transition for her?

The sight of a fishing boat drifting near the near shore reminded me of my recent meeting with Elaine Descuto. She'd been glowing with the news that her Denny was now back in college at University of North Florida. "He still spends weekends crewing on your Granddad's boat," she told me. "I say your grandfather's name every night in my prayers."

"As do I," I told her.

A sudden rupture of the afternoon silence caused me to come upright. A pair of Ski-Doos were flying upriver, tossing huge, watery plumes in their wakes. They swerved dangerously close to the small sailboat, threatening to swamp it as they roared past. My contemplative mood shattered, I held my breath until I saw that, while temporarily thrown off course, the boat had righted itself.

I dropped back onto to the cushions, wondering if the near accident held some metaphoric message. Was my still-uncertain romance with Andy like the little boat, vulnerable to stubborn tides and unforeseeable events? Or was it that sometimes you just had to set sail and trust that the winds would carry you in the right direction?